COOKING GLUTEN, WHEAT AND DAIRY FREE

Michelle Berriedale-Johnson

COOKING GLUTEN, WHEAT AND DAIRY FREE

MICHELLE BERRIEDALE-JOHNSON

GRUB STREET | LONDON

Published in 2011 by
Grub Street
4 Rainham Close
London
SW11 6SS
Email: food@grubstreet.co.uk
Web: www.grubstreet.co.uk

Reprinted 2013, 2014

Design by Sarah Driver
Jacket design by Lizzie Ballantyne
Photography by Michelle Garrett
Food styling by Jayne Cross

A CIP record for this title is available from the British Library

ISBN 978-1-906502-92-8

Printed and bound in Slovenia

Important note: Every effort has been made to ensure that the information in this book is complete and accurate. However neither the publisher nor the author are engaged in rendering professional advice or services to the reader. Professional medical advice should be obtained on personal health matters. This book is not intended to replace treatment by a qualified practitioner. Neither the publisher nor the author accepts any legal responsibility for any personal injury or other damage or loss arising from the use or misuse of the information or advice in this book.

CONTENTS

INTRODUCTION

To the non-medical reader, problems with dairy, gluten or wheat would seem relatively straight forward — but, in fact, we are dealing with at least five different medical conditions — and which one you have could be relevant to what you can eat.

So, let's look at each in a bit more detail.

DAIRY ALLERGY

A dairy or milk protein allergy is an immune response to one or more of the proteins in cow's milk. What this means is that your immune system mistakenly identifies the protein as dangerous and mobilises your body's defences to protect you against it.

A response may be triggered by a very tiny amount of the milk protein — what would be contained in just one drop of milk — and it will usually be immediate, within minutes. Normal cooking does not affect the protein which will be just as allergenic cooked as raw.

You may get a gastric reaction (vomiting or diarrhoea/constipation), a skin reaction (urticaria, hives etc), a release of histamine which will cause swelling, or a respiratory reaction (narrowing of the airways and an asthma attack).

The reaction can be anything from relatively mild to life threatening. For those who are seriously allergic, contact with their allergen can cause an anaphylactic shock in which massive swelling (usually around the mouth and throat) narrows the airways and causes a dramatic drop in blood pressure which, if not treated within minutes with adrenaline, can be fatal. In someone with asthma this kind of shock can also precipitate a fatal asthma attack. Fortunately this is very rare, but the risk cannot be discounted.

Those who react to cow's milk, often but not always, react to the proteins in other animal milks which are largely similar. But if the thought of giving up all animal milks appals, it is worth trying goat, sheep or buffalo milk as you may be one of those who reacts only to the proteins in cow's milk.

Although it may not seem logical, 'dairy' products refers specifically to cow's milk products not the milk or other products of other animals — so if a product is labelled 'dairy free' it means that it is free of cow's milk only, not all animal milks.

what dairy allergics should not eat:
• Any cow's milk products — milk, cream, butter, cheese, yogurt, ice cream.
• Probably any other animal milk products but may be worth checking before crossing them off the shopping list.

DAIRY INTOLERANCE

One can have problems with dairy products without necessarily having a true allergy. Given that cow's milk was designed for baby cows and not for baby, or adult, humans, and that a cow's digestive system is hugely different from a human one, it is not very surprising that some humans have difficulty in digesting cow's milk.

Symptoms of dairy intolerance can include digestive problems, skin problems, breathing problems, behavioural problems (especially in children), headache, glue ear, joint pain, mood swings and almost anything else you can think of.

Those with dairy intolerance are rarely as sensitive as dairy allergics and may be able to eat small amounts of dairy products, especially if they have been further processed either by the natural enzymatic activity that occurs when you make yogurt or cheese, or if they have been cooked.

Those with cow's milk intolerance are quite often able to tolerate the milk and products of other animals.

what dairy intolerants should not eat:

• 'Raw' cow's milk products, more than small amounts of 'processed' cow's milk products (cheese, yogurt, cooked milk etc). However, as each person will be different you will need to establish your own tolerance levels.
• No more than small amounts of other animal milk products but, as above.

LACTOSE INTOLERANCE

All animal milks, including human milk, contain a sugar, called lactose. Infants (of all animal species) make an enzyme in their guts, called lactase, which digests the lactose, or milk sugar, in the milk. Without lactase, the lactose sugar ferments in the gut and causes bloating, wind, diarrhoea and, in the long term, all kinds of other symptoms.

Very rarely an infant will not make any lactase at all. More frequently, their production of lactase may be insufficient to deal with the amount of lactose they ingest in their milk. Most commonly, if an infant (or a child or adult) has a stomach upset and diarrhoea, their stock of lactase will be washed out of their gut and until their gut has had time to make more, they will be temporarily lactase deficient.

Since, in nature, animals only drink milk as infants, the gut will cease to produce lactase once the infant is weaned. However, since the human body is very adaptable, most of us continue to make lactase as long as we go on drinking milk and ingesting lactose sugar. However, since this is a 'make-do' solution, we do not always do it very efficiently. As a result many children and adults will be at least partially lactase deficient and so suffer from what is known as lactose intolerance although, strictly speaking, they are suffering from a lactase deficiency.

To a large extent the lactose sugar in milk is converted into harmless lactic acid by the bacterial activity which takes place when milk is turned into butter, yogurt and cheese. And the harder and more aged the cheese the greater the bacterial activity and the lower the levels of lactose. So many people with lactose intolerance may be able to eat at least some hard cheese and yogurts without ill effect.

what lactose intolerants should not eat:
• Raw animal milks of any kind. Each person should experiment with butter, cheese and yogurt to see how much they can tolerate. For some this will be very little, for some it may be quite a lot.

WHEAT ALLERGY

A wheat allergy, like a dairy allergy, is an immune system response to a protein in the wheat which your body mistakenly recognises as dangerous.

Although relatively rare, a wheat allergy would cause similar symptoms to a dairy allergy (see above) and could, conceivably, cause an anaphylactic shock.

what wheat allergics should not eat:
• Any wheat in bread, cakes, biscuits, pastry, sauces or anywhere else. However, they can eat oats, rye and barley, which greatly expands their gastronomic possibilities.

WHEAT INTOLERANCE

There is a school of thought that believes that many humans, in evolutionary terms, have not really developed beyond the hunter/gatherer stage in which we lived on meat and fish (hunted) and fruits and roots (gathered) and that our digestive systems have not yet adapted to the farmed grains that are the raw materials for the bulk of a modern western diet.

Even if you do not go that far, it is certainly the case that modern western diets, especially those that have adopted the pasta and pizza element of the Mediterranean diet largely to the exclusion of the fruit and vegetable element, are predominantly wheat based. Not only are they wheat based but the wheat on which they are based has been highly refined and processed, losing most of its fibre and many of its nutrients on the way, and acquiring extra gluten — see below.

Given that humans are omnivores, it is not unlikely that basing a diet exclusively on one ingredient (toasted white bread for breakfast, biscuits with coffee, pizza slice for lunch, slice of cake with tea, pasta for supper) will cause both digestive and nutritional problems.

what wheat intolerants should not eat:
• Too many products made from refined white flour. Ideally, no products made with refined white flour at all — try substituting alternative grain flours (see below) or older varieties of wheat such as spelt or kamut which are higher in fibre, lower in gluten and far more nutritious.

GLUTEN INTOLERANCE

Gluten is a glue-like protein which is found in many grains but especially in wheat, rye and barley. It is what holds bread together when the yeast has expanded it so that you get the light soft bread that we all know and love. It is therefore a very useful ingredient in food manufacturing. The more 'glue' you have the easier it is to 'hold products together'.

To maximise its potential, farmers have been encouraged to breed and grow wheat with higher and higher levels of gluten and food manufacturers have used increasingly high levels of gluten in their products. This is especially the case since the invention of the Chorley Wood Bread Process in the 1960s which uses enzymes to speed up the fermentation of the yeast and incorporate higher levels of gluten in bread making.

As a result a diet high in refined wheat products now includes significant quantities of gluten which can, in layman's terms, effectively 'glue up' the digestive system and result in reactions triggered by over consumption.

what gluten intolerants should not eat:

• Products made from refined white wheat flour. Try substituting alternative gluten-free grain flours (see below) or older varieties of wheat such as spelt or kamut which are much lower in gluten.

COELIAC DISEASE

Coeliac disease is also a reaction to gluten but of a different type. Coeliac disease is what is known as an auto-immune disease in which the immune system, as in an allergy, mistakes gluten as dangerous.

When the villi or tiny fronds which line the small intestine and through which we absorb nutrients, come into contact with gluten they become inflamed and then flattened. This means that you can neither absorb nutrients from your food nor digest it properly.

Coeliac disease can develop at any point and can be of varying degrees of severity. It is now thought that the condition has been seriously under diagnosed for years and far from only one in 300 of the population suffering from coeliac disease, it could be as many as one in 70. Moreover, that many people with unresolved digestive and other health problems are in fact undiagnosed coeliacs, but because the symptoms can be so multifarious, they have never been tested for the condition.

Coeliac disease in small children can be very serious as they totally fail to absorb any of the nutrients so essential to growth. It is always to be suspected in any child who is failing to thrive, especially if this is accompanied by digestive problems.

There are now blood tests which can identify coeliac disease although the 'gold standard' of diagnosis remains a biopsy — a small section taken from the gut to be examined under a microscope. This is because in rare instances the blood test can confuse coeliac disease with other unusual but serious digestive conditions. The problem with the biopsy is that for it to show anything, you have to have been eating gluten for three to six months so that the villi are seriously damaged. Many people who suspect gluten as a problem and have already removed it from their diet are unwilling to make themselves ill again merely to confirm something that they think they already know.

However, there are advantages to being a diagnosed coeliac as not only can you access help from your GP but you can get a range of gluten-free foods on prescription. This is less important than it was a few years ago when there were so few alternative gluten-free foods available but since many such foods are still expensive, there are financial benefits to being able to get them on prescription, especially for a child or elderly person who gets them free.

what coeliacs should not eat:

• Any gluten so therefore any product made from wheat, barley or rye.

For more on all of these conditions see the Foods Matter website at www.foods-matter.com

AVOIDING WHAT YOU NEED TO AVOID

The problem for people who are trying to avoid products containing dairy, wheat or gluten is that they are the most commonly used ingredients in food manufacture. This means that you will find it very difficult to buy ready-made foods which do not contain at least one of the ingredients that you must not eat. This is, of course, why you have bought this book — so that you can cook your food for yourself.

In fact, the situation is infinitely better than it was a few years ago as the number of good quality, tasty, ready-made foods available in the shops that genuinely are dairy, gluten or wheat free — and often all three — has mushroomed. For more details on what you can buy see the resources section at the end of this book and the 'Free-from food products' links on the Foods Matter website.

Meanwhile, if you are to stick to a dairy-, gluten- and wheat-free diet, you will need to become an avid reader of labels and ingredients lists — to know what to look for on those ingredients lists, where your forbidden ingredients are likely to turn up and what alternatives to use.

So, below I am listing the different names under which these ingredients can appear, where they may be hiding, what alternatives you can use and any problems your may encounter with the alternatives.

DAIRY PRODUCTS

Don't forget that 'dairy free' on an ingredients list only means cow's milk free, not sheep, goat or other animal milk free. Remember also that dairy products include not only milk but cream, butter, cheese and yogurt — but not eggs.

Dairy products can also be known as:

- Butter
- Casein/caseinates
- Cream — all varieties
- Crème fraîche
- Ghee
- Ice cream
- Lactic acid (E270) but can also be dairy free
- Milk solids
- Whey
- Yogurt

- Buttermilk
- Cheese (including cream, curd and cottage)
- Fromage frais
- Hydrolysed Casein/whey
- Lactalbumin
- Lactose
- Milk of all kinds
- Skimmed milk powder
- Whey protein/sugar

They are likely to be found in:

- Animal fat
- Batter (for pancakes, waffles, fish fingers etc)
- Breads — many enriched breads will include butter and/or milk
- Cheese straws/biscuits
- Crème caramel
- Custard tarts
- Desserts — many different kinds
- Low fat spreads
- Ready meals — most ready meals include butter or milk
- Sauces — all white sauces and many other ready-made sauces
- Vegetable fats

- Artificial cream
- Biscuits — most biscuits include butter or margarine
- Cakes — most cakes use butter and many use milk
- Cheese-flavoured crisps
- Crème patissière/custard
- Chocolate/chocolate products
- Ice creams — most types
- Margarine
- Rice pudding and most other baked puddings
- Scones
- Sweeteners

alternatives to cow's milk and dairy products:

Remember that 'dairy' refers to cow's milk products only (milk, cream, butter, yogurt, cheese, ice cream), not to other animal milks, but if someone is lactose intolerant then they will not be able to tolerate any animal milk as all animal milks contain lactose.

Goat, Sheep and Buffalo Milk, Cream, Butter, Yogurt and Cheese | All of these are now quite easy to obtain and, made in modern hygienic dairies, are mild and pleasant. Many are available both fresh and UHT.

Because of their high fat content goat, sheep and buffalo creams whisk well and can be used in most desserts, milk shakes, ice creams — and cappuccino.

Soya Milk, Cream, Yogurt and Cheese | Soya milk has been a staple vegetarian ingredient for many years so there are many different varieties, both fresh and UHT.

Soya milk comes sweetened and unsweetened, flavoured and plain, fortified and unfortified. Most cook up well in sauces and soups and can be used for cappuccino although a few still separate in hot tea or coffee.

Soya cream works as pouring cream but you cannot whip it. Soya yogurts, both plain and fruit flavoured, are now very good and can be used as an ingredient in a dessert, or as a dessert in their own right.

Hard soya cheeses are not unpleasant although they do not bear much resemblance to 'real' cheese. Soya cream cheese is more successful. You can also get soya cheese slices which melt reasonably well for topping pizzas or burgers.

N.B. Be aware that 30% of those who are allergic to cow's milk are also allergic to soya.

Coconut Milk and Oil | Coconut milk is an excellent cooking milk to which very few people react, but it has a very distinct flavour. It is extensively used in Southeast Asian cooking. It comes in tins and can be used, well stirred, direct from the tin. Coconut cream comes both in tins and as a solid block which needs to be broken down with hot water.

Coconut oil is an excellent butter substitute, although quite strong flavoured and expensive.

Oat Milk | Early brands of oat milk bore a strong resemblance to liquid porridge but more recent ones are quite innocuous. Oat milk works well in savoury dishes and in wholefood-style sweet dishes.

Rice Milk | Rice milk comes plain and flavoured. It is thinner than animal or soya milk and some brands are rather grey and watery in appearance. However it is useful for those who cannot have either animal or soya milks. It is also quite sweet.

Dairy-Free Spreads | There are several dairy-free spreads on the market but scrutinise ingredients carefully as many spreads which appear to be dairy free actually contain whey or casein. Most spreads are flavourless and harmless and can be used in sauces and baking (pastry, cakes etc). They are not good for frying. Coconut oil is a great frying and baking alternative, but expensive.
Avoid spreads using hydrogenated fats if at all possible.

GLUTEN

Gluten is found in:

• Barley	• Rye	• Wheat

But these may also be called:

• Bran	• Bulgar/bulgur
• Cereal binder/filler	• Couscous

- Flour made from barley, rye or wheat
- Semolina
- Malt
- Rusk
- Wheat starch and modified wheat starch

It is likely to be found in:

- Baking powder
- Biscuits (sweet or savoury)
- All breads unless specifically gluten free
- Breadcrumb coatings
- Cereal binder/filler
- Chapatis, poppadoms, naans
- Cheese spread/dips
- Fruit drinks
- Modified starch
- Pancakes and waffles
- Pastry made from wheat, rye or barley
- Pizzas
- Rusk
- Sauces and gravies
- Semolina
- Taramasalata
- Tinned vegetables
- Beer
- Breakfast cereals/muesli
- All bread, cake or pastry mixes unless specifically gluten free
- All buns, muffins, scones, cakes and baked goods unless specifically gluten free
- Confectionery
- Margarines
- Oatcakes
- All pasta or noodles unless specifically gluten free
- Pitta bread
- Ready meals of all kinds
- Salad dressings
- Sausages
- Samosas
- Tinned meat containing preservatives

WHEAT

Wheat can also be known as:

- Bran
- Cereal binder/filler
- Couscous
- Edible food starch
- Flour (plain, self raising, wholemeal, malted etc)
- Modified starch
- Wheat starch
- Semolina
- Bulgar
- Chilton/dinkel
- Durum wheat
- Einkorn/farro
- Graham flour
- Kamut/spelt
- Wheat germ
- Rusk
- Triticum/triticale

It is likely to be found in:

- Baking powder
- Biscuits (sweet or savoury)

- Bottled sauces of all kinds
- All breads unless specifically wheat free
- Cereal binder/filler/protein
- Chapatis, poppadams, naans
- Cheese spread/dips
- Horseradish creams
- Monosodium glutamate (MSG)
- Pancakes/waffles
- All pastry and pastries unless specifically wheat free
- Pizzas
- Rusk
- Salad dressings
- Sausages
- Samosas
- Textured vegetable/vegetable protein
- Breakfast cereals/muesli
- Breadcrumbs and coatings
- Cakes, buns, muffins, scones and all baked goods unless specifically wheat free
- Curry powders
- Instant hot drinks (coffee, tea)
- Oatcakes
- All pasta or noodles unless specifically wheat free
- Pitta bread
- Ready meals of all kinds
- Rye breads and crackers
- Sauces and gravies
- Semolina
- Taramasalata

alternatives to gluten and wheat:

Gluten, in the guise of wheat and wheat flours, starches and thickeners, is very widely used within the food industry both as an ingredient and in the manufacture of ingredients.

This means that great care must be taken, when using anything which is not a primary ingredient, to check the ingredients lists on the packaging against the lists on pages 13-14

Breads and Breakfast Goods | Gluten-free bread flours include combinations of buckwheat, gram (chickpea), corn/maize, millet, potato, rice and tapioca flour.

These are not easy to use as they lack the elasticity and 'setting' quality of gluten. As a result breads may rise (thanks to yeast or raising agents) but promptly fall again to produce brick like loaves.

However, over the last few years it has become possible to buy xanthan gum in powdered form. This is a natural gum which, if added in small quantities to flour for bread and pastry making, makes a reasonable substitute for gluten. Even so, it remains difficult to produce reasonable bread with these flours.

Thankfully a number of companies now produce very acceptable part baked, frozen or long-life breads, rolls, baguettes and croissants. These taste reasonable (if not always brilliant) and look like the original. See Resources, page 234.

Corn Bread | This is made from ground corn or maize meal, not what the UK knows as 'cornflour' which is the purified starch from corn/maize meal. Corn bread is delicious and extensively eaten in the US and North America so most US recipe books will have a number of recipes for it. See recipe on page 210.

Biscuits and Crackers | Pure oat oatcakes and crackers are fine for anyone with a wheat allergy and for most coeliacs; there are also a number of proprietary gluten-free crackers on the market. See Resources, page 234.

Biscuits, Cakes and other Baked Goods | Making good gluten-free cakes and biscuits is far easier than making bread, especially if you are using eggs.

There are now several proprietary gluten-free flours on the market (see p236) which work quite well, especially if you add a little xanthan gum – some of them already include xanthan gum so check the ingredients carefully.

Alternatively combinations of the stronger flours (gram or maize) with the finer, lighter flours (white rice, potato, cornflour/starch or tapioca), in approximately equal quantities, gives a reasonable balance which holds together well without being too strongly flavoured. They are very successful in cakes although biscuits can be rather crumbly unless xanthan gum is added.

You can also use oats or millet flakes (either as they are or whizzed for some minutes in a food processor) in combination with some of the finer flours. Both give quite a coarse, slightly crumbly texture and the oats give lots of flavour – excellent for hearty cakes such as gingerbreads.

There are some excellent Italian and American recipes for cakes made purely with ground corn/maize meal (polenta).

Oats | Oats do not contain gliadin, the protein which affects coeliacs, but a look-alike protein called avelin. Research suggests that this does not affect coeliacs but since there have been no studies on the long term effects of eating oats, very sensitive coeliacs may wish to use them only in moderation.

Care should also be taken as many oats are milled on equipment which also mills wheat so there can be a strong risk of contamination.

Breadcrumbs | You can crumb gluten/wheat-free bread. Alternatively use proprietary gluten-free breadcrumbs.

Pasta | Making pasta at home is laborious even when using wheat flour and a good deal more so if using gluten-free flours. However there are now a large number of gluten-free pastas on the market based on corn, rice, buckwheat and other flours. You will need to experiment with them as some 'bulk' up much more than others and cooking times given on the packs are not always totally reliable. See Resources, page 234.

Pastry | Combination flours, as for cakes and biscuits, work best. 60% gram to 40% rice, made in the normal way, gives a well textured, quite crisp and flavoursome pastry although it is very crumbly. Adding a small amount of xanthan gum (see page 236) helps hold it together.

Pizza and Pizza Bases | Making good gluten-free traditional pizza bases is difficult although the two on page 58 work quite well. There are also a number of proprietary pizza base mixes and pizza bases on the market which are not wonderful but adequate if covered with good toppings. See Resources, page 234.

You can also buy frozen ready-made gluten-free pizzas which are useful for emergencies. See Suppliers List, page 235.

Sausages | Most UK sausages use a substantial amount of wheat-based rusk. However there are a growing number of either pure meat sausages or more traditional sausages using rice-based filler on the market.

Frankfurters, chorizo and other continental sausages may be free of gluten but still check ingredients carefully, especially for dairy products.

Sauces and Thickeners | Cornflour/starch, potato flour and arrowroot all work well as thickeners for sauces, both savoury and sweet. Use as flour but be aware that you will need approximately 30% less by weight of these starches to thicken the same volume of liquid.

Beer | You can now get gluten-free beer, lager and stout. See Resources, page 234.

non-wheat flours

If you do wish to experiment with alternative flours here are a few notes on their properties for which we are grateful to Andrew Whitley, the founder of The Village Bakery. Andrew gives courses on craft and gluten-free baking in Cumbria. For further information call 01968 660449 or check out www.breadmatters.com

Buckwheat flour | Very little binding power and a strong flavour which some people love. Widely used in Russia to make porridge and pancakes (blini). Use in combination with other flours.

Chestnut flour | Good binding properties and very distinctive, sweet flavour which may be overpowering. Good in combination with other flours. Expensive.

Cornflour/starch and Corn/maize meal | Cornflour is the purified starch of the maize meal. A good thickener with good binding properties and useful in combination with other flours in baking — too fine and tasteless on its own.

Corn/maize meal is the whole maize seed ground into flour. Quite coarse and because it oxidises quickly, often leaves a bitter taste. Maize flour is the very finely ground maize meal from which all bran and germ have been removed so it does not oxidise.

Gram/chickpea flour | High in protein, so good for binding. It is widely used for making flat breads in India. However, used on its own gram flour can taste very 'beany' and have a rather claggy mouthfeel. Use in combination with other finer flours such as rice, potato or tapioca.

Lupin flour | Made from the seeds of the sweet lupin which has been bred to remove the bitter alkaloids. Very nutritious and with good binding qualities but strong flavoured.

N.B. 70% of peanut allergics are also allergic to lupin so it is a dangerous flour to use when cooking for food allergics/intolerants.

Millet flour | A fine, bland flour. It goes rancid very quickly making everything taste bitter so needs to be bought from a source with a quick turnover and kept in the freezer. Works best in combination with a strong flour like gram flour.

Potato flour/starch | The flour is the dried and ground potato tuber; the starch is a refined derivative of potatoes. In moderation (not more than 20%) both flour and starch can give some binding and lightness but more than 20% will become gummy and heavy. Very little flavour but good as a thickener.

Quinoa flour | Light, creamy flour from the seeds of the quinoa plant from South America. Not much binding power as a flour and a distinctive, slightly bitter taste — but very nutritious.
   If you cook the grains like rice until they have absorbed as much water as they can then beat them to a sticky mush they will aid binding and moisture retention, but do not use more than 10% of the mush in the dough. Not widely available so expensive.

Rice flour — brown and white | Neither white nor brown rice flour have much binding power but are useful in combination with other stronger flours like gram or maize. Even when finely ground, rice flour can have a gritty texture when baked, and leave a slightly bitter taste. Ground rice (much coarser) can also be used for cakes in much the same way as polenta.

Soya flour | Although excellent nutritionally soya flour, if used at more than 5% of the total weight, gives a very heavy texture and an unpleasant taste to the product. Because of its high protein levels it can have an 'egg substitute' effect in cakes and biscuits (most 'egg replacers' are based on soya) but this does not outweigh its disadvantages.

Tapioca flour | Ground from cassava roots. Very light and bland but a reasonable binding quality. In moderate amounts gives a pleasant chewy texture to breads. If it forms more than 50% of the flour in breads or pastry the texture can become dusty and strange background flavours emerge. Use at 5-10% in breads and up to 40% in pastry or biscuits.

Teff flour | Made from a highly nutritious seed grown mainly in the highlands of Ethiopia. Quite dark and strong flavoured and best used in combination with other lighter flours such as corn or rice.

EATING OUT AND TRAVELLING

It is fine when you are buying your food in packets with neatly listed ingredients or when you are cooking from scratch at home. Eating out in restaurants or with friends and travelling is a whole different matter and you will be dependent on the knowledge and awareness of the restaurant or hotel in which you are eating.

There is an excellent, in-depth guide to eating out with a food allergy from the Anaphylaxis Campaign on the Foods Matter website (www.foodsmatter.com) but meanwhile, here are a few pointers:

1. Warn the restaurant or friends what you can and cannot eat. Always be polite when asking and appreciative of any help you are offered — you are dependent on them for a 'safe' meal.
2. Be specific about what you cannot have and highlight that your allergen may be an ingredient in another dish — the thickener for a sauce for example.
3. It may be worth sending them a list of what you are avoiding — this is especially useful if you are going to be staying for a while in a hotel or if it is for a specific party (such as a wedding) where there will be a lot going on.
4. Offer to take your own food — this may be helpful if you are going to eat with friends who are not confident cooks!
5. If you do not get a chance to warn the eatery in advance, explain clearly to the waiter, or better still, the manager/maitre d'hotel what you cannot eat and ask them if they can cater for you.
6. Be careful of staff who do not appear to understand you or are trying to be helpful by saying 'yes, of course'. If necessary, ask to talk to the chef. But be polite.
7. Unless you are quite confident about the eatery, choose dishes which are unlikely to cause you problems or which will only have a relatively small amount of your forbidden ingredient.
8. If the eatery is seriously unhelpful — go somewhere else!
9. If you are seriously allergic, NEVER eat away from home unless you have your Epipen with you.
10. When travelling always make sure you take some hard-tack rations, just in case you cannot find any suitable foods. Better than starving or feeling ill.

USING THESE RECIPES

Although a number of the recipes in this book do use dairy-free, gluten-free or wheat-free ingredients to create traditional dishes, many of them are recipes which would never include any of these products — just to demonstrate how unnecessary all three ingredients are for a varied, nutritious and delicious diet! I hope that they will encourage you to experiment and to look outside a conventional western diet for ideas. Many cuisines (Japanese, Chinese, Indian, South American) use dairy, gluten and wheat far less than we do — sometimes scarcely at all — so cast your recipe net far and wide!

Quantities are given in metric and imperial but because, apart from in baking, very exact quantities are rarely vital in my recipes, I have rounded the equivalents up or down for easy use. All the recipes serve six people. This is because when I was writing the book my entire family helped in testing the recipes. So I suggest if your family is smaller you reduce the quantites given, or better still, cook the recipe and freeze what is leftover so you always have a meal just a defrost away.

SOUPS, STARTERS AND LIGHT LUNCHES

Carrot and Chilli Soup

Spinach and Bean Curd Soup

Gazpacho

Lentil Soup with Garlic Croutons

Beetroot Soup with Fennel and Horseradish

Cream of Mushroom Soup with Coconut Milk

Yellow Split Pea Soup

Asparagus Soup with Wild Garlic

Celeriac Soup

Curried Butternut Squash Soup

Leek and Salmon Soup with Fresh Dill

Carrot, Tomato and Ginger Soup

Smoked Haddock Soup

Green Pea and Watercress Soup

Celery and Rice Soup with Lemongrass

Sardine Hummus

Aubergine and Nut Butter Pâté

Sardine and Avocado Salad

Smoked Trout and Melon Salad

Crudités with Wasabi Dip

Cauliflower and Anchovy Salad

Potato and Celery au Gratin

Courgettes with Sun-dried Tomato Sauce

Grilled Pear with Watercress and Toasted Cheese

Grilled Cheese-Stuffed Mushrooms

CARROT AND CHILLI SOUP

This is a lovely delicately flavoured soup, given a really smooth and creamy texture by the coconut milk. Most of the red chillies you buy in supermarkets are now quite mild, but take care you do not pick a Scotch bonnet, as two would overwhelm the soup! | Serves 6 | Picture page 21

1 tbsp	olive oil	1 tbsp
2	fresh red chillies, de-seeded and finely sliced	2
500g	carrots, scrubbed and diced	1¼ lbs
200g	approx sweet potato, peeled and diced	7 oz
600ml	wheat/gluten-free vegetable stock	1 pint
800ml	coconut milk	1¼ pints
	juice 2 limes	
1 tsp approx	Tabasco	1 tsp
	sea salt	

1. Heat the oil in a heavy pan and gently fry the chillies for 2-3 minutes.
2. Add the carrots, sweet potato and stock and bring to the boil.
3. Cover and simmer for 30-35 minutes or until the carrots are cooked.
4. Purée in a food processor then return to the pan.
5. Add the coconut milk and lime juice, mix well then season to taste with the Tabasco and sea salt.
6. Reheat to serve.

Note: Be careful not to stand over the chillies as you are frying them as the oils that escape as they cook can really catch in your throat.

SPINACH AND BEAN CURD SOUP

I devised this soup when working on a book of *Festive Feasts* for the British Museum — it could have been served as part of a banquet at the eighteenth century Emperor Qianlong's court. It is quite light and delicately flavoured. | Serves 6

6	dried Chinese mushrooms	6
200g	young fresh spinach	7 oz
400g	firm soya bean curd (tofu) cut into bite-size cubes	14 oz
2 tbsp	sunflower oil	2 tbsp
100g	fresh field mushrooms, sliced thinly	4 oz
2 tbsp	wheat/gluten-free soya sauce or tamari	2 tbsp
2 tbsp	Shaoxing wine	2 tbsp
4	level teaspoons cornflour, mixed with a little water	4
1 litre	good wheat/gluten-free vegetable stock	1¾ pints
	sea salt and freshly ground pepper to taste	
2 tsp	sesame oil	2 tsp

1. Soak the mushrooms in boiling water for 30 minutes then drain, remove the stems and slice very finely.
2. Blanch the spinach in boiling water for 1 minute then rinse in cold water, drain, squeeze dry then chop finely.
3. Blanch the bean curd in boiling water for 10 minutes, then drain and leave to dry.
4. Heat the sunflower oil in a wok over high heat.
5. Add the dried and fresh mushrooms and cook for a minute, stirring.
6. Add the spinach, soya sauce and wine and stir for another minute.
7. Mix the cornflour to a smooth paste with a little of the stock.
8. Add the cornflour, stock, bean curd and salt and pepper to the soup.
9. Bring back to the boil and simmer for 4-5 minutes.
10. Sprinkle with sesame oil and serve at once.

Note: Many Far Eastern dishes are naturally gluten, wheat and dairy free so it is worth trawling through some Chinese, Japanese and Indonesian cookbooks when your culinary inspiration is running low.

GAZPACHO

This is a lovely refreshing summer soup which, with the added vegetables, is quite substantial enough for lunch. If you want to make the soup more filling you can add 50g/2 oz finely chopped ham and 50g/2 oz finely chopped spicy sausage (but check the ingredients of the latter, especially for gluten) along with the chopped vegetables. | Serves 6-8

1 kg	ripe tomatoes, chopped roughly	2 lbs
3	large cloves garlic	3
1	small onion, finely chopped	1
6 tbsp	olive oil	6 tbsp
300 ml	dry white wine	10 fl oz
600 ml	chicken stock	1 pint
	juice 1-2 lemons	
	sea salt and pepper	
50g	each finely chopped celery, green or red pepper and cucumber	2 oz

1. Put the tomatoes in a large pan with the garlic, onion, oil, wine and stock.
2. Bring to the boil and simmer for 1 hour.
3. Purée the soup in a food processor or liquidiser then put through a sieve to remove the tomato pips.
4. Add lemon juice, salt and pepper to taste bearing in mind that flavours get dulled by chilling.
5. Chill the soup and just before serving add the chopped vegetables.

Note: The 'gazpacho' that is normally served in northern Europe is a chilled creamy tomato soup whereas a traditional Spanish gazpacho has a more vigorous flavour and no cream, so much better for those with a dairy problem.

LENTIL SOUP WITH GARLIC CROUTONS

You can use any coloured lentils for this soup although red lentils give it the best colour — and cook fastest. The spices give it a lovely North African flavour — the croutons a delicious crunch. Make sure that you cook the spices gently for a few minutes to bring out the flavour before you add the vegetables.

   You can use the remains of any gluten or wheat-free bread that you have to make the croutons. | Serves 6

2 tbsp	olive oil	2 tbsp
2 heaped tsp	ground cumin	2 heaped tsp
1 heaped tsp	ground coriander	1 heaped tsp
1	large onion, chopped roughly	1
2	large cloves garlic, sliced	2
1	large stick celery, chopped	1
375g	red lentils	13 oz
2 litres	wheat/gluten-free chicken or vegetable stock or water	3½ pints
	sea salt and freshly ground black pepper	

Croutons

8-10 tbsp	olive oil	8-10 tbsp
3	cloves garlic, crushed	3
3	slices of wheat/gluten-free brown bread cut in small cubes	3

1. Put the oil in a deep pan with the cumin and coriander, stir well around and fry very gently for a couple of minutes.

2. Add the onion, garlic and celery and cook gently for 5-10 minutes or until the vegetables are starting to soften.

3. Add the lentils and continue to cook for a few minutes more then add the liquid and a little seasoning.

4. Bring to the boil and simmer gently for 45-60 minutes or until the lentils have all but disintegrated.

5. Purée in a food processor then return to the pan and adjust the seasoning to taste.

6. While the lentils are cooking make the croutons by heating the oil in a wide frying pan.

7. Add the garlic and cook gently for several minutes or until it is lightly cooked through but not burnt.

8. Increase the heat slightly and add the bread cubes.

9. Fry briskly for 5-6 minutes until the cubes are all well browned but not burnt. Remove from the pan onto kitchen paper to drain off any excess oil.

Serve the soup hot with the warm croutons.

Note: If you are a real garlic fan you could also serve the soup with a garlic sauce. Heat 2 tbsp oil in a pan, add 3-4 garlic cloves, crushed, and ½ tsp each ground cumin and coriander. Fry briskly until golden but not burnt and add sizzling spoonfuls to each serving.

BEETROOT SOUP WITH FENNEL AND HORSERADISH

Beetroot and horseradish are a great combination of flavours as the heat of the horseradish counters the sweetness of the beetroot — as anyone who has ever eaten the traditional Jewish dish of gefilte fish with chrain will tell you. | Serves 6

550g	fresh beetroots, topped, tailed, scrubbed and diced	1¼ lbs
1	medium head fennel	1
250g	sweet potatoes, peeled and diced	9 oz
1.2 litres	wheat and gluten-free vegetable stock	2 pints
	sea salt and freshly ground black pepper	
6 tsp	grated horseradish	6 tsp
4 tbsp	plain goat, sheep's milk or soya yogurt	4 tbsp

1. Put the beetroot, fennel, sweet potato and stock into a large pan and bring slowly to the boil.
2. Simmer, with the lid on, for 30-35 minutes or until the beets are cooked, then purée in a food processor.
3. Season to taste and if too thick, add a little extra stock.
4. In a small bowl mix the yogurt into the horseradish until it forms a smooth paste, then season to taste.
5. Serve the soup in bowls with a large spoonful of the horseradish mix swirled into each bowl.

Note: Both beetroot and sweet potato are highly nutritious (as well as delicious) so this soup will also boost your intake of folate, and vitamins A and C.

CREAM OF MUSHROOM SOUP WITH COCONUT MILK

The coconut milk gives a wonderfully creamy texture to this soup, while its flavour melds with, but does not overpower, the flavour of the mushrooms. | Serves 6

6 tbsp	olive oil	6 tbsp
6	small leeks, trimmed and sliced finely	6
350g	chestnut mushrooms, chopped small	12 oz
600ml	coconut milk	1 pint
600ml	gluten/wheat-free vegetable stock	1 pint
	sea salt and freshly ground black pepper	
	juice 1-2 lemons	
100g	oyster or shitake mushrooms, sliced	4 oz
	extra 2 tbsp olive oil	

1. Heat the oil in a heavy pan and add the leeks.
2. Sauté gently for 2-3 minutes, then add the chopped chestnut mushrooms. Continue to cook gently, uncovered for a further 10 minutes.
3. Add the coconut milk and stock. Bring to the boil then reduce the heat and simmer for approximately 20 minutes.
4. Purée in a liquidiser or food processor then return to the pan and season to taste with the salt, pepper and lemon juice.
5. When ready to serve, heat the extra oil in a pan and briskly fry the sliced oyster or shitake mushrooms.
6. Reheat the soup and serve with the extra mushrooms scattered over the top.

Note: You can use any combination of mushrooms that you like for this soup — varying it according to what is available seasonally.

YELLOW SPLIT PEA SOUP

The very excellent flavour of this soup depends on the really long, slow cooking of the onions — so be generous with your time if nothing else! | Serves 6

3 tbsp	olive oil	3 tbsp
3 level tsp	ground cumin	3 level tsp
1 level tsp	ground coriander	1 level tsp
2	medium onions, very finely sliced	2
1	medium carrot, very finely grated	1
300g	yellow split peas	10 oz
2 litres	gluten and wheat-free vegetable stock	3½ pints
	sea salt and freshly ground black pepper	

1. Heat the oil in a heavy pan and add the cumin and coriander.
2. Cook gently for 2-3 minutes then add the onions and carrot and continue to cook very gently, uncovered, stirring regularly, for 45-60 minutes. Make sure they do not burn.
3. Add the split peas and the stock, bring to the boil, cover and simmer for 45 minutes.
4. Season to taste with sea salt and freshly ground black pepper, add extra stock if it is too thick, and serve.

Note: Pulse-based soups are great for those who cannot thicken their soup either with flour or with cream as they are smooth and filling — and nutritious.

ASPARAGUS SOUP WITH WILD GARLIC

This is very much a seasonal soup — to be made in May or June when the English asparagus has just arrived. If you can find some wild garlic (very easy to grow in a shady spot in your garden) it gives it a special flavour. If not, some home-grown chives in a pot will do very well. The simplicity of the ingredients allows the flavour of the asparagus to shine through.

You can serve the soup warm or at room temperature. | Serves 6

550g	fresh asparagus, English if possible	1¼ lbs
1.5 litres	gluten/wheat-free vegetable or chicken stock	2½ pints
200ml	dry white wine	7 fl oz

sea salt and freshly ground black pepper
large handful of wild garlic leaves with flowers if possible or, if you cannot
find wild garlic, fresh chives with flowers

1. Trim the tough ends off the asparagus and cut the spears into shortish pieces and put in a large pan with the stock and white wine.
2. Bring slowly to the boil and simmer, covered, for 30 minutes.
3. Purée in a food processor and season to taste.
4. When ready to serve, reheat the soup gently.
5. Remove the stems and chop garlic leaves quite small.
6. Stir into the soup before serving and scatter the flowers over the tureen or each bowl.

Note: It is so easy to grow herbs such as chives in pots on a balcony or window sill that it is really worth doing as freshly cut herbs are so much more delicious than even the best that you can buy in a shop.

CELERIAC SOUP

Celeriac is a very undervalued vegetable which is a pity as it is delicious and enormously flexible. This has to be the simplest soup recipe ever — but the result is to die for. | Serves 6

675g	bulb of celeriac, trimmed and cut in large cubes	1½ lbs
1	small bulb of garlic, the cloves peeled and halved	1
1.8 litres	wheat/gluten-free vegetable stock	3¼ pints
	sea salt and freshly ground black pepper	

1. Put the celeriac with the garlic and stock in a large pan and bring to the boil.
2. Cover and simmer for 30 minutes or until the celeriac is soft.
3. Purée in a food processor and season to taste. Serve.

Note: Celeriac is a variety of celery with a very developed root and only tiny stalks. It is sometimes known as turnip-rooted celery. It has a similar flavour to celery but gentler without the latter's occasional bitterness. Although rare in the UK, allergy to plants in the celery family is not unusual in continental Europe.

CURRIED BUTTERNUT SQUASH SOUP

This is a lovely creamy, warming soup — even though it does not contain any cream! If you want it to be spicier, you can use some gluten/wheat-free curry paste once the soup is cooked to 'spice it up' a bit more. Just add soup, little by little, to a teaspoon of curry paste in a small bowl then stir into the soup. | Serves 6

4 tbsp	olive oil	4 tbsp
1	large leek, finely sliced	1
3-6 heaped tsp	medium heat gluten/wheat-free curry powder depending on how hot you want your soup	3-6 heaped tsp
1	medium-size butternut squash	1
1 litre	gluten/wheat-free vegetable stock	1¾ pints
	sea salt	

1. Heat the oil in a heavy pan, add the leeks and the curry powder and cook gently, stirring regularly, for 10-15 minutes or until the leeks are soft.
2. Peel the squash and remove the seeds.
3. Cut in cubes and add to the leeks.
4. Continue to cook for a further few minutes then add the stock.
5. Bring to the boil, lower the heat, cover and simmer for 20-25 minutes.
6. Purée the soup in a food processor and season to taste before serving.

Note: Winter squashes, although long a staple in the USA, are relatively recent arrivals in the UK although we have long been familiar with their summer cousins, courgettes and marrows. Butternut squash, with its ability to keep for months and its beautiful golden colour and lovely rich taste, has become a particular favourite. They are also a good source of vitamin C and potassium.

LEEK AND SALMON SOUP WITH FRESH DILL

A light and delicately flavoured soup — lovely for lunch with a freshly baked gluten-free loaf! If you cannot get fresh dill, use 1 heaped tsp of dried dill along with the salmon — but it is much nicer with fresh. | Serves 6

5 tbsp	olive oil	5 tbsp
3	large leeks, very finely sliced	3
400g	salmon fillet, cut into small pieces	14 oz
1.5 litres	gluten and wheat-free fish or vegetable stock	2½ pints
200ml	dry white wine	7 fl oz

	sea salt and freshly ground black pepper	
	juice of 1 large lemon	
large handful	fresh dill	large handful

1. Heat the oil in a heavy pan, add the leeks and cook very slowly for 30-40 minutes or until they are soft.
2. Add the salmon, the stock and wine, salt and pepper and bring slowly to just below the boil, by which time the salmon pieces should be almost cooked. Add the lemon juice and adjust the seasoning to taste.
3. Chop in about half of the dill and mix very gently.
4. Reheat to serve, stirring gently and not allowing the soup to boil.
5. Serve in bowls sprinkled with extra dill.

Note: With their more delicate flavour I find that leeks work better with fish dishes than onions.

CARROT, TOMATO AND GINGER SOUP

This is another of those wonderfully simple but tasty and filling soups. It works equally well hot or cold so is good for winter or summer.

You can just drop a sprig of mint or basil on the top of each bowl, or chop the leaves and stir them into the soup before serving. | Serves 6

550g	carrots	1 ¼ lbs
550g	fresh tomatoes (I used small plum tomatoes)	1 ¼ lbs
2 heaped tsp	powdered ginger	2 heaped tsp
1 litre	gluten and wheat-free vegetable stock	1 ¾ pints
	sea salt and freshly ground black pepper	
	fresh basil or fresh mint	

1. Scrub or peel the carrots and cut in large dice.
2. Halve or quarter the tomatoes.
3. Put all into a pan with the ginger and stock and bring to the boil.
4. Cover and simmer for 20-30 minutes or until the carrots are soft.
5. Purée in a food processor then return to the pan.
6. Reheat and season to taste with sea salt and freshly ground black pepper.
7. Serve decorated with a sprig of fresh basil or fresh mint.

Note: A great soup for boosting your intake of vitamins A and C.

SMOKED HADDOCK SOUP

This is a really substantial, 'North Sea' soup that would be ample for a meal on its own. | Serves 6

450g	smoked haddock (ideally the undyed)	1 lb
600ml	water	1 pint
1	large onion, peeled and chopped roughly	1
400g	celeriac or old potatoes	14 oz
900ml	plain soya or oat milk	1 ½ pints
	sea salt and freshly ground black pepper	
	large handful of chopped fresh parsley (optional)	

1. Put the fish in a saucepan with the water and the onion.
2. Cover and bring slowly to the boil.
3. Turn down the heat and simmer very gently for 10 minutes.
4. Meanwhile, peel and dice the celeriac or potato and put it in a pan with the soya or oat milk. Bring slowly to the boil and simmer for 10-15 minutes or until the vegetables are cooked.
5. If you would like your soup to include actual chunks of fish, remove half of the fish from the water, flake it and set aside.
6. Purée the rest of the fish with the water, the vegetables and the soya or oat milk until quite smooth. (If you want a totally smooth soup then purée all the fish with the vegetables and liquid.)
7. Reheat, add the flaked fish and season to taste with sea salt and freshly ground pepper.
8. Serve sprinkled with parsley, or not, as you choose.

Note: Oat milk, if you have not come across it, is just that — a milk made from oats. The easiest variety to find is called Oatly and comes from Sweden. It is smooth and pleasant and only tastes very faintly of oats. Oatly also make a long-life oat single 'cream' which is very smooth and creamy — really nice on fresh fruit or over a chocolate cake or dessert. Oats are now thought to be safe for all but the most severe coeliacs even though they contain a protein very similar to the wheat protein, gliadin, which causes problems for coeliacs. For more on oats see p18.

GREEN PEA AND WATERCRESS SOUP

If you are making this soup in high summer you can make it with fresh peas — at any other time of the year use frozen petis pois. This recipe retains a good deal of the texture of the skin of the pea. If you prefer it to be totally smooth you need to run the puréed soup through a sieve to remove the pea skins.

The soup can be served hot or cold — although, in the summer, the vivid green colour of the chilled soup is very cooling. | Serves 6

750g	fresh or frozen petit pois	1¾ lbs
250g	fresh watercress plus a few extra leaves to decorate	9 oz
1.5 litres	wheat/gluten-free vegetable stock sea salt and freshly ground black pepper	2½ pints

1. Put the peas in a large pan with all the watercress (stalks and all) apart from what you want to use for decoration.
2. Add the stock and bring slowly to the boil.
3. Simmer for only a few minutes as you want the peas to remaining fresh tasting.
4. Purée very thoroughly in a food processor or liquidiser and then rub through a sieve if you want it to be totally smooth.
5. Season to taste with sea salt and freshly ground black pepper.
6. Chill thoroughly if it is to be served cold.
7. When ready to serve, stir well to re-amalgamate the soup as it will have separated. If it is to be served hot, reheat.
8. Pick off the smaller leaves from the remaining watercress, tearing in half any that are too big.
9. Serve in bowls or a tureen with the extra watercress leaves scattered over the top.

Note: The stalks of herbs such as watercress and parsley are often discarded but, in fact, they have an excellent flavour even if they are a bit tough.

Cook them in your soup or stew then either discard them or purée them as in this soup.

CELERY AND RICE SOUP WITH LEMONGRASS

The very long slow cooking gives this soup great flavour and texture — not unlike your granny's barley soup — but without the gluten. | Serves 6

2 tbsp	olive oil	2 tbsp
1	large onion, finely chopped	1
4	sticks celery, cleaned and finely chopped	4
1	piece of lemongrass, cut in 4 pieces	1
100g	wholegrain rice	4 oz
200ml	dry white wine	7 fl oz
1.75 litres	wheat/gluten-free vegetable stock	3 pints
25g	wild rice	1 oz
150g	fresh spinach, either young leaves or older ones, chopped (optional)	6 oz
	sea salt and freshly ground black pepper	

1. Heat the oil in a large pan and add the onion and celery. Cover and sweat for 20-25 minutes or until they are soft.
2. Add the lemongrass and wholegrain rice and continue to cook for a couple of minutes.
3. Add the wine and stock, bring to the boil, reduce the heat and simmer, covered, for 1 hour.
4. Add the wild rice and continue to cook for a further 30 minutes.
5. Meanwhile, steam the spinach leaves, if you are using them.
6. Season the soup to taste and stir in the spinach just before serving.

Note: The long slow cooking of this soup is essential to release the starches from the rice. It is hard to believe, when you start the cooking, that it will end up as thick and unctuous as it does. But even when cooked, and provided you have used a wholegrain rice, it will retain the texture of the grains.

SARDINE HUMMUS

Hummus is incredibly easy to make and always popular. Adding sardines to the mix is really tasty, gives it a different slant and adds significant nutritional benefit in terms of both calcium and omega 3 fatty acids.

Many people like to include tahini in their hummus so feel free to add some if you wish to. | Serves 6

2 x 400g	tins chickpeas, drained	2 x 14 oz
3-4	cloves garlic, peeled	3-4
½ tsp	ground cumin	½ tsp
	juice 2-3 lemons	
2 x 120g	tins whole sardines	2 x 7 oz
	extra oil olive	
2 tbsp	tahini (optional)	2 tbsp
	sea salt and freshly ground black pepper	

1. Put the chickpeas, garlic, cumin, lemon juice and the sardines with their oil in a food processor and purée till the purée is as smooth as you want it — how smooth or bitty you make it is a matter of taste.
2. If it is too thick add a little extra oil and season to taste.
3. Add the tahini if you are using it and then season to taste.
4. Serve with crudités, gluten-free toast or crackers, rice cakes or whatever you can eat.

Note: This is a great recipe for non-dairy eaters worried about their calcium intake as the sardines, provided they still have their bones, are an excellent source of calcium, as are chickpeas which have almost as much calcium as milk. Other foods with significant levels of calcium include sesame seeds, almonds, tofu, other legumes apart from chickpeas and a number of green vegetables.

AUBERGINE AND NUT BUTTER PÂTÉ

Aubergine pâtés on their own can be very sloppy — and nut and seed butters tend to be very solid — so combining them seemed the ideal answer. I used an almond and hazelnut butter but you could equally well use peanut, cashew, pumpkin seed or sesame, depending on your taste. | Serves 6

1	large aubergine	1
½	head of fresh garlic	½
3 tbsp	nut or seed butter of your choice	3 tbsp
	sea salt and freshly ground black pepper	

1. Wipe the aubergine and cut into large chunks. Peel the garlic cloves and halve. Put both into a steamer and steam for 10 minutes or until the aubergine is quite soft.
2. Transfer to a food processor and add the nut butter. Purée thoroughly and season to taste.
3. Serve with crudités or gluten-free bread or crackers.

Note: Despite the universal popularity of peanut butter, very few people know about the delicious 'butters' that you can make from other nuts and seeds. Because all nuts and seeds contain relatively high levels of fats they make good 'butters' — but are still very healthy as the fats they contain are mainly mono and polyunsaturated fats, not saturated.

SARDINE AND AVOCADO SALAD

Recipes always give you quantities for four or six — but what if you are looking for ideas just for yourself? So here is a suggestion for lunch or dinner for one — which can easily be multiplied up if you want to feed more than just yourself. | Serves 1 or 6

6	thin slices of cucumber, halved or quartered	6
	a handful of sprouted seeds	
2	spring onions, trimmed and chopped (optional)	2
	1 stick celery or ¼ head fennel, finely sliced/chopped	
¹/₈th	iceberg lettuce, chopped	¹/₈th
	small handful parsley, chopped	
1 tbsp	each mayonnaise (check ingredients) and plain sheep, goat or soya yogurt	1 tbsp
1 tbsp	olive oil	1 tbsp
	juice ½ lemon	
	sea salt and freshly ground black pepper	
½	avocado, peeled and sliced	½
2	tinned sardines	2

1. Mix the cucumber, sprouts, spring onions, celery or fennel, lettuce and parsley together.
2. In a separate bowl, mix the mayonnaise and yogurt, olive oil, lemon juice and a sprinkling of salt and pepper.
3. Lay the vegetables out on a plate, lay the avocado and sardines out on top and spoon over the dressing to serve.

Note: Sprouted seeds are believed to be especially nutritious as they are still alive and growing, so full of the many growth enzymes which cannot survive the days of storage and long distance transport to which many shop-bought vegetables are subjected.

SMOKED TROUT AND MELON SALAD

This is a very simple but lovely salad — ideal for a starter or a light lunch.
If you are unable to get fresh dill, substitute with fresh chives or a few fresh
basil leaves rather than using dried dill. | Serves 6

3	whole smoked trout, filleted or 12 smoked trout fillets	3
1½	ogen or charentais melons, skinned and the flesh diced	1½
3	small lemons	3
	a couple of sprigs of fresh dill weed	

1. Lay out the trout fillets on four plates, one fillet down either side leaving room for the melon in the middle.
2. Put the melon flesh in a bowl.
3. Pour over the juice of 2 of the lemons and chop over the dill.
4. Mix the melon well and pile in the middle of each plate.
5. Slice the remaining lemon thinly, cut them half through and twist into butterflies.
6. Decorate each serving with a twisted slice of lemon and serve with thinly sliced gluten-free brown bread or gluten-free crackers.

Note: Dried herbs are fine, in fact sometimes better than fresh ones in cooked dishes (because their flavour is more concentrated) but do not work in uncooked dishes such as salads.

CRUDITÉS WITH WASABI DIP

Crudités make a wonderfully flexible and healthy starter or lunch dish with any kind of dip. The vegetables can be chosen according to the season and be either raw or very lightly blanched.

Wasabi sauce is the green, extremely hot, horseradish sauce served with so many Japanese dishes. If you cannot find wasabi paste you could use finely grated fresh or bottled horseradish but not horseradish sauce as it often includes dairy products. | Serves 6 | Picture page 2

Any selection or combination of the following, washed or wiped and cut into matchsticks, bite-size dice or left whole as appropriate.

3	carrots	3
2	sticks celery	2
1	head fennel	1
	1 red and 1 green pepper	
12	cherry tomatoes	12
12	button mushrooms	12
1	head chicory	1
12	small Brussels sprouts	12
¼	red cabbage	¼
12	spring onions	12
½	head of broccoli or cauliflower	½
250g	goat, sheep or soya cream cheese	9 oz
1 tsp	wheat-free soya sauce or tamari	1 tsp
1 level tbsp	wasabi paste	1 level tbsp
1 tsp	lemon juice	1 tsp
	sea salt and freshly ground black pepper	

1. Prepare the vegetables.
2. Mix the cheese, tamari, wasabi paste and lemon juice together in a bowl then adjust seasoning to taste.
3. Serve with blanched or raw vegetables.

Note: This dip is especially delicious with fresh asparagus in season. Blanch the asparagus stalks in boiling water for just two minutes and then plunge into cold water. It should be quite crunchy but not totally raw.

CAULIFLOWER AND ANCHOVY SALAD

This is a rather unusual salad — based on a Roman recipe! The combination of cauliflower, anchovies and lemon works really well. | Serves 6

6	medium new potatoes, halved	6
1	medium head of cauliflower, broken into florets	1
3 tbsp	olive oil	3 tbsp
6	anchovies plus 2 tbsp oil from the tin	6
2	cloves garlic, crushed	2
	juice 2 lemons	
	freshly ground black pepper	

1. Steam the potatoes for 15-20 minutes until just cooked.
2. At the same time, steam the cauliflower in a separate pan for 10-15 minutes, until just cooked but still slightly crunchy.
3. Heat the oil in a heavy, wide pan and add the anchovies, their oil and the garlic.
4. Cook for several minutes or until the anchovies have partially dissolved.
5. Add the lemon juice and pepper (you should not need any salt), then add the potatoes, cut into large dice, and the cauliflower florets.
6. Toss well in the sauce and leave to marinate for at least 30 minutes before serving warm or at room temperature.

Note: Cauliflower originated in Asia Minor and was not known outside Italy until the 17th century — hence the Roman connection. It is also a good source of the photonutrient sulforaphane, vitamin C and folate.

POTATO AND CELERY AU GRATIN

Smells great and tastes even better. | Serves 6

750g	floury potatoes, scrubbed and halved crossways	1¾ lbs
4 tbsp	olive oil	4 tbsp
3	large sticks celery, chopped small	3
200g	field mushrooms, wiped and sliced	7 oz
	sea salt and freshly ground black pepper	
6-8 tbsp	plain goat, sheep's milk or soya yogurt	6-8 tbsp
75g	Roquefort (blue sheep cheese) or hard soya cheese	3 oz

1. Steam the potatoes for 10-15 minutes or until they are cooked.
2. Meanwhile, heat the oil in a pan and add the celery.
3. Cook for 4-5 minutes then add the sliced mushrooms and continue to cook for a further 4-5 minutes.
4. Cut the potatoes into thin slices and lay half in the bottom of an ovenproof casserole.
5. Season lightly then cover with the celery and mushrooms, season again and top with the remaining potatoes.
6. Spoon the yogurt over the potatoes and sprinkle over the cheese.
7. Brown under a grill, grind over some more black pepper and serve piping hot.

Note: Although no hard soya cheese is ever going to taste as good as a mature cheddar or a cave-aged Roquefort (soft soya cheeses are a much better match for animal milk cheese) they are very much better than they used to be and work quite well in dishes such as this.

COURGETTES WITH SUN-DRIED TOMATO SAUCE

It is a bit of a fiddle grilling the courgettes — but well worth the effort! The sun-dried tomato dip could be used with crackers, crudités or as a dressing for any other salad. | Serves 6

10	sun-dried tomato halves	10
	olive oil	
2	leeks, sliced very finely	2
8	cherry tomatoes, quartered	8
200ml	dry white wine	7 fl oz
12	medium-size courgettes, wiped	12
100ml	water	3 fl oz
pinch	pale muscovado sugar	pinch
	sea salt and freshly ground black pepper	

1. If the sun-dried tomatoes have been preserved in oil, remove from the oil (reserve it) and chop the tomatoes fairly small. If they were just dried, soak for 10 minutes in boiling water then drain and chop.
2. Heat 2 tbsp of the reserved or new oil in a heavy pan and add the sliced leeks; cook gently, uncovered, for 5 minutes.
3. Add sun-dried and cherry tomatoes and the white wine, stir well, bring to the boil, lower the heat, cover and simmer gently for 30-40 minutes.
4. While the sauce is cooking, with a sharp knife or a vegetable peeler, cut the courgettes lengthways into slices as thin as you can manage.
5. Lay them out on a griddle, drizzle with a little oil and grind over some salt and black pepper.
6. Cook briskly under a hot grill until tanned, then turn and repeat the process. Continue until all the slices are cooked.
7. Remove the sauce from the heat and purée in a food processor.
8. Thin with the water (you may need a little extra) and add sugar to taste. You should not need any further seasoning as the courgette slices are already well seasoned.
9. Serve with the courgette slices.

Note: If you are thinking about growing a few of your own vegetables, courgettes are amongst the easiest and most rewarding to grow. A small grow-bag in a tiny patio or even a really large window box could reward you with a fine crop.

GRILLED PEAR WITH WATERCRESS AND TOASTED CHEESE

An excellent lunch dish to make for one – which can very easily be multiplied up for four or six. The combination of the cool pear with the spicy watercress and the flavoursome cheese works really well. | Serves 1 or 6

1 slice	wheat-free dark rye or wholemeal gluten-free bread	1 slice
4	sprigs of watercress	4
6	walnut halves	6
½	fresh pear, peeled and sliced thickly lengthways	½
	2 slices (large enough to cover the pear) or 1 tbsp of Roquefort (blue sheep's cheese), soft blue goat's cheese or soft soya cheese	
	freshly ground black pepper	

1. Toast the slice of bread.
2. Lay the slice of bread on a grill pan and cover with the watercress then the walnut halves.
3. Lay the pear on top and cover it with whichever cheese you are using.
4. Cook under a hot grill till the cheese melts and runs through to the pear.
5. Grind over some black pepper and serve at once.

Note: If you are wheat rather than gluten allergic/intolerant you will be able to eat any of the huge range of rye breads which range from sourdough pumpernickel (very popular in Germany, very sustaining and very addictive) to much lighter, yeast-raised rye breads. However, take care when buying these as many of them use a combination of wheat and rye flour.

GRILLED CHEESE-STUFFED MUSHROOMS

You can use either the very large flat mushrooms (1 per person) for this dish or 2-3 smaller mushrooms for each person, depending on their size.

If you want to use them as a lunch dish you could serve each on a piece of toasted gluten and wheat-free bread — or a slice of wheat-free rye pumpernickel.

The mushrooms are particularly tasty hot, straight from the grill, but are also good cold as finger food or with a salad. | Serves 6 for lunch, a starter or as a cocktail snack

6	very large flat mushrooms or an appropriate number of smaller flat mushrooms	6
3 tbsp	olive oil	3 tbsp
2	medium onions	2
8	rashers back bacon	8
200g	hard goat, sheep or soya cheese	7 oz
	freshly ground black pepper	

1. Drizzle a little oil over the mushrooms and put them under a hot grill, cup side up, for 3-4 minutes.
2. Meanwhile, peel the onions and chop them very finely and cut the bacon rashers into small dice.
3. Heat the remaining oil in a small pan and add the onions and bacon. Cook fairly briskly for 5-8 minutes until the onions are lightly browned and the bacon crisped — but do not burn.
4. Grate the cheese.
5. Mix the cheese into the onion and bacon and pile into the mushroom cups.
6. Put the mushrooms back under the grill for 3-5 minutes or until the cheese has melted and browned — but not burnt. (The goat's or sheep's cheese will melt much faster than the soya cheese, which will become soft without melting in the same way.)
7. Remove from under the grill, grind over some black pepper and serve at once.
8. The mushrooms also taste good cold with a salad.

Note: Katherine Whitehorn famously declared that life was too short to stuff a mushroom — but she might have disagreed over these.

PASTA AND PIZZAS

Spaghetti Bolognese with Chicken Livers

Hemp Pasta Salad

Pasta and Pine Nut Salad

Fresh Salmon and Spinach Pasta

Soba Noodles with Smoked Salmon

Corkscrew Pasta with Savoy Cabbage

Cauliflower or Broccoli Pasta Salad

Hot Pasta Salad

Smoked Fish and Pasta Salad with Horseradish

Basic Pizza Base

'Sort of' Puttanesca Topping

Onion and Pepperoni Pizza Topping

Mushroom and Artichoke Pizza Topping

Wheat and Gluten-free Gnocchi

SPAGHETTI BOLOGNESE WITH CHICKEN LIVERS

This is a much loved stand-by and freezes excellently so it is always worth making extra for the freezer. The chicken livers add a good dose of vitamin A and will go unnoticed by both adults and children who would spurn a chicken liver if offered on its own. | Serves 6

2 tbsp	olive or sunflower oil	2 tbsp
3	bacon rashers, chopped small	3
300g	onions, peeled and chopped	10 oz
120g	carrots, peeled and diced small	5 oz
1	stick celery, chopped small	1
250g	minced beef	9 oz
100g	minced chicken livers	4 oz
2 tbsp	tomato purée	2 tbsp
	sea salt and freshly ground black pepper	
350ml	water or gluten and wheat-free stock	12 fl oz
350-500g	gluten and wheat-free spaghetti (some brands expand in cooking much more than others)	12-18 oz
50g	grated dairy-free cheese (optional)	2 oz

1. Heat the oil in a heavy, deep pan and gently brown the bacon.
2. Add the onion, carrot and celery and continue to cook until they are brown.
3. Add the beef and turn regularly so that it browns evenly.
4. Add the chicken livers, then, after a couple of minutes, the tomato purée.
5. Season lightly with the salt and pepper and add the liquid.
6. Cover the pan and simmer gently for 30-40 minutes.
7. Meanwhile cook the spaghetti according to the instructions on the pack.
8. To serve mix the sauce well into the pasta and serve at once, sprinkled with dairy-free cheese if you are using it.

Note: In the 1980s chicken liver pâté was an essential element in any good dinner party but chicken livers, along with most offal, have sadly fallen out of fashion. This is a shame as most offal is extremely nutritious. Chicken livers, although high in cholesterol, have a negligible amount of saturated fat but are high in protein, iron and vitamin C while a 25g/1 oz portion contains 62% of your daily vitamin A needs.

HEMP PASTA SALAD

The nuttiness of the hemp pasta is delicious in a salad. However, you could also use a buckwheat or brown rice pasta, which would give much the same effect.
| Serves 6

400g	hemp, buckwheat or brown rice spaghetti (see Resources, page 234)	14 oz
4 tbsp	olive oil	4 tbsp
	juice 2-3 lemons	
	sea salt and freshly ground black pepper	
	1 large head fennel, trimmed and sliced into thin matchsticks	
200g	tin water chestnuts, drained and sliced thinly	7 oz
3	small red onions, sliced very finely	3
100g	mixed rocket and lamb's lettuce or other green leaves	4 oz

1. Cook the spaghetti in plenty of salted water for 6-8 minutes or until it is just cooked but still has some bite.
2. Drain and turn into a large bowl with the oil and lemon juice and lots of salt and pepper.
3. Mix in the fennel, water chestnuts and onions. It will be quite difficult to get them well amalgamated with the pasta but worth the effort.
4. Adjust the seasoning to taste.
5. When you are ready to serve, chop and mix in the green leaves and serve at room temperature.

Note: Pasta made with grains other than durum wheat can vary widely in the amount that they 'bulk out' in the cooking so you need to experiment to see how much you will need — corn pastas, for example, expand very much the same amount as wheat whereas hemp or buckwheat expand much less.

PASTA AND PINE NUT SALAD

An excellent salad on its own or as an accompaniment to a meat or fish dish.

If you wanted to make it more substantial you could add some cold chicken breast or thigh cut into fingers. | Serves 4

350g	gluten and wheat-free spaghetti	12 oz
5-6 tbsp	virgin olive oil — I use a well flavoured Greek oil	5-6 tbsp
2 bunches	spring onions, trimmed and chopped	2 bunches
3 large handfuls	fresh parsley or coriander or a combination of the two, chopped	3 handfuls
75g	pine nuts	3 oz
	juice of 1-2 lemons	
	sea salt and freshly ground black pepper	

1. Cook the pasta according to the instructions on the pack.
2. When just al dente, remove from the heat, drain, and turn into a bowl.
3. Mix in 2 tbsp of the oil to prevent it sticking. Allow it to cool slightly.
4. Mix in the chopped spring onions, parsley or coriander, pine nuts and chicken if you are using it.
5. Season liberally with the freshly ground salt and pepper and dress with the lemon juice and extra oil to taste.

Note: Pine nuts, like peanuts, are not, despite their name, nuts. Pine nuts are in fact seeds, peanuts are legumes. Strangely, far more people who are allergic to 'proper' tree nuts (almonds, brazils, hazels etc) can tolerate pine nuts than can tolerate peanuts — yet people who react to pine nuts often also react to peanuts! So be glad that you only have to worry about dairy products, wheat and gluten.

FRESH SALMON AND SPINACH PASTA

A lovely light summer dish — very quick to make. If you cannot get gluten and wheat-free tagliatelle, you could use Japanese soba (buckwheat) noodles, which are also delicious. Alternatively, use a gluten and wheat-free spaghetti.
| Serves 6

6 tbsp	good olive oil	6 tbsp
1	medium onion, chopped small	1
150g	young courgettes, wiped and grated coarsely	6 oz
350g	baby spinach leaves	12 oz
350g	cooked fresh salmon, flaked finely	12 oz
	sea salt and freshly ground black pepper	
	juice of 1-2 lemons	
600g	gluten/wheat-free tagliatelle, spaghetti or soba noodles	1¼ lbs

1. Heat the oil in a heavy pan and gently cook the onion until nearly soft.
2. Add the grated courgettes and continue to cook for a minute or two.
3. Add the spinach to the onion and courgette, cover and cook for a few minutes or until the spinach is wilted.
4. Add the salmon and season to taste with the salt, pepper and lemon juice.
5. Meanwhile, cook the pasta in plenty of lightly salted boiling water according to the instructions on the pack.
6. Once the pasta is done, drain it, spoon it onto a dish or individual plates and spoon over the salmon and sauce.
7. Serve at once.

Note: Gluten and wheat-free pasta can be made from a variety of grains which not only bulk up more or less in the cooking, but take more or less time to cook. The cooking may also be affected by how the pasta was made so always, initially, follow the instructions on the pack. However, we have found that on-pack instructions are not always very accurate so test the pasta regularly so that you do not either under or over cook it.

SOBA NOODLES WITH SMOKED SALMON

Creamy pasta sauces were off the menu for those with dairy allergies but the arrival of soya and oat creams has changed all that. So indulge yourselves... If you cannot get either cream, you could also use a plain thick 'Greek' goat's milk yogurt; sheep and soya yogurts are thinner and will tend to separate when cooked. | Serves 6 | Picture page 47

550g	buckwheat soba noodles (make sure that they are made of buckwheat as thin wheat noodles can sometime also be called, incorrectly, soba noodles)	1¼ lbs
2 tbsp	olive oil	2 tbsp
100g	button mushrooms, finely sliced	4 oz
240ml	dry white wine	8 fl oz
1	heaped tsp of fresh dill, chopped or 1 level tsp of dried dill weed	1 tsp
300ml	soya or oat cream (or 230ml/8floz plain, thick goat's milk yogurt)	10 fl oz
225g	smoked salmon cut into thin matchsticks	8 oz
	a handful of fresh chives	
	juice of 1 lemon	
	sea salt and freshly ground black pepper	

1. Cook the noodles in plenty of fast boiling water according to the instructions on the pack but tasting them to make sure they remain just al dente.
2. Drain, turn into a serving dish or onto plates and keep warm.
3. Meanwhile, heat the oil in a heavy pan and add the mushrooms. Cook for several minutes until they are starting to soften.
4. Add the wine and, if you are using the dried version, the dill. Bring to the boil and simmer for a couple of minutes then remove from the heat and stir in the cream and the smoked salmon.
5. Add the lemon juice and seasoning to taste, spoon over the noodles, sprinkle with the chopped fresh dill, if you are using it, and serve at once.

Note: Buckwheat, or soba noodles are very popular in Japan usually served in a soup or hot broth — often as a fast food in train stations although they will also appear in gourmet restaurants. Do not confuse them with the thick udon noodles which are always made of wheat.

CORKSCREW PASTA WITH SAVOY CABBAGE

In the Italian tradition we normally serve pasta with a more or less substantial sauce but the pasta always remains the major ingredient. However, I also like to use it more as one of several equally important ingredients in a dish — as in this quite filling winter pasta dish where it is level pegging with the Savoy cabbage. As it stands it is a vegetarian dish but you could successfully add some well flavoured meat or fish — 150g/6 oz of spicy sausage, ham, pastrami or smoked mackerel would all be good. | Serves 6

6 tbsp	olive or sunflower oil	6 tbsp
3	medium onions, chopped roughly	3
550g	Savoy cabbage, chopped roughly	1¼ lbs
2 heaped tsp	caraway seeds, bruised with a rolling pin	2 heaped tsp
400ml	vegetable stock	14 fl oz
	sea salt and freshly ground pepper	
150g	spicy sausage, ham, pastrami or smoked mackerel (optional)	6 oz
400g	gluten/wheat-free corkscrews or penne	14 oz

1. Heat the oil in a large pan and gently fry the onions until just soft and lightly tanned.
2. Add the cabbage and continue to cook for a few minutes, then add the caraway seeds, stock and a little seasoning.
3. Simmer for 5-10 minutes or until the cabbage is cooked but still slightly crunchy.
4. If you are using it, mix in the meat or fish.
5. Meanwhile, cook the pasta according to the instructions of the pack, in fast boiling water until just al dente.
6. Drain and mix into the cabbage.
7. Adjust seasoning to taste and serve at once.

Note: Savoy cabbage is a lovely crinkly cabbage with a great flavour whose outer leaves are dark green and inner ones very pale but it is not always available. When it is not you could substitute one of the many varieties of Chinese cabbages — bok choi, pak choi etc.

CAULIFLOWER OR BROCCOLI PASTA SALAD

The ultimate 'swappable' dish. You can serve it hot or at room temperature as a salad, and include cauliflower or broccoli, spinach or peas, ham or chicken and seeds or nuts depending on your taste and your diet. Cold it also makes a great lunch for adults or kids. | Serves 6

	small head of cauliflower or a large head of broccoli, broken into florets	
200g	gluten/wheat-free pasta – spirals, penne or whatever shape that you fancy	7 oz
75g	fresh or frozen spinach leaf or frozen petits pois, defrosted	3 oz
200g	cooked ham or chicken, cut into bite-size pieces	7 oz
2 tbsp	pumpkin seeds, mixed roasted seeds or roasted, salted cashews	2 tbsp
	sea salt and freshly ground black pepper	
	juice 1 large lemon	
3-4 tbsp	virgin olive	3-4 tbsp

1. Steam the cauliflower or broccoli florets for 5-8 minutes until they are just cooked but retain a little crunch.
2. Meanwhile, cook the pasta according to the instructions on the pack and drain.
3. If you are going to have the dish hot, briefly heat the spinach (or peas) and the ham (or chicken) in a microwave or over hot water.
4. Gently mix the florets with the pasta, then mix in the vegetables and meat, and the seeds or nuts.
5. Mix them all well together then season to taste and dress with lemon juice and oil (whether you are serving the dish hot or cold).

Note: Mixed roasted seeds or nuts are a great addition to this sort of salad dish — even a pack of trailmix, if you have nothing else, will make a tasty and nutritious addition to your salad — and will often work in hot dishes too.

HOT PASTA SALAD

Most people either eat their pasta hot, or allow it to get cold and use it in, or with, a salad. However, I really like to combine hot pasta with cold salad ingredients — so that both end up warm. You can use the salad just as a vegetarian salad or you can add cheese (diced goat's, sheep's or soya cheese), fish (tinned sardines or tuna, smoked trout, salmon or mackerel) or meat — ham, chicken strips, salami (having checked the ingredients) or slithers of beef, or even diced tofu. | Serves 6

550g	gluten and wheat-free pasta of your choice — I often use a spaghetti but any other shape is fine	1 ¼ lbs
10	large spring onions or 2 leeks, trimmed and thinly sliced	10
1	large bulb of fennel, sliced very thinly	1
1	green pepper, de-seeded and sliced thinly	1
½	small cucumber, diced	½
2	avocados, peeled and sliced	2
6 handfuls	spinach, lamb's lettuce or watercress	6 handfuls
100g	pine nuts	4 oz
6 tbsp	cold pressed virgin olive oil	6 tbsp
	sea salt and freshly ground black pepper	
	juice 2 lemons	

1. Cook the pasta according to the instructions on the pack.
2. While the pasta is cooking slice the vegetables into a salad bowl. Add the leaves and nuts, and the cheese, meat or fish if you are using them.
3. When the pasta is cooked, drain thoroughly.
4. Return to the pan and add the olive oil and mix well.
5. Mix the salad into the pasta and season to taste with the sea salt and black pepper and lemon juice.

SMOKED FISH AND PASTA SALAD WITH HORSERADISH

You can make this salad with any smoked fish (the strong flavours of mackerel or haddock are particularly good) or with tinned sardines or tinned tuna. | Serves 6

300g	wheat and gluten-free pasta of your choice	11 oz
3	heads fennel, trimmed and sliced	3
2 tbsp	mixed dried sea vegetables	2 tbsp
	(you can get them in most health food stores or delis)	
4 tbsp	olive oil	4 tbsp
400g	smoked mackerel or hot-smoked haddock fillets	14 oz
4 tbsp	grated horseradish (not horseradish sauce)	4 tbsp
5 tbsp	mayonnaise (check ingredients)	5 tbsp
6 tbsp	plain goat, sheep's milk or soya yogurt	6 tbsp
	juice 2 lemons	
	sea salt and freshly ground black pepper	
	plenty of green leaves of your choice	

1. Cook the pasta in fast boiling salted water according to the instructions on the pack, then drain.
2. Meanwhile, steam the fennel for 8-10 minutes or until it is soft.
3. Add the fennel, sea vegetables and oil to the drained pasta and mix well.
4. Break up the fish and mix into the pasta.
5. Mix the horseradish with the mayonnaise, yogurt and lemon juice and season to taste. Use two-thirds of this mix to dress the salad and reserve the rest to serve with it.
6. To serve, pile the green leaves on a dish or in a bowl and the pasta and fish mix in the middle. Serve with the extra sauce.

Note: 'Real' mayonnaise is made from egg, salt, pepper, lemon juice or vinegar and oil so should be fine for anyone on a dairy-free diet. However, if using shop bought you should check the ingredients carefully as either a dairy product or a starch binder might have been used.

BASIC PIZZA BASE

It is now relatively easy to buy gluten or wheat-free pizza bases (see Resources, page 234) but if you are unable to do so — or would prefer to make your own — the two mixtures below make very acceptable thin and crispy bases.

The xanthan gum (see page 236) is not absolutely essential but does help to hold the mixture together. | Enough for 1 x 20cm/8inch pizza base

	Chickpea base	
150g	chickpea (gram) flour	5 oz
50g	rice flour	2 oz
1 level tsp	xanthan gum	1 level tsp
1 level tsp	easy-bake yeast	1 level tsp
½ tsp	salt	½ tsp
1 tbsp	olive or sunflower oil	1 tbsp
100ml	lukewarm water	4 fl oz

1. Sift the chickpea and rice flour and the xanthan gum together.
2. Stir in the yeast, salt and oil then the water.
3. Mix to a smooth dough and knead for a couple of minutes.
4. Put in a bowl, cover with cling film and leave in a warm place for 1 hour to rise. It will not rise as much as a bread but should increase by 30-40%.
5. Heat the oven to 190C/375F/gas mark 5.
6. Roll out the pizza dough on a floured board and transfer to a baking tray.
7. You can bake it at this point, then top it later when you need it — or you can add the topping now.
8. If un-topped, bake for 10-15 minutes or until crisp but not burnt. If topped you will need to cook it for 4-5 minutes longer.

	Buckwheat base	
100g	buckwheat flour	4 oz
75g	rice flour	3 oz
1 level tsp	xanthan gum	1 level tsp
1 level tsp	easy-bake yeast	1 level tsp
½ tsp	salt	½ tsp
1 tbsp	olive or sunflower oil	1 tbsp
150ml	lukewarm water	¼ pint

1. Proceed as for the gram flour base.

PIZZA TOPPINGS

Mozzarella or cheese of some sort is such an integral part of a pizza that being forbidden cheese can look as though it spells the end of eating pizzas. However, this need not be the case. Soya cheese, although it is never going to taste like the real thing, is so much better than it was and can be quite tasty, in relatively small quantities, on top of a well-flavoured pizza. One American company, To-futti (see Resources, page 234) has even come up with a soya mozzarella which melts really well.

But, to be tasty, a pizza topping does not need to contain cheese. Here are some suggestions, all of which are delicious in their own right and all totally dairy free.

'SORT OF' PUTTANESCA TOPPING

Since not everyone is as anchovy mad as I am, anchovy haters could substitute salami for the anchovy in this topping. | Serves 6

2 tbsp	olive oil	2 tbsp
4	large cloves garlic, peeled and crushed	4
2 x 400g	tins plum tomatoes, roughly mashed	2 x 14 oz
	leaves from 1 large sprig fresh rosemary or 1 sprig or 2 tsp dried	
24-30	stuffed green olives, depending on size, halved or sliced	24-30
6	large anchovies, chopped finely	6
	or 6 slices spicy salami (check ingredients) cut into small matchsticks	
	sea salt and freshly ground black pepper	

1. Heat the oil in a heavy, deep pan and gently fry the garlic for a few minutes.
2. Add the tomatoes, rosemary, half the olives and the anchovies or salami.
3. Bring to the boil then reduce the heat and simmer, uncovered, for 30-35 minutes — the tomatoes need to reduce to a thick sauce.
4. Season to taste.
5. When ready to cook, spread over the pizza base, scatter the remaining olives over the top and bake for 15 minutes in a hot oven.

ONION AND PEPPERONI PIZZA TOPPING

I have allowed for a thick layer of onions under the sausage; if you are less of an onion fan, reduce to three large onions. | Serves 6 | Picture page 6

3 tbsp	olive oil	3 tbsp
	4 large or 8 medium onions, peeled and sliced thinly	
100g	sliced spicy sausage or your choice –	4 oz
	but check the ingredients carefully	
	freshly ground black pepper	
	chilli oil (optional)	

1. Heat the oil in a wide pan and add the onions. Cook very gently for 45-60 minutes, stirring regularly, until the onions are quite soft and slightly caramelised.
2. To cook spread the onions over the pizza base and arrange the sausage over the top. Bake for 15 minutes in a hot oven.
3. Grate over some black pepper, drizzle with a little chilli oil and serve.

MUSHROOM AND ARTICHOKE PIZZA TOPPING

The lemon juice is not essential but just adds a little bite. | Serves 6

2 tbsp	olive oil	2 tbsp
150g	chestnut or button mushrooms, wiped and sliced	6 oz
6-8	tinned artichoke hearts, drained and quartered	6-8
	juice 1 small lemon (optional)	
	sea salt and freshly ground black pepper	

1. Heat the oil in a heavy, deep pan and briskly fry the mushrooms for 3-5 minutes or until the juices run. Spoon them over the pizza base.
2. Arrange the artichoke heart quarters over the top.
3. Squeeze over the lemon juice if you are using it and season generously with sea salt and freshly ground black pepper.
4. Bake for 15 minutes in a hot oven.

WHEAT AND GLUTEN-FREE GNOCCHI

Commercially bought gnocchi nearly always contain wheat flour but this recipe, a traditional one from northern Italy uses only potatoes and egg. | Serves 6 as a starter, 4 as a main dish

1 kg	floury, baking type potatoes	2¼ lbs
1	egg, beaten	1
100g	potato flour	4 oz
1 level tsp	salt	1 level tsp

1. Steam the potatoes in their skins till just cooked.
2. Remove and, while still hot, purée in a ricer or through the small disc of a food mill, onto a work surface lightly floured with potato flour.
3. Spread the purée out to cool it then, gradually, add the beaten egg, the salt and most (all, if you need it) of the potato flour.
4. Knead gently until you have a soft dough which is smooth and slightly sticky.
5. Roll into 2.5cm/ 1 inch long sausages.
6. Press a fork down lightly in the middle of each gnocchi.
7. When you are ready to serve them, bring a large pan of lightly salted water to the boil.
8. Cook the gnocchi in batches, by lowering each batch into the water with a slotted spoon. They will sink to the bottom, so stir them lightly to prevent them sticking — very soon after they will float to the top.
9. Count slowly to 10, then remove with the slotted spoon and keep warm while you cook the next batch.
10. Serve with olive oil and the sauce of your choice.

Note: The original of this recipe was given to me by Anna del Conte, the doyenne of Italian cookery writers, any or all of whose books are a delight to read, let alone to cook from.

EGG DISHES

Beetroot and Egg Salad

Tuna Tortilla with Watercress

Egg and Black Rice Salad

Artichoke and Spinach Quiche

Hard-boiled Eggs with Spinach

Hamine Eggs with Aduki Beans

Baked Sweet Potatoes with Eggs

Jersey Royals with Soft-boiled Eggs

Summer Omelette

BEETROOT AND EGG SALAD

Simple, tasty and colourful. You need to use a peppery leaf such as watercress or rocket as a contrast to the smoother and sweeter flavours of the beetroots and eggs. | Serves 6

6	small-medium raw beetroots	6
6	eggs	6
	sea salt and freshly ground black pepper	
6	handfuls of rocket or watercress	6
2 tbsp	plain goat, sheep's milk or soya yogurt, depending on what you can eat	2 tbsp
	juice ½ lemon	
	small bunch of fresh dill	

1. Top and tail the beets, halve them and steam for 15-20 minutes or until a knife goes in easily.
2. Hard boil the eggs, cool and then shell.
3. Arrange the leaves around the outside of a serving dish.
4. Slice the beets into fairly thin rounds, maximum 1cm/¼ inch thick, and arrange the bigger slices around the outside, leaving the end pieces aside.
5. Slice the hard-boiled eggs and once again arrange the larger slices on the plate, reserving the smaller bits.
6. In a bowl mix the yogurt with the lemon juice and season to taste.
7. Chop the remaining bits of beetroot and egg and mix them into the yogurt.
8. Pile into the middle of the dish and decorate with plenty of chopped dill.

Note: In the UK fresh beetroot has only fairly recently come back into favour and been recognised for the delicious and highly nutritious food that it is (for many years it was only ever to be found cooked in a watery, vinegary dressing which entirely killed its natural flavour). Both the root and the leaves are thought to be anti-carcinogenic, and both are high in folate, iron, and potassium. Freshly steamed young beetroots with a little olive oil or goat butter (if you can eat it) and freshly ground sea salt are a real treat.

TUNA TORTILLA WITH WATERCRESS

Delicious hot or cold with a salad or for a picnic but also tasty and filling, sliced, in a lunch box. | Serves 4 as a main course

4 tbsp	olive oil	4 tbsp
2	leeks, finely sliced	2
1	head fennel, finely sliced	1
1 x 400g	tin artichoke hearts, drained	1 x 14 oz
1 x 400g	tin cannellini beans (optional)	1 x 14 oz
100-150g	fresh spinach leaves, torn up roughly	4-5 oz
1	bunch watercress, thick stalks removed	1
2	fresh tuna steaks	2
6	eggs	6
	sea salt and freshly ground black pepper	
	juice 1 lemon	

1. Heat 3 tbsp of the oil in a wide, deep pan and add the leeks and fennel. Cook gently for 5-10 minutes or until they are quite soft. Quarter the artichoke hearts. Add these along with the beans and mix gently but thoroughly into the vegetables. Add the spinach and watercress, cover the pan and allow them to wilt for 3-4 minutes over the heat. Gently mix them so that the leaves are well distributed.

2. Meanwhile, add the remaining oil to a separate pan, heat, and briskly sear the tuna steaks on both sides. Remove from the pan and cut into bite-size chunks.

3. Add the chunks of tuna to the vegetables in the pan and season with sea salt, freshly ground black pepper and lemon juice. Beat the eggs in a separate bowl.

4. Add 2 tbsp cold water and season. Pour the egg mixture into the vegetable pan and mix well. Increase the heat and cook briskly for 3-4 minutes or until the egg starts to set. If possible move the pan under a hot grill to finish cooking the eggs and lightly toast the top of the tortilla. Serve hot or cold.

EGG AND BLACK RICE SALAD

Black Nanjing rice is very exotic (to be found in delis and upmarket food stores) but you can make the dish equally well with a wholemeal brown rice or even with a white rice. However, the colour contrast between the black rice and the yellow and white eggs is very effective.

If you cannot eat soya you can use a soya/gluten-free stock instead of the miso although the flavour will be different. | Serves 6

6	eggs	6
1	dried red chilli, chopped small	1
200g	mini tomatoes, halved or quartered	7 oz
50g	sun-dried tomatoes, chopped	2 oz
1 tsp	cumin seeds, lightly crushed in a bowl with the end of a rolling pin	1 tsp
200g	black Nanjing rice	7 oz
1¼ litres	miso (made with 1 tbsp miso and 1¼ litres boiling water)	2¼ pints
1 x 400g	tin water chestnuts, drained and halved horizontally	1 x 14 oz

1. Hard boil the eggs.
2. In a wide pan heat the chilli pieces for a few minutes but do not allow to burn. Add the fresh tomatoes and cook briskly for a few minutes to soften the tomatoes and draw out their liquid.
3. Add the sun-dried tomatoes and cumin seeds and continue to cook for another few minutes.
4. Add the rice, stir around and then add half of the liquid. Bring back to the boil and simmer fairly briskly for 20-30 minutes, topping up the liquid as needed.
5. When the rice is cooked, add the water chestnuts and season with sea salt and freshly ground black pepper, if it needs it.
6. To serve, pile the rice in the middle of a serving dish. Shell and halve the eggs and arrange them around the rice.

Note: Nanjing 'black' rice comes from the coastal region at the base of the Yangtze river. The rice is unmilled and it is the rice bran, rather than the grain that is black. It is very dramatic to look at and has a quite strong, slightly smoky flavour.

ARTICHOKE AND SPINACH QUICHE

A quiche is a complete no-go area for anyone with dairy and wheat or gluten sensitivities, as a 'normal' quiche contains substantial quantities of all of them. However, you can make a very satisfactory quiche filling with non-dairy milks, and gluten-free pastry with one of the many alternative flours. | Serves 6 | Picture page 63

Pastry

300g/12 oz flour — you can use your own favourite gluten-free flour, a proprietary mix or my favourite — 200g/7 oz gram flour with 100g/4 oz rice flour — well sifted

150g	goat's butter or dairy-free spread	6 oz
50-75ml	ice cold water	2-3 fl oz

Filling

3	rashers of back bacon	3
½ tbsp	olive oil	½ tbsp
4	tinned artichoke hearts	4
large handful	fresh baby spinach leaves	large handful
4	eggs	4
400ml	goat, sheep, soya or oat milk	14 fl oz
	sea salt and freshly ground black pepper	

---

1. Put the flour in a food processor with the butter or spread and whizz till it has the texture of breadcrumbs.
2. Add the water and whizz again briefly.
3. Remove from the processor, roll into a ball and wrap in clingfilm and chill for 15 minutes.
4. Meanwhile heat the oven to 180C/350F/gas mark 4.
5. Roll out the pastry and line a 20cm/8 inch flan dish. If the pastry crumbles just use pieces to patch.
6. Line with greaseproof paper, weight with beans and bake blind for 15 minutes.
7. Remove the paper and beans and continue to cook for a further 15 minutes or until the pastry is crisp.
8. Cut the bacon into small dice.
9. Heat the olive oil in a pan and fry the bacon pieces briskly until they are crisp and tanned but not burnt.
10. Drain the artichoke hearts and cut into quarters. Mix the artichoke hearts, spinach and bacon well and strew over the bottom of the flan dish.
11. Beat the eggs in a bowl and add whichever milk you are using.
12. Season with sea salt and freshly ground black pepper.
13. Pour the milk mixture over the vegetables and bacon in the flan dish and bake for 30 minutes or until the flan is slightly risen and firm to the touch. Allow to cool slightly before serving.

HARD-BOILED EGGS WITH SPINACH

A very traditional combination, given a little spice by the slightly bitter chicory. Lovely as a summer lunch dish. | Serves 6

1 kg	fresh spinach	2½ lbs
25g	goat's butter or dairy-free spread	1 oz
	sea salt, freshly ground black pepper and ground nutmeg	
6	eggs	6
2 tbsp	plain goat, sheep's milk or soya yogurt	2 tbsp
	juice ½ lemon	
1	head chicory, finely chopped	
	large handful fresh chives, chopped small	

1. Cook the spinach in 2cm/½ inch of water and drain thoroughly.
2. Add the butter or spread, stir well and season with salt, pepper and nutmeg.
3. Meanwhile, hard boil the eggs. When cooked, shell and slice.
4. In a bowl mix the yogurt with the lemon juice and season to taste.
5. Mix in the chicory and chives.
6. Arrange the spinach in the base of a serving dish with the eggs over it.
7. Spoon over the dressing and serve at once.

Note: Although baby spinach leaves can now be found in the salad chillers of most supermarkets, their flavour is a pale shadow of the more mature field spinach usually only available through farmers' markets and organic boxes. If you can get the latter you will soon taste the difference.

HAMINE EGGS WITH ADUKI BEANS

This recipe is based on one from North Africa for very slow cooked eggs with fava beans. Try to cook it at least a day before you want to eat it to allow the flavours time to mature. | Serves 6

200g	dried aduki beans	7 oz
6	large eggs	6
2	medium onions	2
6	large cloves garlic	6
3 tbsp	olive oil	3 tbsp
2 level tsp	cumin powder	2 level tsp
150g	red lentils	5 oz
1.2 litres	miso or gluten/wheat-free vegetable stock	2 pints
	sea salt and freshly ground black pepper	
2	large handfuls fresh parsley, ideally flat leaf	2

1. Soak the beans in plenty of cold water for 4-5 hours.
2. Cook the eggs very slowly (2-3 hours at a bare simmer) in plenty of water with a few onion skins or coffee grounds to tint them lightly. Allow to cool in the water and then peel and discard the shells.
3. When the beans have been soaked, discard the water and put them in a deep pan covered in fresh cold water. Bring to the boil and simmer, uncovered, for 45 minutes then drain.
4. Meanwhile, peel the onions and garlic and chop finely in a food processor.
5. Heat the oil in a deep, heavy pan and add the cumin. Stir well then add the minced onion and garlic. Cook very gently for 20-30 minutes or until the vegetables are quite soft.
6. Add the lentils, stir well then add the stock. Bring to the boil and simmer, uncovered for a further 30 minutes or until the lentils are cooked and mushy.
7. Add the aduki beans and the eggs and stir very gently so as not to damage the eggs.
8. The dish should be very juicy so if you think it needs extra liquid, add extra stock or miso at this stage.
9. Season lightly and set aside in a larder or fridge for up to 24 hours.
10. To serve, reheat the pan very gently. Adjust the seasoning to taste and serve with lots of freshly chopped parsley.

BAKED SWEET POTATOES WITH EGGS

You can serve this dish either as a supper or lunch dish (with the eggs) or as a vegetable (without the eggs). It is also a good dish for children who love the sweetness of the potato — and can dip gluten-free bread 'soldiers' into the eggs. | Serves 6

1 kg	sweet potatoes, peeled and sliced/diced	2¼ lbs
3-4	large cloves garlic, peeled	3-4
1 tbsp	pumpkin or walnut oil	1 tbsp
	(if you find them difficult to get, olive or sunflower oil will be fine but not as tasty)	
1 tbsp	maple syrup	1 tbsp
	sea salt and freshly ground black pepper	
2 tbsp	sunflower seeds, roughly chopped in a food processor	2 tbsp
6	eggs	6

1. Peel and dice the sweet potato and peel the garlic cloves.
2. Put them both in a steamer and steam for 15-20 minutes or till both are quite soft.
3. Meanwhile, heat the oven to 180C/350F/gas mark 4.
4. When soft, purée the sweet potato in a food processor along with the oil and maple syrup.
5. Season to taste with sea salt and freshly ground black pepper.
6. If you want to serve the purée as a vegetable, add the sunflower seeds and reheat.
7. If you want to serve it with eggs, spoon it into an ovenproof casserole and make six indentations in the purée.
8. Break an egg into each then sprinkle the sunflower seeds over the eggs.
9. Bake for 15-20 minutes or until the eggs are just set and serve at once with a green salad or vegetable.

Note: Despite their name, sweet potatoes are botanically quite different to 'normal' potatoes — the former belong to the *Convolvulaceae* family, the latter to the *Solanacaea*. Not only are sweet potatoes quite delicious, they are also rich in complex carbohydrates, protein, vitamins A and C, and, unlike normal potatoes, very rarely cause allergic reactions.

JERSEY ROYALS WITH SOFT-BOILED EGGS

The Jersey Royal potato season is so short that it is worth making the most of it – although the dish will taste good with any new potatoes.

If you wish you can dress the leaves with a little cider vinegar and virgin olive oil but I felt that the egg yolk was sufficient. This makes a lovely lunch or light supper dish. | Serves 6

750g	Jersey Royal new potatoes	1¾ lbs
6 handfuls	each of fresh rocket and fresh watercress	6 handfuls
12	spring onions	12
	sea salt and freshly ground black pepper	
6	eggs	6

1. Scrub the potatoes, halve any large ones and steam them for 10-15 minutes or until cooked.
2. Meanwhile, break up the rocket and watercress leaves and trim and slice the spring onions. Mix them all together.
3. Season lightly with sea salt and freshly ground black pepper.
4. Boil the eggs for 4-5 minutes depending on the size – you want the white to be cooked but the yolk still runny.
5. Remove from the boiling water and plunge into cold water to stop them cooking any further.
6. Pile the green leaves into the middle of six plates. Arrange the new potatoes around the outside of the leaves. Carefully shell the eggs and break each one in half over the leaves so that the yolk spills out.
7. Grind over a little more black pepper and serve at once.

Note: The Jersey Royal, the very first new potato of the season with its unique flavour, was first known as the Jersey Royal fluke. In the 1870s a Jersey farmer called Hugh de la Haye was given an unusual potato with 15 eyes. He planted it and the following season, it produced very early, particularly well-flavoured kidney-shaped potatoes. De la Haye started to export his potatoes to London where they had a huge success; by the late 1890s, a usual crop export of Jersey Royals would be in the region of 60,000 tonnes – at 140 shillings per tonne! Today the Jersey Royal is the only potato that can be exported from the island.

SUMMER OMELETTE

Very delicious, very easy, very flexible (you can add or subtract ingredients as you feel inclined) and as good cold as hot. However, if making for six, you may need to use two pans. | Serves 6

6 tbsp	olive oil	6 tbsp
3	medium onions, sliced thinly	3
2	sticks celery, washed and chopped	2
½ each	of a red, green and yellow pepper, sliced thinly	½ each
6-8	mushrooms, sliced	6-8
1	medium courgette, grated coarsely	1
150g	baby spinach leaves	6 oz
large handful	parsley	large handful
10	eggs	10
	sea salt and freshly ground black pepper	
4 slices	chicken or ham, cut into small pieces	4 slices
150g	sheep's milk or soya feta, crumbled (optional)	5 oz

1. Heat the oil and add the onions, celery and peppers and cook gently till they are starting to soften.
2. Add the mushrooms and courgettes and continue to cook till the latter are softening, then add the spinach and parsley and stir around for a minute till the spinach wilts.
3. Heat a grill.
4. Beat the eggs in a bowl, season, add the meat and cheese and immediately tip into the pan and stir round well to mix.
5. Increase the heat slightly and cook for 2 minutes or until the egg is starting to set.
6. Move to under a grill for a further 2 minutes or until the top is cooked.

Note: This is an excellent dish for a lunch box or picnic as it is very nutritious and quite filling, tastes as good cold as hot and does not get squashed.

FISH

Smoked Mussel and Shrimp Pilaff

Tuna with Tomato Concasse

Celery Scallops with Arame Quinoa

Haddock and Egg Pie

King Prawn Gumbo

Stir-fried Tuna with Chilli

Moules Marinière

Red Cabbage with Smoked Salmon

Lemon Sole Stuffed with Seaweed and Wild Rice

Smoked Mackerel and Potato Salad

Baian Seafood Stew

Sardine Potatoes

Fillets of Salmon and Cod with Coconut Milk and Lemongrass

Baked Trout with Oregano and Green Bean Pasta

Fish Soup

Prawns in Coconut Milk

Quinoa Stuffed Trout Fillets

Anchovy and Mushroom Risotto

Smoked Haddock Burgers in Aubergine 'Buns'

SMOKED MUSSEL AND SHRIMP PILAFF

A useful dish that works as well hot as cold. You should be able to get tinned smoked mussels or oysters in delicatessens or better stocked supermarkets and dried shrimp in any Chinese supermarket. Since it is quite a filling dish, serve it just with a green leaf salad. | Serves 6

75g	dried shrimp	3 oz
4 tbsp	olive oil	4 tbsp
4 x 85g	tins smoked mussels or oysters	4 x 3 oz
12	large spring onions, trimmed and chopped	12
2 heaped tsp	ground cumin	2 heaped tsp
1 heaped tsp	ground coriander	1 heaped tsp
2 heads	chicory, chopped	2 heads
200g	small button mushrooms, wiped and halved	7 oz
500g	red Camargue or wholegrain brown rice	1¼ lbs
1 litre	gluten-free fish stock or water	1¾ pints
400ml	dry white wine	14 fl oz
	sea salt and freshly ground black pepper	
	juice from 2 lemons	
2 handfuls	fresh flat parsley or coriander	2 handfuls

1. Soak the shrimp in boiling water for 4 minutes then drain.
2. Heat the olive oil, plus the oil from the fish cans, in a wide pan.
3. Add the spring onions with the cumin and coriander and cook for a couple of minutes.
4. Add the chicory and continue to cook for another 3-4 minutes.
5. Add the mushrooms, cook for another few minutes, then add the shrimp and the rice.
6. Stir well, fry the rice for a couple of minutes and then add the fish stock or water and wine. Bring to the boil and simmer briskly, uncovered, for 20-25 minutes or until the rice is nearly cooked and the liquid nearly absorbed.
7. Add the smoked mussels or oysters and season lightly.
8. Simmer gently for another few minutes then turn off the heat and leave for several hours for the flavours to amalgamate.
9. Before serving, add the lemon juice and adjust the seasoning to taste.
10. Chop the parsley or coriander and stir into the pilaf.
11. Serve warm or at room temperature.

Note: Although neither oysters nor mussels contain any omega 3 fatty acids, prawns do, and all three are very good sources of selenium, vitamin B12 and zinc while the wholegrain rice contains thiamin, niacin, vitamin B6, iron, magnesium and potassium — so this is a seriously nutritious dish!

TUNA WITH TOMATO CONCASSE

Cooking fish in a casserole is a very easy, and a very tasty, way to do it especially for a relatively firm fish such as tuna.

Including the sun-dried tomatoes in the vegetable combination allows them to rehydrate slowly and deepens the flavour much more effectively than soaking them in boiling water. | Serves 6

4 tbsp	olive oil	4 tbsp
2	medium onions, peeled and sliced	2
6	cloves garlic, peeled and thinly sliced	6
3	sticks celery, washed and chopped	3
2	medium red peppers, trimmed and thinly sliced	2
50g	sun-dried tomatoes, cut small	2 oz
450g	cherry or plum tomatoes, halved	1 lb
	sea salt and freshly ground black pepper	
6	frcsh tuna steaks or fillets	6
	juice 1 lemon	

1. Heat the oil in a wide pan and add the onions, garlic, celery and peppers, and cook gently for 15 minutes or until the vegetables are softening.
2. Meanwhile, season the tuna thoroughly on both sides with sea salt and freshly ground black pepper.
3. Add the sun-dried and fresh tomatoes to the vegetables and continue to cook gently, uncovered, for a further 15-20 minutes or until the tomatoes are entirely broken down.
4. Add the tuna steaks or fillets to the vegetables, bed them well down, cover the pan and cook for a further 6-8 minutes or until the fish is cooked through.
5. Squeeze over the lemon juice, adjust the seasoning to taste and serve with new potatoes or rice and a green salad.

Note: A concasse is a French term usually applied to tomatoes which are peeled and then chopped to a particular size so to use it in this context is stretching it somewhat — but does make the dish sound more interesting!

CELERY SCALLOPS WITH ARAME QUINOA

This recipe was originally devised for someone who had very wide ranging salicylate intolerance (a condition which bars you from eating most fruits and vegetables). Celery, iceberg lettuce and sea vegetables were about the only vegetables that she could eat. In fact, the combination worked so well that it became one of our favourite recipes. | Serves 6

½ tsp	sea salt	½ tsp
250g	quinoa	9 oz
2 heaped tbsp	dried arame (Japanese seaweed)	2 heaped tbsp
	10-15 grinds black pepper	
12 sticks	celery, washed and sliced crossways	12 sticks
¾	of a medium iceberg lettuce, chopped roughly	¾
	200ml/6 fl oz white wine or 100ml/3 fl oz medium dry sherry and 100ml/3 fl oz water	
24	fresh scallops	24
	pumpkin oil	

1. Add the sea salt to a pan of fast boiling water then add the quinoa with the arame and black pepper.
2. Boil briskly, uncovered, for 7-10 minutes or until the quinoa is soft but still has some texture. Drain and keep warm.
3. Meanwhile, steam the celery pieces over boiling water for 8 minutes or until they are softening but still have a little crispness.
4. Add the lettuce, mix well together and continue to steam for a further 5 minutes.
5. At the same time, heat the wine or sherry and water in a pan and add the scallops.
6. Simmer very gently for 4-5 minutes or until they are just cooked.
7. Arrange the quinoa around the edge of a serving dish or on individual plates.
8. Pile the celery and lettuce mixture in the middle and arrange the scallops on the top. Grind over a little extra black pepper and drizzle over a little pumpkin oil. Serve at once.

Note: Arame is a seaweed which can be bought, dried, in thin black fronds. It is very popular in Japanese cooking and is mild and pleasant in flavour. It can be added to soups, stews, vegetables or grains as they cook. Like most seaweeds it is very nutritious being particularly high in calcium, iron and iodine.

HADDOCK AND EGG PIE

A good old-fashioned fish pie. But none the worse for that. You can use either fresh or smoked haddock for this pie but if you use the latter, try to make sure that it is naturally smoked and not dyed. | Serves 6 | Picture page 75

1½ kg	old potatoes, scrubbed and cut in large pieces	3½ lbs
3 tbsp	olive oil	3 tbsp
4	medium onions, sliced	4
6	eggs	6
700g	haddock fillets, fresh or smoked	1½ lbs
450ml	goat's, sheep's, soya or oat milk	15 fl oz
3 tbsp	goat's butter or dairy-free spread	3 tbsp
	sea salt and freshly ground black pepper	
1½ heaped tsp	arrowroot or cornflour	1½ heaped tsp
	sea salt and freshly fround pepper	

1. Steam the potatoes in their skins until quite soft.
2. Meanwhile, heat the oil in a wide pan and gently cook the onions for 15-20 minutes or until they are quite soft and lightly tanned.
3. While the potatoes and onions are cooking, put the haddock into a pan with the milk, bring to the boil and simmer gently for 10 minutes or until it is cooked.
4. Hard boil the eggs.
5. Mash the potato with 2 tbsp of goat's butter or dairy-free spread, depending on what you can eat, season lightly and stir in the cooked onions, mixing well. Keep warm.
6. Remove the fish from the milk, remove the skin and set the flesh aside.
7. Shell the eggs, cut them up and mix them gently into the fish.
8. Put both in the bottom of a pie dish and keep warm.
9. Make a paste with the arrowroot or cornflour and a little of the cooking milk, then add the rest of the milk and heat gently, stirring, until it thickens slightly.
10. Season to taste and pour over the fish.
11. Spread the potato and onion mixture on the top, dot with the remaining butter or spread and brown lightly under a grill.
12. Serve at once with a green vegetable.

Note: Arrowroot is the fine starch made from the roots or rhizomes of the large perennial herb plant found mainly in tropical climates. It is totally gluten free and very useful for thickening sauces and soups. You can also use it as a flour but it is too fine to use successfully on its own and is usually better mixed with a coarser flour such as maize meal or gram flour.

KING PRAWN GUMBO

A gumbo is the traditional soup-cum-stew of the southern states of the USA. Essential to any gumbo are the 'holy trinity' of onions, celery and bell peppers in a strong, thick sauce with meat or shellfish. In this gumbo we use the soft vegetables to create the thick sauce (but you can add any other ingredients you like). | Serves 6

6 tbsp	extra virgin olive oil	6 tbsp
2	small red onions, sliced thinly	2
3-6	red chillies, depending on how hot you want the gumbo, pips removed and finely sliced	3-6
2	sticks of celery	2
18	small okra, topped, tailed and sliced	18
2	red bell peppers	2
1	orange bell pepper, sliced	1
½	medium butternut squash, peeled and diced	½
3	yellow courgettes, (if you can get them, if not use green) wiped, topped and tailed and sliced	3
18	whole cherry tomatoes	18
600g	king prawns	1½ lbs
12 tbsp	patna or basmati or any long grain rice sea salt and freshly ground black pepper large handful of fresh coriander	12 tbsp

1. Heat the oil in a heavy, lidded pan and add the onions, chillies, celery, okra, and bell peppers and cook briskly for a few minutes, stirring well.
2. Reduce the heat and continue to cook for a further 10 minutes until the vegetables are softening.
3. Add the diced squash, courgettes and tomatoes, cover the pan tightly and reduce the heat.
4. Simmer, covered, for 30-40 minutes or until the squash and courgettes are cooked through — the soft vegetables should have semi-disintegrated into a thick, flavoursome sauce.
5. Add the prawns and some seasoning and continue to simmer for a further 5 minutes just to cook the prawns.
6. Meanwhile, cook the rice in plenty of fast boiling water for 8-10 minutes or until it is just cooked. Drain, rinse and keep warm.
7. Adjust the seasoning of the gumbo to taste and, just before serving, sprinkle with lots of coarsely chopped coriander.
8. Serve with the rice and a green salad. (Cont. on page 82)

Note: Okra is a traditional vegetable of the Deep South, brought by the slaves from their native Africa. Many people don't like it because, as it cooks, it releases a thick sticky substance that they find 'slimy'. However, if you continue to cook the okra, it loses its 'sliminess' and releases delicious, quite delicate flavours.

STIR-FRIED TUNA WITH CHILLI

If you cannot get fresh tuna, you can make this dish with tinned although it will not be as tasty. Some people like their fresh tuna (like their steak) almost raw, others prefer it cooked through so you will need to adapt your cooking time to suit you and your guests. | Serves 6

3 tbsp	sunflower oil	3 tbsp
3	fresh green chillies, carefully seeded and finely sliced	3
3	large cloves garlic, peeled and thinly sliced	3
25g	knob of fresh ginger, peeled and cut into fine matchsticks	1 oz
1	red pepper, de-seeded and thinly sliced	1
1	head fennel, trimmed and thinly sliced	1
500g	fresh tuna, cubed	1 ¼ lbs
9	spring onions	9
2 x 220g	tins water chestnuts, drained and halved horizontally	2 x 7 oz
75g	cashew nuts	3 oz
	wheat-free soya sauce or tamari	
	freshly ground black pepper	
	large handful fresh coriander, chopped	

1. Heat the oil in a wide pan or wok and briskly cook the chillies, garlic and ginger for a couple of minutes, making sure they do not burn.
2. Add the red pepper and fennel, reduce the heat slightly and continue to cook for another 3 minutes.
3. Add the fresh tuna and continue to cook briskly for a further 3-6 minutes depending on how cooked you like it.
4. Meanwhile, slice the spring onions lengthways and cut in half.
5. Add the water chestnuts, cashew nuts and spring onions and cook for a final minute to warm everything through slightly.
6. Season to taste with tamari and black pepper and serve at once sprinkled with the fresh coriander.

Note: The stronger chillies release powerful vapours when they are fried so take care that you do not stand over the pan or you can find yourself being choked by chilli fumes.

MOULES MARINIÈRE

Once an 'r' comes back into the month, shellfish such as oysters and mussels suddenly appear in the fishmongers. Moules marinière is always thought to be off the menu for dairy allergics/intolerants as the classic recipe includes lot of cream. However, you can make a delicious soup/sauce without any cream and these days, if you want to add a creamy touch, you can use one of the recently developed soya or oat creams which will be totally safe. | Serves 6

2½ kg	fresh mussels in their shells	6 lbs
2 tbsp	olive oil	2 tbsp
2	large onions, finely chopped	2
2	cloves garlic, peeled and crushed	2
600ml	dry white wine	1 pint
	salt and freshly ground black pepper	
3 tbsp	chopped parsley	3 tbsp
200ml	soya or oat cream (optional)	7 fl oz
	crusty fresh gluten-free baguette	

1. Clean the mussels thoroughly, scraping off as many of the barnacles as possible and removing the beard or byssus from the pointed end. They should all close firmly when tapped, if not, throw them out; it means they are dead and must not be eaten as they will make you thoroughly ill.
2. Heat the oil in a large wide pan and add the onions and crushed garlic. (If you do not have a big enough saucepan to fit all the mussels, split them in two and cook them in two pans.)
3. Cook the onions and garlic gently for 4-5 minutes or until the onions begin to soften.
4. Add the wine and the mussels, shake the pan vigorously with the lid on then simmer for 5 minutes.
5. Take off the heat and transfer the mussels to a hot tureen or individual plate. Add the cream if you are using it.
6. Spoon over the sauce — do not pour the juices from the saucepan or the sand that inevitably remains in the mussels will get transferred too. If you want to use the juices you must pour the juices through a sieve with an extremely fine mesh.
7. Sprinkle over the chopped parsley and serve at once.
8. Serve with a hot baguette which has been briefly refreshed in the oven.

Note: A number of manufacturers are now offering gluten-free baguettes, rolls and other fancy breads most of which can be stored in the freezer until needed — see Resources, page 234.

RED CABBAGE WITH SMOKED SALMON

This is an unusual combination with a rather Russian flavour. Use smoked salmon off cuts rather than slices as it is the flavour of the fish that you want in this dish. | Serves 6

2 level tsp	dill seeds	2 level tsp
4 tbsp	sunflower oil	4 tbsp
5	medium red onions, peeled and sliced	5
1	small-medium red cabbage, sliced very thinly	1
200ml	gluten and wheat-free vegetable stock	7 fl oz
12	spring onions, trimmed and chopped	12
200g	mangetout	7 oz
450g	smoked salmon off cuts	1 lb
	juice 2 lemons	
	sea salt and freshly ground black pepper	
	handful parsley, chopped	

1. Put the dill seeds in a bowl and bruise them gently with the end of a rolling pin.
2. In a heavy based pan heat the oil and add the onions. Fry gently for 5-10 minutes or until they are starting to soften.
3. Add the cabbage and the vegetable stock.
4. Bring to the simmer, cover and cook for 10-15 minutes or until the cabbage is also starting to soften.
5. Add the chopped spring onions, the mangetout (halved if they are very big) and the smoked salmon pieces.
6. Cook for a further 4-5 minutes to allow the flavours to amalgamate then season to taste with the salt, pepper and lemon juice.
7. Add the parsley and serve warm or at room temperature.

Note: If you wanted to add an even more Russian note to this dish you could stir in a couple of tbsp of plain goat's, sheep's milk or soya yogurt, depending on what you can eat, along with the seasoning.

LEMON SOLE STUFFED WITH SEAWEED AND WILD RICE

This is an attractive dinner party dish and not as much trouble as it looks. | Serves 6

6 tbsp	olive oil	6
3	medium leeks, finely sliced	3
1	medium head fennel, chopped very finely	1
2	handfuls mixed dried sea vegetables	2
3 tbsp	wild rice	3 tbsp
600ml	fish or vegetable stock	1 pint
6 tbsp	basmati or Jasmine rice	6 tbsp
1	egg	1
	juice 2 lemons	
6	large fillets of lemon sole, skinned	6
450ml	white wine or fish stock	15 fl oz
200g	green beans, trimmed and halved	7 oz
4	courgettes, wiped and sliced	4
200g	fresh spinach or chard, chopped	7 oz
	parsley to decorate	

1. Heat 2 tbsp of oil in a deep pan and gently sweat two of the leeks and the fennel, covered, for 5-10 minutes or until they are starting to soften.
2. Add the sea vegetables, the wild rice and 500ml/18 fl oz of stock. Bring back to the boil and cook, uncovered, for 10 minutes.
3. Add the white rice and continue to simmer until all the rice is cooked, adding more stock or water if it is needed.
4. Heat the oven to 180C/350F/gas mark 4.
5. Remove from the heat, cool slightly and then stir in the egg, the lemon juice and seasoning if needed.
6. Use around half of the rice to stuff the fillets of sole and place the rolls in an ovenproof or microwave dish.
7. Roll the rest of the rice into teaspoon-size balls.
8. Add 300ml/10 fl oz of white wine or fish stock to the fish and cover.
9. Bake for 30 minutes or till the fish is cooked. Keep warm.
10. Bake the rice balls for 20 minutes to crisp their surface. Keep warm.
11. Meanwhile, in another pan, heat the remaining oil and add the remaining leek. Cook gently for 10 minutes, then add the green beans, courgettes, spinach and the remaining stock. Cover and cook gently for 10-15 minutes or until the vegetables are all cooked but retain a little crunch. Season to taste.
12. To serve place the sole rolls around the outside of a dish and pile the vegetables in the middle. Dot the rice balls, around the dish, pour over the juices from both the fish and the vegetables, decorate with parsley and serve at once.

SMOKED MACKEREL AND POTATO SALAD

This is a great summer salad, very tasty but very easy to prepare. Dress it while the vegetables are still warm so that they absorb the flavours of the lemon juice and oil. | Serves 6

550g	new potatoes	1¼ lbs
200g	fine green beans	7 oz
350g	smoked mackerel, peppered or	12 oz
	not, or a combination of the two	
	sea salt and fresh coarsely ground black pepper	
	juice of 1-2 lemons	
4-6 tbsp	good virgin olive oil	4-6 tbsp

1. Scrub the potatoes and steam for 15-20 minutes or until they are cooked through. Remove and halve or quarter them, depending on size.
2. Meanwhile, top and tail the beans and steam them for 5-7 minutes or until they are just cooked but still slightly crunchy.
3. Remove and cut in half.
4. Skin and break up the smoked mackerel into bite-size pieces.
5. Mix the potatoes, beans and smoked mackerel gently together so that the potatoes do not get too broken up. Turn into a serving dish.
6. Sprinkle with coarse sea salt, lots of coarsely ground black pepper, the lemon juice and the oil.
7. Serve at room temperature with a green salad.

Note: Although mackerel is very nutritious — an excellent source of omega 3 fatty acids, selenium, and vitamins B6 and B12 — and very flavoursome, many people find it rather oily, strong in flavour and difficult to cook. Smoked mackerel fillets, however, need no cooking and taste less oily though very flavoursome. Although they are usually served cold in salads, they can also be served warm (as in this dish) or hot with a strong-flavoured vegetable such as red cabbage.

BAIAN SEAFOOD STEW

Use this recipe to make a spectacular dish for a summer dinner party — but make sure that your guests have plenty of napkins as it is not the easiest thing to eat. I used kombu but you could use any other dried Japanese seaweed. | Serves 6

3 red mullet heads and 3 mackerel heads to make stock — you can either get the fishmonger to give you his discarded fish heads or use the fish for some other dish (If you do not want to make your own fish stock you can use a proprietary one but make sure that it is wheat/gluten free)

3 tbsp	olive oil	3 tbsp
2 sticks	celery, chopped very small	2 sticks
6	large sprigs fresh coriander, well washed	6
9	grinds fresh black pepper	9
50g	dried kombu or other dried seaweed, chopped fairly small and softened for 10 minutes in a little water	2 oz
	sea salt	
450ml	medium white wine	15 fl oz
1 kg	very well washed, fresh mussels in their shells (If you cannot get fresh mussels you can use 350g/12 oz frozen although the flavour is not as good)	2 lbs
150g	fresh brown shrimps, cooked	6 oz
6	fresh or frozen scallops, each one cut in four pieces	6
6	langoustines, ready cooked	6
50g	pine nuts, lightly browned in the oven or under the grill	2 oz

1. Make the fish stock by putting the fish heads in a pan and adding 1¾ litres/3 pints of water. Bring it to the boil and boil briskly for 10 minutes. Remove from the hob and strain — reserve the stock and discard the heads. Alternatively, make up 1¾ litres/3 pints of stock.
2. Heat the oil in a large pan and add the celery.
3. Chop the roots and stems of the coriander (keep the leaves for garnish) finely and add them to the celery with the pepper. Cook them gently for about 10 minutes or till the celery has softened.
4. Add the drained seaweed with the stock and the salt, bring to the boil and simmer for 15 minutes or till the seaweed is cooked.
5. Meanwhile, heat the white wine in a separate pan and, as soon as it is boiling, add the well-scrubbed mussels. Cover them and cook them very briskly for 4-5 minutes or till they have all opened widely. Discard any that do not.
6. If you are using frozen mussels add them to the wine and gradually bring the pot back to the simmer.

7. Add the cooked mussels and wine along with the shrimps, scallops and langoustines to the pot. Continue to cook gently for 5 minutes.
8. Add the pine nuts and the chopped coriander leaves, adjust the seasoning to taste and serve at once.

Note: This recipe is based on one I found in Apicius' book of 'formulae' — the only cookery book which has survived since the Roman era. Baiae was a popular ancient Roman seaside resort near Naples, which is, presumably, where Apicius found the recipe.

SARDINE POTATOES

This is an amazingly simple and delicious way to boost your intake of omega 3 fatty acid and calcium — and works really well for children as well. You can make it just for one or increase the quantities according to the numbers you have to feed. | Serves 1 or 6

1	large baking potato per person	1
2	tinned sardines per person, with bones	2
	(you could also use sardines in tomato sauce for variety)	
2	chopped anchovies per person (optional) or sea salt to taste	2
	freshly ground black pepper	
	juice from ½ lemon per person, approx.	

1. Heat the oven to 180C/350F/gas mark 4.
2. Bake the potatoes for 45 minutes-1 hour depending on size.
3. You can also speed the process up by part microwaving them but be sure that you give them some time in the oven so that you get a good crispy skin. Microwaved potatoes are almost impossible to stuff because their skins are too soft and thin.
4. When cooked, split the potatoes and scoop the insides into a warmed bowl.
5. Mash the potatoes with the sardines and anchovies, if you are using them. Season to taste with the salt, pepper and lemon juice and return the stuffing to the potato skins.
6. Serve at once with a green vegetable or salad.

Note: Tinned sardines are a great food for those on a dairy-free diet as, provided you use the ones with bones, they are a great source of calcium — half a tin of sardines providing roughly the equivalent amount of calcium as half a pint of milk and approximately a quarter of your daily calcium need.

FILLETS OF SALMON AND COD WITH COCONUT MILK AND LEMONGRASS

A very simple dish with a Far Eastern flavour. Using the two different fish makes for an attractive colour combination but you could use just salmon, just white fish or an alternative fish such as monkfish. | Serves 6

2 tbsp	sunflower oil	2 tbsp
2	heads fennel, trimmed and sliced very thinly	2
4	heads Little Gem lettuce or 2 small Cos lettuce, chopped	4
1	stick lemongrass, bruised with a rolling pin	1
15	cardamom pods, bruised with a rolling pin	15
9 heaped tbsp	Jasmine rice	9 heaped tbsp
3	175-200g / 6-7 oz fillets of salmon	3
3	175-200g / 6-7 oz fillets of cod or haddock	3
2	lemons, sliced	2
1 x 400ml	tin coconut milk	1 x 14 fl oz
	sea salt and freshly ground black pepper	

1. Heat the oil in a wide pan, add the fennel and lettuce, lemongrass and cardamom pods and stir well.
2. Cover and sweat gently for 10-15 minutes.
3. Meanwhile, put the rice in a large saucepan and add sufficient water to cover the rice with around 2cm/¾ inch to spare. Bring the rice to the boil uncovered, then cover and simmer for around 20 minutes or until the rice is cooked through. Add a little extra water if it dries up before it is cooked.
4. Allow to stand for 5 minutes after it is cooked and then fluff with a fork.
5. While the rice is cooking, lay the fish fillets over the lettuce, cover with the lemon slices, grind over a little sea salt and black pepper, then pour over the coconut milk.
6. Cover the pan and simmer gently for a further 10-15 minutes or until the fish is cooked. Adjust the seasoning to taste.
7. Remove the lemongrass and serve with the rice and a green vegetable or a green leaf salad.

Note: Lemongrass is widely used in Thai and Vietnamese cooking. It is quite pungent with a light lemon flavour. You can buy the roots, which should look fresh, not dry and brittle, in supermarkets and Asian stores; they can be stored in a plastic bag in the fridge for up to three weeks. To get the best flavour, bruise the root with a rolling pin before use.

BAKED TROUT WITH OREGANO AND GREEN BEAN PASTA

The oregano gives this dish a nice Mediterranean flavour. | Serves 6

6 tbsp	olive oil	6 tbsp
2	medium leeks, very thinly sliced	2
2	small heads fennel, very thinly sliced	2
1	medium head chicory, very thinly sliced	1
2 heaped tsp	dried oregano	2 heaped tsp
24	cherry tomatoes	24
	2 large or 3 medium trout, cleaned — with or without their heads	
1	lemon, sliced	1
	sea salt and freshly ground black pepper	
500g	gluten/wheat-free penne	1 ¼ lbs
4 tbsp	olive oil	4 tbsp
12	spring onions, trimmed and chopped	12
18	button mushrooms, sliced	18
12	green beans, cut in thirds	12
3	handfuls fresh spinach, chopped	3
	juice 1 lemon	

1. Heat the oil in a heavy pan, add the leeks, fennel, chicory and oregano and sweat over a low heat for 15-20 minutes.
2. Cut the tomatoes into quarters and add to the pot.
3. Continue to cook slowly, uncovered for a further 15 minutes.
4. Heat the oven to 180C/350F/gas mark 4.
5. Transfer the vegetables to the bottom of an ovenproof casserole large enough to take the fish.
6. Lay the fish out on top of the vegetables, with the lemon slices down the middle of each. Sprinkle with sea salt and freshly ground black pepper, cover and bake for 25-35 minutes depending on the size of the fish.
7. Meanwhile, cook the pasta according to the instructions on the pack then drain and reserve.
8. Heat the oil in a heavy pan and add the spring onions and mushrooms.
9. Cook for a few minutes then add the beans and the chopped spinach.
10. Cook for another few minutes. The beans should be starting to soften slightly but still be crunchy.
11. Mix the vegetables into the pasta and season with sea salt, freshly ground black pepper and lemon juice.
12. Serve the trout on the cooking vegetables on a large platter surrounded by the pasta.

FISH SOUP

For this soup-cum-stew to have the best flavour, you must allow time to cook the vegetables and anchovies really slowly. It tastes better if you can cook it up to the point when you would add the fish ahead of time. When you are ready to serve it, reheat the soup gently and add the fish. This allows you to get the full flavour of the slow-cooked vegetables while still retaining the fresh flavour of recently cooked fish. | Serves 6

3 tbsp	olive oil	3 tbsp
50g	tinned anchovies with their oil, chopped small	2 oz
3	medium onions, peeled and sliced finely	3
3	cloves garlic, peeled and sliced	3
1½	large heads fennel, trimmed and sliced finely	1½
12	cherry tomatoes, quartered	12
2 litres	gluten/wheat-free fish or vegetable stock	3 pints
250ml	dry white wine	8 fl oz
3	large old potatoes, scrubbed and diced	3
675g	mixed boned and skinned fish of your choice –	1½ lbs

such as ⅓ haddock, ⅓ salmon and ⅓ mussels but you could
also include haddock, tuna, shrimps, prawns, clams, or whatever you like
sea salt and freshly ground black pepper

1. Heat the olive oil and the oil from the tin of anchovies in a large heavy pan and add the onion, garlic, fennel and chopped anchovies.
2. Cook very slowly for 15 minutes.
3. Add the tomatoes and continue to cook very slowly until the onions are very soft but scarcely coloured – this could take another 15-20 minutes.
4. Add the stock, wine and potatoes, bring to the boil, cover and simmer gently for a further 20 minutes or until the potatoes are cooked.
5. You can set the soup aside at this point if you wish.
6. When you want to serve the soup, reheat the vegetables and stock while you prepare the fish, cutting any firm fleshed fish into bite-sized cubes. (Do not cut them too small or they will disintegrate.)
7. When the soup has reached the boil, reduce the heat, add the fish and cook for 3-4 minutes very gently (do not boil or the fish will fall apart).
8. Adjust the seasoning to taste and serve at once.

Note: This is a pretty substantial soup and would certainly be enough for a main meal.

PRAWNS IN COCONUT MILK

Very quick, very easy and very tasty. | Serves 6

6 heaped tbsp	Patna or other long grain rice	6 heaped tbsp
½ tsp	sea salt	½ tsp
3-4	small red or green chillies	3-4
1	small head radicchio, sliced very finely	1
3	small heads pak choi or similar Chinese greens, sliced finely	3
400ml	full-fat coconut milk	14 fl oz
	juice 3 limes	
550g	fresh prawns	1¼ lbs
	white pepper	

1. Heat a large pan of cold water, add the salt and when it comes to the boil, add the rice.

2. Simmer for 8-10 minutes or until the rice is cooked without being mushy. Drain and keep warm.

3. Meanwhile, seed the chillies and cut them into very thin matchsticks.

4. Dry fry in a pan or wok taking care not to stand right over them as the fumes from the oil can choke you.

5. Add the sliced radicchio and pak choi with the coconut milk. Bring to the boil and simmer for a couple of minutes only.

6. Add the lime juice and the prawns and continue to simmer for a further 2-3 minutes or until the prawns are cooked.

7. Adjust the seasoning to taste and serve immediately with the rice and a green salad.

QUINOA STUFFED TROUT FILLETS

It is slightly fiddly rolling up the trout fillets with their stuffing but the result is worth the effort. | Serves 6

150g	quinoa grains	6 oz
700ml	gluten/wheat-free fish or vegetable stock	1 ¼ pints
	grated rind of one large lemon and one large lime	
	large handful flat-leaf parsley	
	sea salt and freshly ground black pepper	
6	rainbow trout, filleted	6
200ml	dry white wine	7 fl oz

1. Heat the oven to 170C/325F/gas mark 3.
2. In a small pan simmer the quinoa in the stock for 10-15 minutes or until it is soft but not mushy.
3. Add the lemon and lime rind and the parsley.
4. Taste and add salt and pepper if it needs it — the stock may already be well seasoned.
5. Lay the trout fillets out on a board and cut in half, lengthways.
6. Put a spoonful of the stuffing at one end of each fillet and roll it as neatly as you can.
7. Lay the fillets side by side in an ovenproof dish, sprinkle over any stuffing that remains and pour over the white wine.
8. Cover the dish and bake for 35-45 minutes or until the fish is cooked.
9. Serve with a green vegetable or salad.

Note: Quinoa is a delicious gluten/wheat-free, and highly nutritious, South American seed. The protein in quinoa contains all of the eight essential amino acids making it a 'complete protein', almost unique for a grain alternative. The texture of quinoa (pronounced 'keenoah') is a cross between couscous and rice and can be used as a substitute for either. You can buy it in some supermarkets and most health-food stores.

ANCHOVY AND MUSHROOM RISOTTO

Unlike a pilaff a risotto should be eaten quite 'wet' with plenty of the deliciously flavoured cooking juices. | Serves 6

3 tbsp	olive oil	3 tbsp
1	large leek, trimmed and thinly sliced	1
10	anchovies, chopped	10
250g	mushrooms, ideally a selection of different ones	9 oz
400g	Arborio risotto rice, rinsed under cold water	14 oz
1 litre	wheat/gluten-free vegetable stock	1¾ pints
300ml	dry white wine	½ pint
2	largish courgettes, wiped	2
200-400ml	water	7-14 fl oz
	sea salt and freshly ground black pepper	

1. Heat the oil in a wide, heavy pan and add the leeks and anchovies.
2. Fry gently for 5-10 minutes or until they are softening.
3. Wipe and slice the mushrooms, add to the leeks and continue to cook for a further 5-8 minutes.
4. Add the rice, stir gently and cook for a couple of minutes or until the rice is starting to become transparent.
5. Add the stock and wine, bring to the boil and cook reasonably quickly for 8-10 minutes or until the liquid is absorbed.
6. Meanwhile, grate the courgettes on a coarse grater.
7. When the first lot of liquid is absorbed, add the courgettes and extra water bit by bit until the rice is totally cooked but enough liquid remains to make a little 'sauce'.
8. Remove from the heat and season to taste.
9. Serve with a good green salad.

SMOKED HADDOCK BURGERS IN AUBERGINE 'BUNS'

The usual burger solution for those on gluten or wheat-free diets is to look for a gluten-free burger bun, of which there are several — see Resources, page 234. However, this is a rather different solution — aubergine 'buns'.

Grilling the aubergine is a bit time-consuming but can be done while you are making the fillings and it is very tasty.

If you prefer to be more traditional, make the burgers larger, grill briskly on both sides and serve in normal burger buns. | Serves 6

Aubergine burger 'buns'
6-8 aubergines — enough to give you 48 reasonable-size slices
about the thickness of your little finger — 2 'buns' per person
sea salt and freshly ground black pepper
olive oil

1. Heat the grill.
2. Fill the grill tray with aubergine slices over which you have dribbled a little olive oil and plenty of ground sea salt and black pepper.
3. Grill until lightly browned on one side then turn over and repeat the process on the other side. The slices should be soft to the knife.
4. Set aside and repeat the process with the next batch of slices.

Hot-smoked haddock filling

	1 generous tbsp olive oil	
1	large onion, chopped very fine in a food processor	1
100g	quinoa grains	4 oz
600ml	gluten/wheat-free vegetable stock	1 pint
400g	hot-smoked haddock	14 oz
2 tbsp	grated horseradish (not horseradish sauce)	2 tbsp
	sea salt and freshly ground black pepper	

1. Sweat the onion in the oil very slowly until it is totally soft then add the quinoa. Stir well then add the stock.
2. Bring to the boil and simmer gently until the liquid is absorbed and the quinoa is very soft.
3. Meanwhile, break up the smoked haddock into flakes. Add it to the quinoa along with the horseradish. Adjust the seasoning to taste. Make into small patties the size of your aubergine slices.
4. To serve, sandwich the haddock mixture between two slices of aubergine and reheat, lightly covered, in a moderate oven for 15 minutes.

Note: Smoking has become a lot more sophisticated with the arrival of 'hot smoking'; a process by which the food is slowly cooked in the smoke above the fire whereas in cold smoking the smoke is passed through the food at room temperature. To preserve food which has been cold smoked it usually also needs to be salt cured in order to kill harmful bacteria. This process results in much stronger flavours.

CHICKEN AND GAME

Slow-cooked Chicken with Sweet Potato

Chicken and Courgette Pie

Chicken and Chilli Stir Fry

Coq au vin with Celeriac Purée

Chicken and Pomegranate Salad

Roast Chicken with Aubergine and Tomato Sauce

Chicken Breasts with Ginger

Redbush Tea Chicken and Avocado Salad

Chicken Salad with Pumpkin Oil

Duck à la Mode

Casserole-roasted Pheasant with Butternut Squash

Spicy West Indian Chicken Casserole

Chicken Korma with Coconut Milk

Roast Haunch of Venison

Khoresh with Pomegranate

Duck Breasts with Apple and Ginger

SLOW-COOKED CHICKEN WITH SWEET POTATO

A very simple dish to cook which derives its flavour from the long, slow cooking — overnight in a slow cooker is ideal. | Serves 6

3 tbsp	olive oil	3 tbsp
4	medium onions, finely sliced	4
4	medium-size sweet potatoes, peeled	4
4 heaped tsp	dried mixed herbs	4 heaped tsp
½ tsp	sea salt and plenty of freshly ground black pepper	½ tsp
2 x 400g	tins of chopped tomatoes	2 x 14 oz
1 x 2 kg	chicken	1 x 4lbs

1. Heat the oil in a heavy casserole in which you will be able to fit the chicken.
2. Add the onions and cook gently for 5-10 minutes or until they are softening.
3. Meanwhile, dice the sweet potatoes and then add them to the onions.
4. Add 3 teaspoons of mixed herbs and the salt and pepper.
5. Cook for a further 10-15 minutes or until the sweet potatoes are also quite soft.
6. Add the tomatoes, stir well then place the chicken on top of the vegetables.
7. Sprinkle the remaining mixed herbs over the chicken and grind over a little more sea salt and black pepper.
8. Cover the dish and bring to a very low simmer.
9. Cook over a very low heat for 2-3 hours or until the flesh is falling off the chicken.
10. Alternatively transfer to a slow cooker and cook overnight.
11. Serve from the casserole or cooker with baked potatoes and a green vegetable.

Note: If you do not want to use a whole chicken you could use chicken breasts, thighs or drumsticks for this dish but you would need to reduce the cooking time to 1-1½ hours.

CHICKEN AND COURGETTE PIE

This dish can be served as a casserole or as a pie — you just need to add a pastry top to create the latter. | Serves 6

400g	of your favourite gluten-free pastry or use the recipe on p122	14 oz
12	shallots	12

3 tbsp	olive oil	3 tbsp
400g	piece celeriac root	14 oz
1	medium chicken or 6 chicken joints	1
1	fresh lime	1
400ml	coconut milk	14 fl oz
	sea salt and freshly ground black pepper	
3	courgettes	3
150g	fresh baby spinach leaves or larger leaves torn into small pieces	5 oz
25g	corn or potato flour	1 oz
1	egg (f you are making the pie)	1

1. Peel the shallots and put in a wide pan (big enough to take the chicken joints) with the oil and cook gently.
2. Peel the celeriac and cut into small dice (the size of your thumbnail), add to the pan and continue to fry gently for another 5 minutes.
3. If you are using a whole chicken, joint it then add the joints to the pan and fry until lightly tanned on all sides.
4. Peel the skin from the lime and cut it into very thin matchsticks.
5. Add the lime peel and the coconut milk and season well, cover the pan and simmer for 30 minutes.
6. Meanwhile, clean the courgettes and slice them thickly.
7. Add them to the pan along with the fresh spinach and continue to simmer, covered, for another 15 minutes.
8. If you are topping the pie with pastry, heat the oven to 180C/350F/gas mark 4.
9. In a small bowl mix some of the cooking liquid into the corn or potato flour until it makes a smooth paste.
10. With a slotted spoon remove the chicken and vegetables into a pie dish.
11. Add the remaining cooking liquid to the corn or potato flour, return to the pan and cook gently for a few minutes, stirring continually, until it thickens.
12. Season to taste with salt, pepper and some of the lime juice and pour over the chicken and vegetables.
13. If you are serving as a casserole, serve with an extra green vegetable and rice or a mashed root vegetable.
14. To turn it into a pie, roll out the pastry. Top and decorate the pie with pastry leaves or balls and brush with beaten egg.
15. Bake for 25-35 minutes or until the top is brown and crisp and serve with an extra green vegetable and rice or a mashed root vegetable.

CHICKEN AND CHILLI STIR FRY

Fresh ginger root is fairly easy to find, in Indian or West Indian shops if not in the supermarket, but if you cannot find it you can still use ground ginger.

The stir fry can be served with lots of rice or rice noodles. | Serves 6

	1 knob fresh ginger (approx. 40g/1½ oz) or 1½ tsp ground ginger	
2-3	fresh or dried red chillies (depending on how hot you want your stir fry)	2-3
4	cloves garlic	4
3 tbsp	sunflower oil	3 tbsp
9	large spring onions, chopped roughly	9
2	small red peppers, seeded and thinly sliced	2
3	chicken breasts, sliced into thin matchsticks	3
2 tbsp	tamari or other wheat/gluten-free soya sauce	2 tbsp
300g	tin bamboo shoots, drained	11 oz
200g	mangetout, halved	7 oz
	large handful of fresh coriander, chopped	

1. Peel the fresh ginger and slice into thin matchsticks.
2. De-seed and slice the chillies into very thin strips.
3. Peel and slice the garlic thinly.
4. Heat the oil in a wok or wide frying pan and add the ginger, chillies and garlic and cook briskly, without burning, for a minute.
5. Add the spring onions and red pepper. Continue to cook for a further 3 minutes.
6. Add the chicken and the tamari, continue to cook briskly for a further couple of minutes then reduce the heat and cover the wok.
7. Cook more gently for 8-10 minutes or until the chicken is cooked.
8. Add the bamboo shoots and mangetout, cook for a further couple of minutes to warm the bamboo shoots and mangetout, but not long enough for the latter to lose their colour.
9. Serve at once with lots of fresh coriander and rice or rice noodles.

COQ AU VIN WITH CELERIAC PURÉE

To get the best out of this recipe you need to leave yourself a couple of days so that it can marinate in the wine for at least 24 hours and then be cooked very slowly. In a classic coq au vin, the cooking juices would be thickened with a beurre manié but I prefer the slightly cleaner taste of the unthickened juices.

Jerusalem artichokes have a quite short season, quite a strong flavour and can have an alarming effect on the digestion so you may prefer just to use the celeriac and potatoes or sweet potatoes. | Serves 6

1	large leek, trimmed and finely sliced	1
2	sticks celery, washed and chopped small	2
2	carrots, washed and sliced in thin rounds	2
20	button mushrooms, halved or sliced	20
	2 sprigs thyme (or 2 tsp dried) and 4 bay leaves	
150g	dried chestnuts (optional)	6 oz
500ml	red wine	18 fl oz
250ml	gluten/wheat-free chicken or vegetable stock	8 fl oz
2½ kg	chicken	5 lbs

1. Mix the vegetables, herbs and the chestnuts, if you are using them, together in a bowl large enough to hold the chicken.
2. Heat the wine and stock in a pan, or in a microwave for 3 minutes — do not boil.
3. Pour over the vegetables and mix well. Push the chicken well down into the marinade, cover and leave in a cool place (a larder or fridge) for 12 hours. Turn the chicken over in the marinade and leave for another 12 hours.
4. Transfer the chicken to a heavy pan or casserole and pour over the marinade and vegetables. Cover and bring slowly to the boil. Turn down immediately and cook very slowly — scarcely simmering — for 3-4 hours. Leave to cool in the pan. To serve you just need to reheat the chicken in its juices and serve with the purée and a green vegetable.

CELERIAC PURÉE

2	large onions, peeled and thickly sliced	2
3 tbsp	olive oil	3 tbsp
1 kg	celeriac	2 lbs
700g	potatoes or sweet potatoes	1 ½ lbs
450g	Jerusalem artichokes (optional)	1 lb
2 tbsp	goat's butter or dairy-free spread	2 tbsp
	sea salt and freshly ground black pepper	

1. Fry the onions gently in the oil until quite soft and well tanned — this will take 20-25 minutes. Meanwhile peel the celeriac, sweet potatoes and artichokes (if you are using them) or scrub the potatoes.
2. Cut in large dice and steam till soft then mash with the butter or spread and a little sea salt and black pepper.
3. Beat in the onions and adjust the seasoning to taste.
4. Serve with the chicken and a green vegetable.

CHICKEN AND POMEGRANATE SALAD

Fresh pomegranate seeds are ideal for this dish and are now available in a number of supermarkets as well as Middle Eastern stores but, if you cannot find any fresh ones, you can use dried seeds (also from a Middle Eastern store), soaked in boiling water for 10-15 minutes. | Serves 6

1	medium-large chicken	1
	onion, carrot, celery, mushrooms, bouquet garni	
1	large pomegranate	1
300ml	plain sheep's, goat's milk or soya yogurt	½ pint
	juice 1 large lemon	
	sea salt and freshly ground black pepper	
4 tbsp	boiling water	4 tbsp
	green leaves	

1. Put the chicken in a large pan with the vegetables and bouquet garni.
2. Cover and bring slowly to the boil.
3. Simmer for 45-60 minutes or until the chicken is cooked.
4. Allow to cool then remove from the pot.
5. Remove the flesh from the chicken (discarding the skin), cut into bite-sized pieces and set aside.
6. Return the bones to the pot and cook for another hour to make wonderful chicken stock.
7. Meanwhile, de-seed the pomegranate. This is a fiddly job (I suggest you wear rubber gloves if you do not want your fingers stained black) but well worth it.
8. Add the yogurt to the pomegranate seeds in a bowl.
9. Stir well then add the lemon juice and seasoning to taste, plus the boiling water.
10. Pour ¾ of this dressing over the chicken reserving the rest to spoon over just before serving.
11. When ready to serve, arrange green leaves on a dish, with the chicken on top. Spoon over the remaining sauce and serve at once.
12. Serve with fresh gluten-free bread and more leaves.

Note: Pomegranates, which are native to Iran and right across to the Himalayas have been grown through the Mediterranean for thousands of years. They were introduced to California in the mid-eighteenth century by Spanish settlers. Pomegranate juice is particularly high in three polyphenols (a potent form of antioxidant) — tannins, anthocyanins, and ellagic acid. These are present in many fruits but not in such quantities. Pomegranates are also high in vitamin C and potassium.

ROAST CHICKEN WITH AUBERGINE AND TOMATO SAUCE

The tomatoes in this sauce have a wonderfully intense flavour. | Serves 6

	sea salt and freshly ground black pepper	
	1 large or 2 small chickens	
4 tbsp	olive oil	4 tbsp
4	medium onions, peeled and chopped in a food processor	4
4	large cloves garlic, peeled and chopped in a food processor	4
2 heaped tsp	each dried thyme and oregano	2 heaped tsp
5 tbsp	tomato purée	5 tbsp
1 kg	fresh plum tomatoes, halved	2 lbs
6 tbsp	white wine	6 tbsp
2 tsp	muscovado sugar	2 tsp
2	large aubergines plus extra olive oil	2
	basil, parsley or coriander to decorate	

1. Heat the oven to 180C/350F/gas mark 4.
2. Grind some sea salt and black pepper over the chickens and roast them for 1½-2 hours or until quite cooked. Keep warm.
3. Meanwhile, heat the oil in a wide pan and add the onions, garlic and herbs.
4. Cook gently for 10-15 minutes or until the onions have softened.
5. Add the tomato purée, tomatoes, wine and sugar and mix well.
6. Bring to the boil and simmer, uncovered, for 45 minutes or until they have cooked down to a thick sauce. Season to taste and keep warm.
7. While the tomatoes are cooking, slice the aubergines thinly and heat a grill or griddle. Grind sea salt and black pepper over the aubergine slices and dribble with olive oil.
8. Grill briskly until they are nicely browned then turn the slices over and repeat the process. Set aside and keep warm.
9. To serve, lay the aubergines out on a warmed serving dish. Spoon the tomato sauce onto them as a bed for the chicken.
10. Slice the chicken, arrange over the tomato and decorate with basil, parsley or coriander before serving with new potatoes and a green salad.

CHICKEN BREASTS WITH GINGER

This is a very simple and very tasty dish but you must allow the chicken to marinate for 3-4 hours for the flavours to mature. | Serves 6

6	small chicken breasts	6
50g	piece of fresh ginger	2 oz
	juice of 3 limes or 2 large lemons	
	sea salt and freshly ground black pepper	
3	large yellow peppers	3
4 tbsp	olive oil	4 tbsp

1. Skin the chicken breasts and cut them into bite-sized matchsticks.
2. Peel the ginger and cut into very thin matchsticks.
3. Mix the ginger and chicken well together in a bowl, season well with sea salt and freshly ground black pepper, pour over the lime or lemon juice.
4. Cover and leave in a cool place to marinate for 3-4 hours.
5. De-seed the peppers and cut into long, thin strips.
6. Heat the oil in a heavy pan and slowly cook the peppers, stirring regularly, until very soft — this will take 20-30 minutes.
7. Remove the peppers with a slotted spoon, drain as much oil as possible from the peppers back into the pan, and set the peppers aside.
8. With a slotted spoon, remove the chicken and ginger from the marinade, reserving the latter.
9. Reheat the oil and briskly fry the chicken and ginger, without burning, for 3-4 minutes or until cooked. Add the marinade and stir together for another minute.
10. Remove from the heat, mix in the peppers thoroughly and serve warm or at room temperature with lightly cooked broccoli or a green salad.

Note: Although I believe that, if you can afford it, all organic meat really does taste better than non organic, I do think that organic chickens are dramatically more flavoursome than non organic. However, if you cannot always afford them, this is a good dish to make with non organic chicken as the ginger gives the meat lots of extra flavour.

REDBUSH TEA CHICKEN AND AVOCADO SALAD

The redbush tea gives a pleasantly smoky flavour to the sauce and is very refreshing. | Serves 6

3	redbush tea bags	3
3	chicken breasts, skin removed	3
1	medium or 2 small leeks, very thinly sliced	1
2 tsp	fresh green peppercorns	2 tsp
3 tbsp	plain sheep's, goat's milk or soya yogurt	3 tbsp
	juice 1 small lemon	
	sea salt and freshly ground black pepper	
2	ripe avocados	2
	a good selection of green leaves — lettuce, lamb's lettuce, watercress, rocket, parsley etc	

1. Put the teabags in a bowl and pour over 250ml/8 fl oz boiling water — leave to steep for 5-10 minutes then discard the bags.
2. Slice the chicken breasts into thick matchsticks and put in a pan with the tea, the thinly sliced leeks and the peppercorns.
3. Bring to the boil then simmer gently, covered for 5-8 minutes or until the chicken is cooked.
4. Remove the chicken and leeks with a slotted spoon and reserve the cooking juices.
5. In a bowl stir the yogurt till smooth then add the cooking and lemon juices and season to taste with salt and pepper.
6. Peel the avocados and slice.
7. Mix the avocados gently into the chicken and dress with the sauce. There will be too much sauce so reserve the rest for dressing the leaves.
8. To serve pile the leaves on a dish, pile the chicken and avocado mixture in the middle and then pour over the remaining dressing before serving.

Note: Fans of *The Number 1 Ladies Detective Agency* will need no introduction to redbush tea — but for the rest of the world...
   Rooibos, pronounced 'roy-bosh' is for 'red bush', a broom-like plant from the leaves of which you can make a herbal tea — an excellent alternative for those who need to avoid 'normal' tea. It is high in antioxidants, and, in South Africa, is often used to soothe irritated skin and digestive complaints.

CHICKEN SALAD WITH PUMPKIN OIL

The pumpkin oil and balsamic vinegar combine to make a really delicious dressing for the chicken. Serve with new potatoes and the cucumber salad on p146. | Serves 6

3 tbsp	olive oil	3 tbsp
4	medium onions, very finely sliced	4
	the cooked breast and thigh meat from one large chicken	
	sea salt and freshly ground black pepper	
4 tbsp	balsamic vinegar	4 tbsp
8 tbsp	toasted pumpkin seed oil	8 tbsp
	baby spinach and red chicory leaves	
	nasturtiums to decorate (optional)	

1. Heat the oil in a heavy, wide pan then add the sliced onions and stir thoroughly so that the onions are well broken up.
2. Fry VERY gently, over a very low heat, for 40–45 minutes. The onions should very gradually change colour and dry out but must not burn.
3. Slice the chicken meat and lay a third of it out in a pie dish.
4. Grind over a little sea salt and black pepper and sprinkle over a quarter of the onions.
5. In a separate bowl mix the balsamic vinegar and the pumpkin oil and spoon a third over the chicken.
6. Place another layer of chicken in the bowl and repeat the procedure twice.
7. You should end up with a good handful of onions left — lay them aside.
8. Leave the chicken to marinate for 3-4 hours.
9. To serve, arrange the spinach leaves and chicory in a dish.
10. Spoon over the chicken, pouring any remaining marinade over the top. Sprinkle over the remaining onions and decorate.

Note: 'Real' balsamic vinegar is made from sweet white Trebbiano grape pressings that are boiled down to a dark syrup and then aged in oak kegs, with a vinegar 'mother'. The ageing can go on for many years (up to 100) over which time the vinegar is moved to smaller and smaller kegs of different woods — chestnut, cherrywood, ash, mulberry, and juniper. As it ages, moisture evaporates thickening the vinegar and concentrating the flavour. All of which explains why 'real' balsamic vinegar is so expensive and why you should be dubious about the quality of cheap ones.

DUCK À LA MODE

This recipe is from an 18th century recipe book and was intended for wild duck. However, it tastes excellent with the domesticated variety. | Serves 8

2	medium ducks with giblets	2
3 tbsp	olive oil	3 tbsp
2	medium onions, peeled and chopped roughly	2
1	medium carrot, scrubbed and diced	1
2	rashers of streaky bacon, chopped	2
4	mushrooms, chopped	4
1 heaped tbsp	corn or potato flour	1 heaped tbsp
175ml	red wine	6 fl oz
900ml	gluten and wheat-free chicken or vegetable stock or water	1½ pints
	2 sprigs parsley and 2 bouquet garni	
	freshly ground black pepper	
50g	goat's butter or dairy-free spread or 3 tbsp olive oil	2 oz
2 tbsp	seasoned corn or potato flour	2 tbsp
4	anchovy fillets, chopped very small	4
4	shallots or small onions, peeled and chopped very small	4
300ml	Marsala or sweet red wine	½ pint
	large bunch fresh herbs — parsley, thyme, bayleaves	
2	lemons	2

1. Remove the giblets from the ducks. Set the liver aside.
2. Heat the oil in a heavy pan and add the onions, carrot, bacon and mushrooms.
3. Fry briskly for 5-10 minutes, stirring frequently to prevent it burning, or until the vegetables are well tanned.
4. Add whichever flour you are using and continue to cook and stir for a further few minutes until the flour is also lightly browned.
5. Gradually add the wine, stirring continually, and then the stock or water.
6. Add the giblets, parsley and bouquet garni. Bring to the boil, reduce to a simmer and cook at a gentle simmer for an hour.
7. Strain the gravy and season with black pepper and with sea salt if it needs it.
8. Joint the duck into 4 breasts and 4 legs, removing any excess fat or skin. You can use the carcase and wings to make an excellent duck soup.
9. Heat the butter, spread or oil in one large or two smaller heavy lidded pans.
10. Briskly fry the duck joints until they are lightly browned on all sides.
11. Remove onto kitchen paper and pat dry. Throw out the excess fat or reserve for other purposes.

12. Wipe the inside of the pan or pans with kitchen paper. Roll the joints well in the seasoned flour and return them to the pans.

13. Chop the duck liver very small and add to the pans along with the chopped anchovies and onions.

14. Add 600ml/1 pint of the gravy and the Marsala along with the herbs, well tied together. Ensure that the liver, onion, anchovy and herbs are well submerged in the sauce. Bring to the boil, cover and reduce to a simmer for 40 minutes.

15. Remove the herbs and adjust the seasoning to taste.

16. Grate the rind from the lemons and add to the sauce. Squeeze the juice and add gradually to your own taste.

17. Serve the duck joints with the sauce spooned over the top and lightly steamed new potatoes and a green vegetable.

CASSEROLE-ROASTED PHEASANT WITH BUTTERNUT SQUASH

Game birds need careful cooking and just plain roasting can often produce a tough bird. Casserole roasting allows you to cook the birds slowly in well-flavoured juices, which will help even the toughest of birds. | Serves 6

2 tbsp	oil	2 tbsp
30	shallots or button onions, peeled	30
550g	butternut squash, cubed	1 ¼ lbs
5	sprigs fresh thyme	5
3	pheasant or other game birds, plucked and cleaned	3
	freshly ground black pepper and sea salt	
450ml	Marsala or other sweet red wine	15 fl oz

1. Heat the oil in a heavy lidded casserole.

2. Fry the shallots and squash briskly for 5-10 minutes until they are lightly tanned all over.

3. Lay the thyme on top and the birds over the thyme.

4. Grind a little black pepper and sea salt over the birds then pour over the Marsala.

5. Cover tightly and simmer very gently for 1½-2 hours.

6. Serve with new or roast potatoes or brown rice and a green vegetable.

Note: Marsala wine was produced in the west of Sicily and, in the 19th century, was fortified with brandy so that it would survive long sea voyages back to northern Europe. It was especially popular during prohibition in the USA as Marsala bottles looked quite medicinal so were less risky to acquire than some other forms of wine. Marsala is particularly popular in Italian cooking.

SPICY WEST INDIAN CHICKEN CASSEROLE

This is a very hot and 'sunny' casserole, exotically flavoured with the banana. Serve with lots of fluffy white rice and a fresh green salad. | Serves 6

4	large cloves garlic	4
2-3	fresh or dried red chillies	2-3
3 tbsp	olive or sunflower oil	3 tbsp
1 heaped tsp	ground coriander	1 heaped tsp
2	large red peppers, de-seeded and sliced	2
200g	okra, sliced	7 oz
550g	chicken meat, cut in bite-size pieces	1 ¼ lbs
675g	tinned tomatoes	1 ½ lbs
1 tsp	salt	1 tsp
½ tsp	black pepper	½ tsp
2	medium-large bananas	2

1. Peel and slice the garlic and de-seed and chop the chillies.
2. Heat the oil in a deep, heavy pan and add the garlic, chillies, coriander, peppers and okra.
3. Stir well and cook gently for 10 minutes.
4. Add the chicken and tomatoes, salt and pepper. Stir well.
5. Bring to the boil, reduce to a simmer, cover and cook for 30-35 minutes or until the chicken is cooked through.
6. Peel and slice the banana thinly. Add to the chicken mixture and stir in thoroughly, but gently. Return to the heat for a further 5 minutes.
7. Adjust seasoning to taste.
8. Serve with rice, a green salad and extra hot sauce.

Note: Do not forget to wash your hands thoroughly after handling chillies and not to touch your eyes until you have done so.

CHICKEN KORMA WITH COCONUT MILK

A chicken korma is a rich, creamy, lightly spiced dish that, in the west, is normally made with cream or yogurt but which traditionally can equally well be made with coconut milk. In fact, the coconut milk gives it, if anything, an even softer and silkier texture than using more conventional animal-milk cream. Serve the korma with plenty of white rice and a good green salad. | Serves 6 | Picture page 97

4 tbsp	olive or sunflower oil	4 tbsp
3 level tsp	ground ginger	3 level tsp
3 level lsp	ground cumin	3 level tsp
400g	onions, peeled and sliced thinly	14 oz
600ml	coconut milk	1 pint
25g	ground almonds	2 oz
4	large chicken breasts cut into thick strips	4
300g	small young potatoes, scrubbed and sliced thickly	11 oz
	sea salt and freshly ground black pepper	

1. Heat the oil in a heavy, deep pan and add the spices. Cook gently for a couple of minutes.
2. Add the onions and cook gently, stirring regularly, for 8-10 minutes or until they are starting to soften.
3. Mix the coconut milk into the ground almonds and add to the mixture.
4. Add the chicken and potatoes and season lightly.
5. Bring slowly to the boil, cover, reduce the heat and simmer gently for 30 minutes or until the chicken and potatoes are both cooked.
6. Adjust the seasoning to taste and serve with plenty of white rice and a good green salad.

Note: A korma is a northern Indian dish dating from the 18th century. Like much north Indian cooking, the spices are delicate rather than fiery and the texture creamy.

ROAST HAUNCH OF VENISON

This recipe was originally developed for the book of 'festive feasts' I wrote for the British Museum and was billed as part of Hiawatha's wedding feast! The acidity of the cranberries and the vinegar will help to break down any toughness in the meat. | Serves 6

100g	fresh cranberries	4 oz
	1 level tsp ground allspice or 2 tsp allspice berries	
6 tbsp	maple syrup	6 tbsp
6 tbsp	red wine vinegar	6 tbsp
1.75 kg	joint of venison	4 lbs
6	streaky bacon rashers	6
900g	young greens – spinach, watercress, pak choi, lettuce, parsley, chard, or any combination thereof	2 lbs

1. Lightly crush the cranberries with the allspice, maple syrup and wine vinegar in a food processor.
2. Put the venison into a bowl large enough to hold it and pour over the cranberry mixture making sure that all the venison is covered.
3. Cover and leave in a cool larder or the top of a fridge for at least 24 hours.
4. Heat the oven to 170C/325F/gas mark 3.
5. Transfer the venison to a roasting tin and pour the marinade around the bottom. Cover the joint with the bacon rashers and a piece of aluminium baking foil.
6. Bake for 2-2¼ hours, removing the foil about 1 hour before it is cooked. Serve with the juices.
7. Just before you are ready to serve the venison, wash and chop the greens roughly.
8. Steam or boil them for a couple of minutes in a few centimetres/ ½ inch of water. They should be just wilted. Serve with the venison.

Note: Deer were a plentiful and common food for American Indians in the 19th century. They believed that when they ate the flesh of brave animals some of the animal's courage was transferred to the eater. The liver and kidneys were regarded as a source of instant energy and since they could be eaten raw, were sometimes used as a 'pick-me-up' after a long hunt. Because they were so nourishing and easy to eat, the remains would be taken back to the camp as a gift for the elderly members of the tribe.

KHORESH WITH POMEGRANATE

This is a wonderfully rich khoresh designed for wild duck or pheasant, but which tastes almost as delicious with chicken or farmed duck. You should be able to get the pomegranate juice and seeds in a Middle Eastern or Greek delicatessen. Serve with chilau rice (see p155) and follow with a green salad. | Serves 6

3 tbsp	olive oil	3
	1 or 2 ducks (depending on size), 3 pheasants or a chicken – jointed	
2	medium onions	2
350g	coarsely chopped walnuts or pecans	12 oz
1	piece cinnamon stick	1
1 heaped tbsp	brown sugar	1 heaped tbsp
	sea salt and freshly ground pepper	
450ml	pomegranate juice	15 fl oz
50g	pomegranate seeds, fresh or dried, optional	2 oz
	juice of ½-1 lemon	

1. Heat the oven to 160C/325F/gas mark 3.
2. Heat the oil in an ovenproof casserole and brown the jointed bird(s) thoroughly on all sides. Remove from the pan and set aside.
3. Brown the onions in the same oil then return the birds to the pan.
4. Add the nuts, dried pomegranate seeds (if using fresh they should be added later) cinnamon, sugar, seasoning and the pomegranate juice.
5. Cover the casserole and cook gently for 1½-2 hours or till the meat is really tender and falling off the bone.
6. Carefully remove the bird or birds from the casserole and put on a baking tray.
7. Increase the heat of the oven to 180C/350F/gas mark 4.
8. Return the birds to the oven for 15 minutes to slightly crisp the skin.
9. Meanwhile, skim the excess fat from the sauce (if you are using a duck there will be a great deal) and save it for other uses.
10. Add the fresh pomegranate seeds, if you are using them.
11. Adjust the seasoning of the sauce to taste, adding as much lemon juice as you find necessary to set off the sweet richness of the sauce.
12. Serve the birds with chilau rice (p155) with the sauce spooned over it. Follow with a green leaf salad.

Note: A khoresh is a delicate Persian stew – a combination of meats, or fish with vegetables, fresh or dried fruits, grains, and sometimes nuts. The seasoning is subtle and the flavours are achieved by long slow cooking.

DUCK BREASTS WITH APPLE AND GINGER

Duck can be quite a rich meat so the ginger and sharp apples provide a good contrast. | Serves 6

2	medium Bramley or other sharp cooking apples	2
75g	peeled fresh ginger	3 oz
6	large duck breasts with skin	6
	sea salt and freshly ground black pepper	
1 tbsp	goat's butter or olive oil	1 tbsp
2	large sprigs rosemary	2
300ml	ginger wine	10 fl oz
150ml	water	5 fl oz

1. Peel, quarter and slice the apples and slice about half of the peeled ginger root finely.

2. Lay the duck breasts out, on the counter, skin down, and season with salt and freshly ground black pepper.

3. Lay a layer of apple slices down one of the breasts and top with a layer of ginger slices. Cover this with a second duck breast, skin side up. Tie the breasts together with string and grind more black pepper over the top. Repeat with the remaining four breasts.

4. Heat the goat's butter or oil in a wide heavy pan and lay the three pairs of breasts in the pan. Fry briskly, without burning for 4-5 minutes or until the skin is nicely brown. Turn over carefully, grind more black pepper over the upturned side and fry for another 5 minutes.

5. Lay the sprigs of rosemary between the breasts and add the ginger wine and water to the pan, bring to the boil, lower the heat, cover the pan and simmer very gently for 20 minutes.

6. Meanwhile, cook the remaining apple with the remaining ginger, in large pieces, and 100ml/4 fl oz water until the apple is totally soft. Add the remaining water if it looks as though it is drying up. Allow to cool and then discard the ginger pieces. Remove the breasts from the pan and keep warm.

7. Chill the cooking liquid briefly to help separate the fat, then remove the fat and keep for roasting potatoes!

8. Add the cooking juices to the puréed apple, reheat and adjust the seasoning if required.

9. Remove the string and carefully slice the duck breasts thickly. Lay out in a serving dish and serve with the sauce and a green vegetable or salad.

MEAT

BEEF
Yorkshire Puddings
Spicy Enchiladas
Beef Tajine with Chickpeas and Cumin
Beef and Chilli Stir Fry
Steak Pies
Pot Roast with Red Cabbage
Minced Beef Casserole with Spinach
Steak with Garlic
Beef Casserole with Ginger

LAMB
Leg of Lamb with Puy Lentils
Lamb's Kidneys Provençal with Camargue Rice
Roast Leg of Lamb (or Mutton) with Garlic
Roast Lamb with Mushroom Cream
Laurent's Lamb Couscous with Quinoa
Ginger Lamb and Lentil Stew
Sun-dried Tomato and Lamb Kidney Risotto
Lamb Chops with Olives and Courgettes

PORK
Casseroled Ham with Lentils
Portuguese Loin of Pork
Garbanzo Stew
The Emperor's Sliced Pork with Garlic
Ham Kebabs
'Carbonnadoed' Pork Ribs
Red Cabbage with Spicy Sausage
Sausages with Mashed Roots

YORKSHIRE PUDDINGS

The secret to making Yorkshire puddings is to ensure that the oven and the oiled tray into which you pour the batter are really hot. | Makes 12 individual puddings

50g	gram (chickpea) flour	2 oz
50g	rice flour or 100g/4 oz of your favourite gluten-free flour	2 oz
1	egg	1
	sea salt and freshly ground black pepper	
120ml	plain unsweetened soya or oat milk	4 fl oz
90ml	water	3 fl oz
2 tbsp	sunflower oil	2 tbsp

1. Heat the oven to 190C/375F/gas mark 5.
2. Put the flours, egg and milk, with a pinch of salt and a grind of black pepper, in the food processor and whizz thoroughly.
3. Pour a couple of drops of sunflower oil into the bottom of 12 individual mince pies tins or one flat baking dish.
4. Put in the oven for a couple of minutes to heat until the oil is smoking.
5. Pour the batter into the individual holders or into the tin and return it to the oven at once.
6. Bake for 20 minutes or till the puddings are risen and golden.
7. Serve at once with beef, with gravy — or with jam.

Note: In the days when meat was scarce, the Yorkshire pudding would be cooked under the roast so that the juices from the roast dripped onto it. You would then have a good helping of the pudding before the meat so that you were not too hungry when you got to the meat and didn't eat too much. If there was any pudding left over, it was eaten as a dessert with jam.

SPICY ENCHILADAS

Your enchiladas will taste better if you cook the filling a day in advance to allow the flavours time to 'mature'.

Taco shells made just of corn should naturally be gluten free but you need to check the ingredients carefully as some may include wheat flour. | Serves 6

	1 pack of 12 corn taco shells (check ingredients)	
3 tbsp	olive/sunflower oil	3 tbsp
250g	minced beef	9 oz
2	medium onions, chopped roughly	2
2	cloves garlic, peeled	2
2 tbsp	tomato purée	2 tbsp
1 x 240g	tin tomatoes	1 x 8 oz
2-4	fresh red chillies (depending how hot you want your enchiladas), de-seeded and chopped	2-4
	sea salt and freshly ground black pepper	
1 x 400g	tin red kidney beans, drained	1 x 14 oz
	handful chopped parsley	
½	iceberg lettuce, shredded	½
	Optional garnish: grated goat's, sheep's or soya cheese	

1. Heat the oil and fry the minced beef until it is browned.
2. Meanwhile, put the onions, garlic, tomato purée, tinned tomatoes and the chilli into the food processor and purée.
3. Add the mixture to the beef, bring back to the boil, season lightly, cover and simmer for 30-40 minutes.
4. Add the kidney beans and continue to simmer, uncovered for a further 15 minutes. Cool and set aside for 24 hours.

To serve
5. Reheat the filling and sprinkle in some chopped parsley.
6. Shred the lettuce.
7. Heat the taco shells in a microwave on full power for 30 seconds or in a pre-heated moderate oven for 2-3 minutes.
8. Put a lining of lettuce in each taco shell, then spoon in the meat filling and, if you are using it, sprinkle over some grated goat's, sheep's or soya cheese.

BEEF TAJINE WITH CHICKPEAS AND CUMIN

A tajine is the traditional all-in-one stew of North Africa, cooked long and slowly and tasting delicious. Tajines vary depending on which part of North Africa you are in but the essential element which gives them their flavour is the long, slow cooking. The ingredients are sometimes sautéed first but not always. A slow cooker is ideal for tajine cooking. | Serves 6

4 tbsp	olive oil	4 tbsp
2 heaped tsp	ground cumin	2 heaped tsp
4	medium onions, chopped	4
4	cloves garlic, crushed	4
650g	stewing beef, trimmed and cut in large pieces	1½ lbs
350g	cooked or tinned chickpeas	12 oz
400g	young potatoes, scrubbed and halved or quartered	14 oz
	water	
	salt and pepper	
3	handfuls of fresh parsley or coriander leaves	3

1. Heat the oil in a pan just big enough to hold the meat and the vegetables.
2. Add the cumin and cook for a minute.
3. Add the onions, garlic and the beef and cook briskly for a couple of minutes only just to brown the beef.
4. Add the potatoes and chickpeas, a little salt and pepper and enough water to just cover the meat and vegetables.
5. Bring slowly to the boil, cover tightly and then cook very slowly for 2-3 hours or overnight in a slow cooker. The meat should be falling apart by the time the tajine is cooked.
6. Adjust the seasoning to taste and serve with plenty of freshly chopped parsley or coriander.
7. Serve with plenty of salad and maybe a gluten-free flat bread.

Note: The traditional tajine pot consists of a flat, circular base with low sides and a large domed or cone-shaped lid which sits inside the base unit. It is specially designed so that the condensation that forms during the cooking drips back into the food thus keeping it moist. It is made of heavy clay which is sometimes, but not always, glazed. When the food is cooked the domed lid can be lifted off and the food served from the base.

BEEF AND CHILLI STIR FRY

Stir fries are quick and easy and almost infinitely adaptable. Including the garlic, onions, chilli, ginger and soya sauce will give a Far Eastern flavour to any combination of meats, fish or vegetables but this method of cooking works no matter what the ingredients.

You can serve the stir fry with rice but it will probably not need any other vegetables as there are so many already in it. You can use either red or green chillies, depending on how hot you want your dish — the red are usually quite mild, the green a lot hotter. Remember to wash your hands well after handling the chillies. | Serves 6

3 tbsp	stir fry, olive or coconut oil	3 tbsp
6	cloves garlic, peeled and sliced	6
1-2	red or green chillies, seeds removed, thinly sliced	1-2
50g	peeled fresh ginger, cut into thin matchsticks	2 oz
3	small raw beetroot, well scrubbed and cut into thin, wide strips	3
20	button mushrooms, halved	20
1	large green pepper, de-seeded and thinly sliced	1
3 tbsp	wheat/gluten-free soya sauce or tamari	3 tbsp
1 tsp	miso dissolved in 200ml/7 fl oz boiling water	1 tsp
4 large handfuls	curly kale, tough stems removed, washed and chopped roughly	4 large handfuls
400g	fillet or other tender cut of beef, cut into matchsticks no thicker than a pencil	14 oz
20	spring onions, trimmed, halved lengthways if they are big, and cut in 5cm/2 inch pieces	20
	extra soya sauce, sea salt and freshly ground black pepper to taste	

1. In a wok or wide frying pan heat the oil and add the garlic, chillies and ginger.
2. Fry briskly but without burning for a couple of minutes then add the beetroot, mushrooms and green pepper and continue to fry briskly for a further 5 minutes.
3. Add the soya sauce and the dissolved miso, stir well, cover the wok, reduce the heat and cook for 10 minutes or until the beetroot is starting to soften.
4. Add the curly kale, stir well in and cover again.
5. Continue to cook for another couple of minutes then remove the cover, add the beef and onions and increase the heat.
6. Cook briskly for a couple of minutes until the beef is lightly cooked then remove from the heat.
7. Adjust the seasoning to taste and serve at once.

Note: Miso is the Japanese equivalent of a western Bovril or Marmite — a thick paste made from fermented soya beans and salt which can be used as a spread, a drink, a soup or a stock for cooking. There are many varieties of miso but all are highly nutritious and, provided they have been made properly and are not too salty, absolutely delicious.

STEAK PIES

I devised two versions of this steak pie, one with Marsala and one with gluten-free beer. Both were delicious so I am giving you the recipes for both.

Because different gluten-free flours have different textures they often absorb different amounts of liquid so, if you are using your own gluten-free flour combination for the pastry, you may need to be flexible about the amount of water you need to add. | Serves 6

	Pastry for both pies	
100g	gram (chickpea) or maize flour	4 oz
50g	rice flour	2 oz
	or 150g/6 oz of your favourite gluten-free flour	
1/2 tsp	xanthan gum	1/2 tsp
75g	goat's butter or dairy-free spread, cut up into small pieces	3 oz
90ml	cold water	3 fl oz
1	egg (optional)	1

1. Whizz the flours with the xanthan gum and butter or spread in a food processor until the texture of breadcrumbs.
2. Add most of the water, whizz again briefly. If the pastry is holding together remove from the processor, roll into a ball and chill. If it is still too dry add a little more water and whizz again before rolling and chilling.

WITH MARSALA AND SWEET POTATO FILLING

Marsala, which is a rich, sweet red wine, combines beautifully with the sweet potato and the beef.

550g	stewing beef, trimmed and cubed	1¼ lbs
400g	sweet potato, peeled and diced into large cubes	14 oz

2 tbsp	well seasoned cornflour or potato flour	2 tbsp
200ml	Marsala	7 fl oz
200ml	gluten/wheat-free beef or vegetable stock	7 fl oz

1. Heat the oven to 160C/325F/gas mark 3.
2. Roll the cubed beef and the sweet potato in the flour and lay out in the bottom of a pie dish. Add the wine and the stock, cover the dish tightly and bake for 1½ hours or until the beef is really tender.
3. To complete the pie, increase oven temperature to 180C/350F/gas mark 4.
4. Roll out pastry between 2 well-floured sheets of clingfilm.
5. Wet the edges of the pie dish and line with a thin piece of pastry.
6. Wet this in turn, remove one layer of clingfilm and carefully lift the pastry lid onto the pie. Remove other sheet of clingfilm. Press down the edges with your fingers. If the pastry tears cover the tears with pastry leaves or balls 'stuck' in place with a dab of water.
7. Decorate the pie with leaves or balls and brush generously with beaten egg.
8. Return to the oven for a further 25-30 minutes or until the pastry is cooked and lightly tanned.
9. Serve with lots of fresh green vegetables.

WITH BEER

You can use just one or several vegetables with your beef in this version of the pie. My favourite combination is mushroom and leek but feel free to be inventive.

550g	stewing beef, trimmed and cubed	1¼ lbs
2 tbsp	well seasoned cornflour or potato flour	2 tbsp
12-15	largish button mushrooms or 200g/7 oz	12-15
	peeled and diced sweet potato or potato, or 12	
	shallots, peeled but left whole, or 2	
	medium leeks, peeled and cut in thick slices	
400ml	gluten-free beer or stout (see Resources on page 234)	14 fl oz

1. Heat the oven to 160C/325F/gas mark 3.
2. Roll the cubed beef and whichever vegetables you are using in the potato or cornflour and spread it out in the bottom of a pie dish. Add the beer, cover the dish tightly and bake for 1½ hours or until the beef is really tender.
3. Complete the pie as above and serve with lots of fresh green vegetables.

POT ROAST WITH RED CABBAGE

This is a really hearty, north European dish, full of flavour and designed to keep out the winter chill. | Serves 6

1 kg	pot roast or rolled topside of beef	2¼ lbs
9	small red onions, peeled but kept whole	9
1	head fennel, chopped roughly	1
6	small, whole beets, scrubbed and topped and tailed	6
¼	medium red cabbage, sliced	¼
2 heaped tsp	coriander seeds, bruised with a rolling pin	2 heaped tsp
	several stalks fresh parsley	
4	bay leaves	4
	sea salt and freshly ground black pepper	
1 litre	wheat and gluten-free stock	1¾ pints
300ml	red wine	½ pint

1. Put the beef in the middle of a heavy casserole.
2. Surround it with the onions, fennel, beets and red cabbage.
3. Sprinkle over the coriander seeds and add the parsley and bay leaves and a little seasoning.
4. Pour in the stock and red wine.
5. Cover the pot and slowly bring to the boil.
6. Turn down the heat and cook very slowly for 2-3 hours or in a slow cooker overnight.
7. Allow to get completely cold and remove any extra fat which has risen to the top and set.
8. To serve, reheat and adjust the seasoning if it needs it.
9. Serve with baked or mashed potatoes and a green vegetable.

MINCED BEEF CASSEROLE WITH SPINACH

This is a really tasty casserole and can be adapted to your own taste in mustard — seriously hot or mild and flavoursome. However, check the mustard ingredients carefully — good French mustard should be gluten/wheat free while classic English mustard is made with wheat flour. | Serves 6

3 tbsp	olive oil	3 tbsp
3	medium onions, finely chopped	3
3	large carrots, scrubbed and cut into thin rounds	3
30	button mushrooms, wiped, kept whole or cut in half	30
600g	minced beef	1¼ lbs
4-6 tbsp	French or wholegrain mustard — as hot or mild as you like	4-6 tbsp
180ml	red wine	6 fl oz
240ml	water or gluten/wheat-free stock	8 fl oz
	sea salt and freshly ground black pepper	
340g	fresh leaf spinach	12 oz

1. Heat the oil in a heavy pan and add the onions and carrots. Cook briskly, but without burning, for 10 minutes.
2. Add the mushrooms and cook for a further 5 minutes.
3. Add the beef and cook briskly for another few minutes then add the mustard and mix well in.
4. Add the red wine, water or stock and some sea salt and freshly ground black pepper.
5. Bring to the boil, lower the temperature, cover and simmer gently for 1-1½ hours.
6. Adjust seasoning to taste.
7. Wash the spinach. If using baby leaves leave them whole; if using larger leaves you will need to tear them into small pieces.
8. Add the spinach to the casserole and continue to cook for 3-4 minutes or until the spinach is just wilted.
9. Serve at once with lots of rice, baked or mashed potatoes or another root vegetable.

Note: Mustard should be made from the seeds of black, brown or white mustard plants, steeped in alcohol and vinegar and then puréed with salt, pepper and herbs. In wholegrain mustard the seeds are not puréed at all, giving it a much grainier texture; in smooth mustards (such as English) they are entirely pulverised. Wholegrain mustards should not contain any wheat or gluten but smooth mustards, such as English, often do.

STEAK WITH GARLIC

This is so simple that it scarcely justifies being a recipe but so good that I would like people to enjoy it.

---

1 steak per person, cut of your choice – I prefer to go for a rib eye or rump which may be slightly less tender than a fillet but which has a deeper flavour
freshly ground sea salt and freshly ground black pepper
4 cloves of garlic per person

---

1. Lay the steak out on a plate and grind over a little sea salt and black pepper.
2. Crush 2 cloves of garlic in a garlic press and spread over the steak.
3. Turn the steak and repeat the process on the other side. Leave for 1-2 hours to absorb the flavours.
4. Grill, barbecue or fry to your taste and serve with baked potatoes and a green vegetable or salad.

Note: Sea salt is obtained by evaporating sea water and can have very different flavours, and mineral content, depending on where it has been gathered. Table salt is usually refined from mined rock salt and is pure sodium chloride. Table salt just makes food salty, good sea salt adds layers of flavours of its own as well as bringing out the flavour of the food with which it is used.

BEEF CASSEROLE WITH GINGER

This is a lovely warming dish for a chilly day in early autumn. The ginger is not aggressive but gives an unusual flavour. | Serves 6

12	shallots	12
50g	piece root ginger	2 oz
4 tbsp	olive oil	4 tbsp
900g	stewing beef	2 lbs
2 level tbsp	cornflour	2 level tbsp
	sea salt and freshly ground black pepper	
300ml	red wine	10 fl oz
250ml	gluten and wheat-free beef or vegetable stock	8 fl oz
250g	green beans	9 oz
350g	gluten and wheat-free penne	12 oz

1. Peel the shallots. Peel the ginger and cut into thin matchsticks.
2. Heat 2 tbsp of the oil in a deep pan and add the shallots and ginger and fry moderately briskly for 4 minutes.
3. Meanwhile, trim the beef and cut into bite-size pieces.
4. Season the cornflour and toss the beef in it until each piece is well covered.
5. Add to the pan and fry briskly for 3-4 minutes or until the flour is turning brown.
6. Add the wine and the stock, stirring well to make sure that you get all the burnt bits off the bottom of the pan.
7. Reduce the heat, cover the pan and simmer gently for 1 hour.
8. Trim the beans and cut into short pieces. Add to the beef and continue to cook gently for another 15 minutes or until the beans are softened but still slightly crispy.
9. Meanwhile, heat a large pot of salted boiling water and cook the pasta according to the instructions on the pack.
10. Drain, add the extra oil, mix well then arrange around the outside of a large serving dish.
11. Pile the beef with all its juices in the middle and serve at once.

Note: The easy availability of root ginger in the west has enormously broadened its use. When I was a child the only ginger we knew was powdered and was used in gingerbread. We certainly never thought of using it in savoury dishes where it adds the most delicious flavour to almost anything.

LEG OF LAMB WITH PUY LENTILS

This dish is better if the flavours are allowed to mature for at least 24 hours so, ideally, cook it the day before you want to eat it. | Serves 6

2 tbsp	virgin olive oil	2 tbsp
6 tbsp	Puy lentils	6 tbsp
3	medium leeks, trimmed and halved	3
2	medium-sized parsnips, halved lengthways, cut in rounds	2
10	button mushrooms, halved or quartered	10
2 tsp	each dried marjoram and thyme	2 tsp
2	bay leaves	2
½ tsp	each ground coriander and salt	½ tsp
1 tsp	black pepper corns	1 tsp
1	small leg of lamb	1

6	cloves garlic, peeled	6
200ml	red wine	7 fl oz
500ml	gluten/wheat-free vegetable/chicken stock	18 fl oz
1 x 400g	tin haricot beans, drained	1 x 14 oz

1. Put the oil in the bottom of a heavy casserole with the lentils, leeks, parsnips, mushrooms, herbs and spices and mix well together.
2. Cut six slits in the lamb and insert the garlic cloves then place it on top of the vegetable and lentil mixture.
3. Add the red wine and stock and bring very slowly to the boil.
4. Simmer very gently for 2 hours. Alternatively bake the casserole in a low oven (160C/325F/gas mark 3) for 2½ hours.
5. Remove the casserole from the oven and lift out the lamb.
6. Set it aside and gently mix the haricot beans into the vegetables.
7. Return the lamb to the casserole and set aside to cool. Leave in a cool place for 24 hours.
8. Before serving reheat the casserole over a low heat or in a medium oven for 35-40 minutes.
9. Adjust the seasoning to taste and serve with green vegetables.

Note: Puy lentils, known in France as the 'pauper's caviar', are small, round, dark green lentils which have lots of flavour and remain firm after cooking so are great for salads. They were originally grown in the volcanic soils around Puy in the Auvergne although they are now also grown in Italy and the USA.

LAMB'S KIDNEYS PROVENÇAL WITH CAMARGUE RICE

This is a deliciously colourful and nutritious dish hailing from the sunny south of France. | Serves 6

	Rice dish	
3 tbsp	olive oil	3 tbsp
3	leeks, finely sliced	3
350g	red Camargue or wholegrain brown rice	12 oz
1 litre	wheat/gluten-free vegetable stock	1¾ pints
50g	lightly toasted pine nuts	2 oz
	sea salt and freshly ground black pepper	

1. Heat the oil in a wide pan and gently cook the leeks for 10 minutes.
(While they are cooking, start cooking the vegetables for the kidneys see below.)
2. Add the rice, stir around for a few minutes then add the stock.
3. Bring to the boil and simmer, uncovered, for 15-20 minutes or until the rice is cooked. Add extra liquid if needed.
4. Add the pine nuts, season to taste.

Kidneys

6 tbsp	virgin olive oil	6 tbsp
3	large onions, peeled and sliced	3
4	large cloves of garlic, peeled and thinly sliced	4
4	medium yellow, orange or red peppers, deseeded and sliced	4
4	heaped teaspoons of dried oregano	4
100g	sun-dried tomatoes	4 oz
500ml	medium sherry or half sherry and half Marsala	18 fl oz
12	lamb's kidneys, trimmed and sliced	12

1. Heat the oil in a wide pan and add the onions, garlic, peppers and oregano.
2. Cook gently for 20-25 minutes or until all the vegetables are quite soft.
3. Meanwhile, chop the sun-dried tomatoes and put them in a bowl with the sherry or sherry and Marsala.
4. Heat them gently together without boiling, for 3 minutes.
5. Add the kidneys to the onion and pepper mixture and continue to fry gently for 3-4 minutes. Add the tomatoes and sherry and mix well.
6. Continue to cook for a further 4-5 minutes and season to taste with sea salt and freshly ground black pepper.
7. Serve with the rice and a green vegetable.

Note: Red rice is a quite new and deliciously nutty variety of rice grown in the Camargue — the huge river delta between the two arms of the Rhone river just south of Arles on France's Mediterranean coast.

ROAST LEG OF LAMB (OR MUTTON) WITH GARLIC

Many years ago when I was working on a Victorian cookbook I came across this wonderful recipe from Edward Abbott, a wealthy Tasmanian doing the Grand Tour. The book is now, sadly, out of print but the recipe lives on! Mr Abbott says of the dish:

'When the *gigot à l'ail* [leg of lamb with garlic], which we had specially requested, was placed on the table it appeared to be a *gigot aux haricots* [leg of lamb with haricot beans], but the meat was delicious and the beans were certainly superior to and bearing a different flavour from any haricots we had ever tasted before....... We summoned the landlord and demanded why we had not been served what we ordered but were assured that the dish that we had just eaten, and enjoyed, was indeed *gigot à l'ail* and what we had mistaken for beans, was garlic.'

In the original recipe the cloves of garlic were blanched three times but 21st century garlic is far milder than 19th century garlic so one blanching will be quite enough.

12	heads of garlic	12
1	medium leg of lamb (or mutton) – approx 2 kg/4½ lbs	1
	sea salt	
1 tbsp	gluten/wheat-free flour	1 tbsp
150ml	red wine	5 fl oz
pinch	dark brown sugar	pinch

1. Peel all the garlic heads – a longish business but there is no way round it.
2. Put the cloves of garlic in a pan covered with light salted water, bring to the boil and simmer for 3 minutes.
3. Spread the cloves over the bottom of a baking tray but keep them close together so that they remain under the meat and get dripped on by the cooking juices, otherwise they will dry out.
4. Place the lamb or mutton on a rack above the garlic cloves and roast in a medium oven (180C/350F/gas mark 4) for 20 minutes per 450g/ lb.
5. When cooked remove to a warmed serving dish and pile the garlic cloves around the meat.
6. Drain any excess fat from the tin then add the flour. Stir and cook over a gentle heat for a few minutes then gradually add the red wine and enough water to thin to a gravy consistency.
7. Serve with the lamb and appropriate vegetables – roast potatoes and green beans would be appropriate.

ROAST LAMB WITH MUSHROOM CREAM

The combination of cooking apple and rosemary gives this dish a lovely fresh flavour. Serve with a mashed root vegetable (such as celeriac) and a lightly cooked green vegetable — mangetout or fine green beans would be good. | Serves 6

1½ kg	boned and rolled leg or shoulder of lamb	3 lbs
	sprig of fresh rosemary (or 1 teaspoon dried)	
3 tbsp	virgin olive or sunflower oil	3 tbsp
2	small onions, finely chopped	2
200g	button mushrooms, stems removed and thinly sliced	7 oz
1	medium cooking apple, peeled, cored and finely chopped	1
1 level tbsp	cornflour	1 level tbsp
500ml	gluten/wheat-free vegetable or chicken stock	18 fl oz
120ml	oat or soya cream	4 fl oz
2-3 tbsp	good quality French mustard (check ingredients)	2-3 tbsp
	sea salt and freshly ground black pepper	

1. Heat the oven to 180C/350F/gas mark 4.
2. Sit the lamb on top of the rosemary in a baking tray and bake for 1 hour to 1 hour and 20 minutes depending on how rare you like your lamb.
3. Meanwhile heat the oil in a heavy pan and gently cook the onions with the mushrooms and apple till all are quite soft.
4. Add the cornflour, stir around for a couple of minutes, then gradually add the stock.
5. Bring back to the simmer and cook for a few minutes, stirring all the while, till the sauce thickens slightly.
6. Add the oat or soya cream and 2 tbsp of the mustard. Taste for flavour and add more mustard, salt or pepper to suit your palate. Set aside till the lamb is cooked.
7. Just before serving, remove the lamb from the oven, remove as much fat as you can from the juices in the roasting tin and add these to the 'sauce'. Reheat.
8. Pour the 'sauce' into a preheated flattish serving dish, cut the strings from the lamb and place in the middle of the sauce to serve.

Note: Cornflour is an excellent thickener for sauces, although, since it is rather more efficient at the job than wheat flour, one needs to be careful not to use too much. If you are corn intolerant, arrowroot is a good alternative.

LAURENT'S LAMB COUSCOUS WITH QUINOA

In the 1980s Laurent, from Morocco, ran the most wonderful couscous restaurant on an insignificant little parade of shops in north London, but enthusiasts would come from all over the city. Alas, Laurent has long since retired, but his recipe lives on in a wheat and gluten-free version.

Although quinoa does not have exactly the same texture as couscous and does not 'fluff up' in quite the same way, it is a close enough equivalent to work very well. | Serves 6

4 tbsp	olive or vegetable oil	4
2 heaped tsp	ground cumin	2 heaped tsp
4	cloves garlic, crushed	4
4-6	carrots, depending on size, scrubbed and cut in thick rounds	4-6
2	medium leeks, trimmed and cut in thick slices	2
2	sticks celery, cut in thick slices	2
	1 large red and 1 large green pepper, trimmed and cut in large dice	
700g	lamb (a boned shoulder will do excellently), trimmed and cubed	1½ lb
3	merguez or other spicy sausages (check ingredients) cut in thick slices	3
1 x 400g	tin peeled chopped tomatoes	1 x 14 oz
500ml	gluten/wheat-free vegetable or chicken stock	18 fl oz
	sea salt and freshly ground black pepper	
2	medium courgettes, sliced thickly	2
350g	white cabbage, chopped coarsely	12 oz
150g	mangetout, halved	6 oz
1 x 400g	tin chickpeas, drained	1 x 14 oz
1 tsp	harissa, Tabasco or hot sauce (check ingredients)	1 tsp
900ml	gluten/wheat-free vegetable or chicken stock	1½ pints
300g	quinoa	11 oz

1. Heat the oil in the bottom of a large pan and add the cumin and garlic.
2. Cook gently for a couple of minutes then add the carrots, leeks, celery and pepper. Continue to cook for another 5 minutes.
3. Add the lamb and sausages, fry for a minute or two, then add the tomatoes, the stock and a little seasoning.
4. Bring to the boil, cover and reduce the heat. Simmer for 40 minutes.
5. Add the courgettes, cabbage, mangetout, chickpeas and whichever hot sauce you are using. Re-cover and continue to simmer for a further 15 minutes.
6. Meanwhile, bring the remaining stock to the boil in a separate pan and add the quinoa. Cook briskly, uncovered for 8-10 minutes, or until the quinoa is

cooked and most of the liquid absorbed.

7. Adjust the seasoning of the 'stew' to taste and then serve in a big dish with the quinoa piled in the middle and the stew round the outside.

8. Serve with harissa to be added to taste.

GINGER LAMB AND LENTIL STEW

This is a really lovely 'one-pot' meal, satisfying but not too heavy. | Serves 6

4 tbsp	olive oil	4 tbsp
24	shallots	24
50g	knob of ginger, peeled and cut into matchsticks	2 oz
4 heaped tsp	ground cumin	4 heaped tsp
600g	stewing lamb, trimmed and cubed	1¼ lbs
400g	green lentils	14 oz
600ml	stock	1 pint
500ml	red wine	18 fl oz
400g	baby tomatoes	14 oz
1	largish green/white cabbage	1
	sea salt and freshly ground black pepper	

1. Heat the oil in a heavy pan and add the shallots, ginger and cumin.

2. Fry gently for 3-5 minutes.

3. Add the lamb and continue to cook for a few minutes more.

4. Add the lentils, stock, red wine and tomatoes, bring to the boil, cover and simmer for 1 hour, checking the liquid level periodically.

5. Chop the cabbage and add to the pot.

6. Cook for a further 8-10 minutes or until the cabbage is just cooked but still slightly crunchy.

7. Season to taste and serve in soup bowls with a spoon.

SUN-DRIED TOMATO AND LAMB KIDNEY RISOTTO

A very tasty and creamy risotto — and a great way to get the unenthusiastic to eat offal. | Serves 6

4	rashers back bacon	4
2	largish onions	2
4 tbsp	olive oil	4 tbsp
150g	button mushrooms, sliced	5 oz
18	sun-dried tomatoes	18
500g	risotto rice	18 oz
1 litre	liquid made up of the tomato soaking liquid and gluten/wheat-free chicken or vegetable stock	1¾ pints
300ml	dry white wine	½ pint
6	lamb's kidneys	6
3 tbsp	plain goat's, sheep's milk or soya yogurt sea salt and freshly ground black pepper	3 tbsp

1. Cut the bacon into small dice and peel and chop the onions finely. (If you are using a food processor, do not turn it into mush.)
2. Heat the oil in a large wide pan and add the bacon and onions.
3. Cook briskly but without burning for 4-5 minutes then add the mushrooms and continue to cook for a further 5 minutes.
4. Meanwhile, chop the sun-dried tomatoes into large pieces and soak in a small bowl in enough boiling water to cover them.
5. Add the rice to the pan and stir around.
6. Drain the tomatoes, reserving the liquid, and add them to the pan.
7. Make the liquid up to 1 litre/1¾ pints with the stock and add to the pan along with the wine. Stir well.
8. Bring to the boil then reduce the heat and simmer briskly for 10-15 minutes or until the rice is cooked and the liquid almost absorbed, stirring occasionally to prevent sticking.
9. The risotto should remain quite liquid — not dry like a pilaff — so add extra stock if it is drying out.
10. While the rice is cooking, trim and cut the kidneys into medium-size pieces about 6 per kidney. Add these to the risotto and continue to cook for 3-4 minutes — the kidneys should remain pink in the middle.
11. Add the yogurt and season to taste. Serve at once with a plain green salad.

Note: Sun-drying tomatoes on hot tile roofs was the way that Italians preserved tomatoes for winter storage, although today they have become a gourmet ingredient. Twenty pounds of fresh, ripe tomatoes will dry down to just one pound when they are sun-dried. Sun-dried tomatoes have the same nutritional value as fresh ones: high in lycopene, antioxidants and vitamins.

LAMB CHOPS WITH OLIVES AND COURGETTES

Lamb chops and cutlets can be very dry so this is a good way to cook them, complete with their own sauce. | Serves 6

4 tbsp	olive oil	4 tbsp
3	medium leeks, cleaned and finely sliced	3
3	sticks celery, cleaned and sliced	3
6	large cloves garlic, peeled and sliced	6
	6 small or 3 large courgettes, wiped and grated	
36	stuffed green olives, halved	36
6	chump or loin chops	6
	sea salt and freshly ground black pepper	
2	large sprigs of fresh rosemary or 2 tsp dried	2

1. Heat the oil in a heavy casserole and add the leeks, celery and garlic.
2. Cook gently, without burning, for 5-10 minutes or until they are quite soft.
3. Add the courgettes and the olives and continue to cook for a further 3-4 minutes.
4. Lay the lamb on top of the vegetables and grind over some salt and pepper.
5. Lay the rosemary sprigs over the lamb.
6. Cover the pan tightly and simmer very gently for 30-40 minutes depending on how pink you like your lamb.
7. Serve from the pan with a root and a green vegetable, depending on what you can eat.

CASSEROLED HAM WITH LENTILS

This recipe is for a warming winter casserole — one of those one-pot meals which only involve putting all the ingredients into a pot and letting it get on with it. | Serves 6

6	small onions, peeled but left whole	6
1	large parsnip, peeled and sliced	1
1	large sweet potato, peeled and diced/sliced	1
½	a medium butternut squash, peeled and diced	½
3	large handfuls of fresh spinach (you could also used frozen leaf)	3
1 tsp	freshly ground black pepper	1 tsp

6 heaped tbsp	Puy lentils	6 heaped tbsp
1 kg	piece fresh gammon	2¼ lbs
1 heaped tsp	gluten and wheat-free hot mustard	1 heaped tsp
1 litre	water	1¾ pints

1. Put all the ingredients apart from the mustard and water into a heavy fire-proof pot. Mix the water into the mustard and pour over the ingredients in the pot.
2. Bring slowly to the boil, cover and simmer very gently for at least 2 hours. Leave to cool in the pot.
3. Remove any excess fat and reheat.
4. Adjust the seasoning to taste if it needs it.
5. To serve, remove the piece of gammon from the pot and carve/cut into slices. Serve with the vegetables and cooking juices.

Note: Historically a 'side of gammon' was the whole, cured side of the hog including the hams, loins and the shoulders. Today the word gammon is used mostly for the hams. Gammons are cured using the 300-year-old Wiltshire cure which can take up to six weeks of soaking, or 'pickling' in a brine solution containing just enough sugar to counter some of the harsh taste of the salt but not enough to mask the natural taste of the cured ham.

PORTUGUESE LOIN OF PORK

This is a popular dish in all the coastal regions of Portugal where the *almejas* or clams are both abundant and cheap. The nearest English equivalent to such clams is a cockle but mussels are less fiddly to deal with, easier to get fresh and would taste just as good. You could of course cheat and use frozen cockles or mussels though the dish would not look as pretty. If you don't want to use loin of pork substitute chops. In Portugal the dish is served with lots of sauté potatoes and large wedges of lemon. | Serves 6

8-10	large cloves garlic, peeled	8-10
1 level tsp	sea salt	1 level tsp
3-4	dried chillies (depending on size), chopped small	3-4
900g	approx. loin of pork, sliced into 6 or 6 good pork chops	2 lbs
500g	old potatoes, scrubbed	1¼ lbs
4 tbsp	olive oil	4 tbsp

	40 fresh mussels or 60 cockles or 450g/1lb frozen	
1	onion, chopped finely	1
	several sprigs parsley, chopped	
300ml	water or water and white wine mixed	½ pint
2	lemons	2

1. Crush the garlic with the salt and chillies using the point of a tough knife. Spread the mixture over both sides of the pork and set aside for 24 hours in a larder or fridge.
2. Boil the potatoes and then slice thickly.
3. Clean the mussels or cockles thoroughly if they are fresh, discarding any which do not close when tapped and cutting off the beards.
4. Defrost the frozen ones if you are using them and drain them thoroughly, reserving the defrosted juices.
5. When ready to cook the dish, grill the pork under a high heat till it is cooked through and well browned on the outside.
6. While the pork is cooking, sauté the potato slices briskly on both sides in the oil until they are crisp and brown.
7. Meanwhile heat the wine and water with the onion and parsley till it is boiling. Drop in the cockles or mussels, cover with a tight fitting lid and cook over a very high heat till all the shells have opened — any which refuse to do so should be thrown out as it means they could be bad.
8. Lay the pork chops out on a serving dish and spoon over the seafood. Surround with the potatoes and serve with wedges of lemon.
9. If you are using frozen fish, heat the defrosted juices with the onion and parsley and a little extra white wine. Add the defrosted molluscs and heat gently till they are hot. Serve as above.

Note: In Portugal the pork would be cooked in a clay oven but it could also be cooked on a barbecue making this a delightfully summery southern dish.

GARBANZO STEW

A real Spanish peasant stew. If you do not want to use pork you could use a cheap joint of lamb/mutton (scrag end, breast etc), in which case you will need salt along with the black pepper. | Serves 6 | Picture page 117

300g	dried chickpeas	11 oz
750g	bacon hock or salted belly pork	1¾ lbs
4	large cloves garlic, peeled	4
4	large carrots, scrubbed	4
1 tsp	black pepper	1 tsp
4	bouquet garni	4
3 tbsp	olive oil	3 tbsp
3 litres	water	5 pints
500g	potatoes, scrubbed	1¼ lbs
400g	green cabbage	14 oz

1. Soak the chickpeas overnight in enough water to cover; drain.
2. Cut the meat, with fat, into medium-size cubes.
3. Slice the garlic (thinly) and the carrots (thickly).
4. Put all into a large pot and add the black pepper (you should not need any salt), the bouquet garni, oil and water.
5. Cover loosely, bring slowly to the boil and simmer for 2-3 hours or until the chickpeas are cooked.
6. Cut the potatoes in fairly large dice and add to the pot. Cook for a further 20 minutes.
7. Slice the cabbage coarsely and add to the pot. Cook for a further 10 minutes. Add salt to taste if needed and serve.

Note: Chickpeas (known as garbanzo beans in Spain) are one of our oldest foods, the earliest traces of which, in the Middle East, date from over 7,500 years ago. They come in various colours — although the most common are creamy yellow — are hugely versatile, much used in North African and Indian cooking (think hummus and channa masala), are very nutritious and make great gluten-free flour.

THE EMPEROR'S SLICED PORK WITH GARLIC

This is another of the recipes I devised when working on the British Museum's book *Festive Feasts* (see Spinach and Bean Curd Soup on page 23). It too could have been served at Emperor Qianlong's court. The pork is mouth-wateringly tender and absorbs the flavours of the sauce beautifully. You need to cook it several hours in advance to give the meat time to absorb fully all of the many flavours of the sauce. | Serves 6

800g	lean loin of pork, boned and rolled	1¾ lbs
6	spring onions, trimmed and chopped	6
2	thick slices of ginger root, peeled	2
400ml	water	14 fl oz
3 tbsp	peanut oil	3 tbsp
6	large cloves garlic, peeled and chopped finely	6
1 heaped tsp	each sea salt and muscovado sugar	1 heaped tsp
2 tbsp	rice vinegar	2 tbsp
2 tbsp	wheat/gluten-free soya sauce or tamari	2 tbsp
2 tsp	chilli oil	2 tsp

1. Put the pork in a heavy pot with the spring onions, ginger and water.
2. Bring to the boil and simmer, covered, for 45 minutes.
3. Remove the pork and cool slightly.
4. Keep the cooking water for stock; discard the onions and ginger.
5. Slice the pork thinly along the grain and lay the slices out on a serving dish.
6. Heat the peanut oil in a wok and stir fry the garlic for a minute.
7. Remove from the heat and mix in the sea salt, sugar, rice vinegar, soya sauce and chilli oil. Spoon over the pork slices and leave to marinate for a couple of hours.
8. Serve at room temperature with green salad.

Note: Traditional soya sauce is made by fermenting soya with kôji, a type of yeast, in giant urns under the sun; although today most soya sauces are fermented in controlled environments. Soya sauce should not contain any wheat or gluten but always check the ingredients as the cheaper varieties may do so.

HAM KEBABS

A great kebab for the barbecue but it does work just as well under a grill or in a hot oven. | Serves 6

750g	piece of unsmoked gammon	1¾ lbs
2 level tsp	ground cumin	2 level tsp
	grated peel and juice 3 large limes	
3 tbsp	maple syrup	3 tbsp
	vegetables and fruit for the kebab sticks — I used red and yellow peppers, courgette and fresh pineapple but feel free to use whatever you prefer or is in season	

1. Cut the ham into bite-size cubes.
2. Mix the cumin with the lime peel and juice and the maple syrup in a bowl just big enough to take the ham.
3. Add the ham, mix well, cover and leave to marinate for 24 hours, turning every now and then so all the ham gets bathed in the marinade.
4. Cut up the vegetables and fruit that you are using and thread them onto kebab sticks with the ham pieces.
5. Cook on a barbecue or under a grill basting with the remaining marinade.

'CARBONNADOED' PORK RIBS

This recipe comes from Robert May's *Accomplish't Cook*, published in 1660, but it tastes just as good now as it did then. | Serves 6

1.5 kg	approximately pork ribs	3½ lbs
	sea salt	
2 tbsp	fennel seeds, lightly crushed	2 tbsp
	freshly ground black pepper	
	red wine vinegar	

1. Spread the ribs out on a baking tray.
2. Sprinkle with the sea salt and the fennel seeds and leave for at least 1 hour.
3. Transfer to the barbecue and cook thoroughly — 15-20 minutes depending on the size of the ribs.
4. Serve the ribs with freshly ground black pepper and red wine vinegar, which 'each diner should sprinkle over the meat to their own taste'.

RED CABBAGE WITH SPICY SAUSAGE

A really dramatic looking — and tasting — dish. You can serve it hot or cold, as a dish on its own or an accompaniment to a roast meat. | Serves 6

2 tbsp	hemp or olive oil	2 tbsp
8	stalks celery	8
2 tsp	fennel seeds, lightly bruised	2 tsp
350g	finely sliced red cabbage	12 oz
120ml	red wine	4 fl oz
350g	chorizo or other spicy sausage (check the ingredients carefully) cut into 2.5cm/1 inch chunks	12 oz
	sea salt and freshly ground black pepper	
	sprig of fennel leaf or parsley to decorate	

1. Heat the oil in a heavy pan and add the celery and fennel seeds.
2. Cover and sweat over a low heat for 20-25 minutes or until the celery is quite soft.
3. Add the red cabbage, the wine and the sausage, cover the pan again and continue to sweat over a low heat for a further 20 minutes. The cabbage should still retain a little bit of crunch.
4. Season to taste with sea salt and freshly ground black pepper although, depending on the sausage you have used, you may not need much of either. Serve the dish hot, warm or cold, as a main course or as a substantial salad.

Note: Chorizo is a traditional sausage eaten all over Spain and made from chopped pork with garlic, chilli and paprika (which gives it its characteristic red colour). It is usually cured, although a 'soft' chorizo can be made by marinating the pork in the spices. It can come both hot (*picante*) and mild or sweet (*dulce*) so check when you buy! It should not contain any fillers (gluten) but, as always, check the ingredients.

SAUSAGES WITH MASHED ROOTS

Conventionally, 'mash' means mashed potatoes but in fact there is no reason why you should not mash any root vegetable or any combination of root vegetables. The combination in this recipe works really well but feel free to experiment with other root vegetables. Just remember that if you are using 'normal' potatoes and a food processor, less than 50% of the total mix should be potato or the mixture with go very gluey. | Serves 6

1	medium celeriac, peeled and cubed	1
1	medium sweet potato, peeled and cubed	1
1	medium parsnip, scrubbed and cubed	1
1	large potato, scrubbed and cubed	1
8-12	gluten/wheat-free sausages of your choice	8-12
1tbsp	goat's butter or dairy-free spread	1 tbsp
1 tbsp	goat's, oat or soya cream (optional)	1 tbsp
	sea salt and freshly ground black pepper	

1. Put the root vegetables in a steamer and steam until quite soft — this will probably take around 20 minutes.
2. Start frying, or grilling, the sausages.
3. Tip the vegetables into a food processor, add the butter or spread and whizz for several minutes.
4. Add the cream if you are using it and season to taste.
5. Serve with the sausages.

Note: Although the traditional British 'banger' contains rusk or breadcrumbs as a filler, many of the more exotic sausages now available are made from pure meat from almost any animal. Gluten-free 'conventional' sausages made with rice or a corn 'rusk' are also relatively easily available — see Resources on page 234.

SALADS, VEGETABLES & VEGETARIAN DISHES

Green Pepper and Flageolet Bean Salad
Cucumber and Artichoke Salad
Red Cabbage and Butter Bean Salad
Alternative Tabbouleh
'Vigorous' Bean Salad
Broccoli and Butter Bean Salad
Celeriac and Beetroot Remoulade
Brown Rice with Fennel
Artichoke and Red Onion Risotto
Nori Rice
Ginger, Puy Lentil and Cashew Nut Loaf
Chilau Rice
Simple Tomato Sauce
Red Cabbage and Butter Bean Bake
Baked Shallots with Cherry Tomatoes
Beetroot with Quinoa and Red Cabbage
Beetroot with Pak Choi and Black Olives
Creamed Turnips with Aubergine
Tofu 'Moussaka'
Stir Fries
Stewed Cucumber with Onions
Cashew and Sprout Stir Fry
Herby Parsnip, Corn and Tomato Bake
Warm Parsnips with Okra and Coriander
Quinoa with Chard and Pine Nuts
Swede and Chickpea Mash
Lentil-stuffed Peppers
Many Cabbages!
Green Thai Tofu Curry
Vegetable Pie
Sautéed Sprouts with Walnuts

GREEN PEPPER AND FLAGEOLET BEAN SALAD

This can be served as a salad (without the tofu) or as a vegetarian dish (with it). Since tofu naturally absorbs flavours well, marinating or smoking it is very successful. There are several different brands available in most health food stores. | Serves 6 | Picture page 145

6 tbsp	olive oil	6 tbsp
6	medium leeks, sliced thickly	6
4	medium-large green peppers, trimmed and sliced	4
1 x 400g	tin flageolet beans, drained	1 x 14 oz
75g	pumpkin seeds	3 oz
250g	marinated or smoked tofu (optional)	9 oz
	sea salt and freshly ground black pepper	
	plenty of chopped fresh parsley or coriander	

1. Heat the oil in a heavy pan and sweat the leeks with the green peppers for 35-40 minutes or until they are quite soft.
2. Add the flageolet beans, pumpkin seeds and tofu, if you are using it.
3. Continue to cook for a further 5 minutes.
4. Season to taste and then allow to cool to room temperature.
5. Just before serving add a good handful of chopped fresh parsley or coriander.

Note: Flageolet beans are small immature kidney beans that were first bred in France in the 19th century. They are hard to find, fresh, outside France but relatively easily available tinned. Flageolet beans come in a variety of colours but I think the green ones have the best flavour. In France they are traditionally served with lamb but work very well in any dish.

CUCUMBER AND ARTICHOKE SALAD

A refreshingly different cucumber salad. Serve with cold meats or a rich fish such as smoked mackerel or salmon. | Serves 6

1	large cucumber	1
1 x 400g	tin artichoke hearts, drained	1 x 14 oz
75g	alfalfa sprouts	3 oz
	sea salt and freshly ground pepper	
2 tbsp	cider (or wine) vinegar	2 tbsp

1. Cut the cucumber into relatively small cubes, discarding any over-seedy sections, and put in a bowl.
2. Cut the artichoke hearts into eighths and mix into the cucumber.
3. Add the alfalfa sprouts, pulling them gently apart so that they are well distributed.
4. Season with salt and pepper and sprinkle over the vinegar before serving.

Note: Fresh artichokes will be heavier due to higher water content. Small artichokes have more tender leaves and larger ones have bigger hearts. Choose artichokes with tight, undamaged leaves, and don't choose artichokes for supper unless you are happy to linger over them — they are not fast food!

RED CABBAGE AND BUTTER BEAN SALAD

A great simple salad which can be eaten with cold meats or on its own.
| Serves 6 | Picture page 145

2 tsp	caraway seeds	2 tsp
2 x 400g	tins butter beans	2 x 14 oz
⅔	of a small red cabbage	⅔
3-4 tbsp	plain goat's, sheep's milk or soya yogurt	3-4 tbsp
2 tbsp	cider vinegar	2 tbsp
	sea salt and freshly ground black pepper	

1. Bruise the caraway seeds with the base of a rolling pin then put them into a bowl or a saucepan.
2. Add the butter beans with the liquid from the tin, stir well and heat over a low heat or in a microwave (2 minutes on high) until they are warm but have not started to cook.
3. Leave them for 20-30 minutes to allow the beans to absorb the flavour of the caraway seeds then discard the liquid and most of the seeds.
4. Meanwhile, slice the red cabbage very thinly and mix with the beans.
5. Mix the yogurt and vinegar and season with salt and pepper.
6. Use to dress the salad then serve.

Note: Cider vinegar (made from fermented apples) is recommended as being helpful for a whole range of health problems from arthritis to diabetes — and warts! Whatever its health properties, it is delicious — much more so, in my book, than wine vinegar (made from grapes).

ALTERNATIVE TABBOULEH

Couscous is a sad loss for many on gluten- or wheat-free diets but both quinoa (see Laurent's Lamb Couscous with Quinoa on page 132) and some of the whole grain rices make good alternatives. In this recipe I have used the lovely nutty red rice from the Camargue district of southern France. If you cannot find Camargue rice, use a good wholegrain brown rice.

A traditional tabbouleh would not include nuts or seeds but use them if you want to make the dish a bit more substantial. | Serves 6

1	medium onion, finely chopped	1
300g	red Camargue rice	11 oz
2	small leeks, trimmed and finely sliced	2
2	sticks celery, finely chopped	2
50g	pine nuts (optional)	2 oz
50g	sunflower seeds (optional)	2 oz
	large handful flat or curly parsley, finely chopped	
	large handful fresh mint, finely chopped	
	sea salt and freshly ground black pepper	
	juice of 1-2 lemons	
3-4 tbsp	virgin olive oil	3-4 tbsp

1. Cook the onion and rice in plenty of fast boiling water for 10-12 minutes or until the rice is just cooked.
2. Drain and set aside.
3. Mix in the leeks, celery, nuts and seeds (if you are using them) and the parsley and mint.
4. Season and dress to taste with lemon juice and oil.
5. Serve alone or as part of a mezze.

Note: Tabbouleh, a classic Middle Eastern dish, is usually served with pitta bread although the more traditional accompaniment in the Middle East would be a lettuce leaf — much better for those on gluten- and wheat-free diets.

'VIGOROUS' BEAN SALAD

Why the name of this recipe? Because there is serious eating in this salad so you feel really vigorous after you have eaten it. It is a bit of a 'cheat' salad as I use all tinned beans although there is nothing to stop you cooking them fresh if you prefer. Dressing the beans when they are warm allows them to really absorb the flavours of the dressing.

You can serve this on its own or as an accompaniment to roast meat or fish.
| Serves 6

1 x 400g	tin butter beans	1 x 14 oz
1 x 400g	tin aduki beans	1 x 14 oz
1 x 400g	tin haricot beans	1 x 14 oz
1 x 400g	tin flageolet beans	1 x 14 oz
4	cloves garlic (optional)	4
1-2 tbsp	dried sea vegetables	1-2 tbsp
6	spring onions, trimmed and cut small	6
1 x 400g	tin artichoke hearts, drained, and quartered	1 x 14 oz
2	large handfuls parsley, chopped fairly roughly	2
	sea salt and freshly ground black pepper	
1-2	lemons	1-2
4-6 tbsp	olive oil	4-6 tbsp

1. Open and drain most of the liquid out of the tins of beans. Mix them well in a large bowl.
2. Peel the garlic, if you are using it, slice the cloves finely and mix them into the beans.
3. Heat the beans gently in a microwave or over a low heat until they are about blood temperature then remove from the heat.
4. Mix in the dried sea vegetables, spring onions, artichoke hearts and parsley, season generously and dress with the lemon juice and oil to taste.
5. Leave to cool to room temperature to serve.

Note: Pulses and legumes eaten with grains form a high quality protein and are low in fat. These beans and peas are to be found widely in cans, but the dried versions will last for years on your shelf without losing their high nutrient value.

BROCCOLI AND BUTTER BEAN SALAD

A lovely summer salad which is substantial enough for lunch on its own. If you want to make more of a main dish of it you can add whatever sort of cheese you can eat or some salted roasted cashews. | Serves 6

225g	trimmed broccoli florets	8 oz
550g	cooked butter beans (freshly cooked or tinned)	1¼ lbs
	juice of 1 lemon or 2 tbsp cider vinegar	
3 tbsp	olive oil	3 tbsp
	sea salt and freshly ground black pepper	
100g	lamb's lettuce or watercress leaves	4 oz

1. Steam the broccoli florets for a couple of minutes only — you want them to remain slightly crunchy.
2. Turn the broccoli into the serving dish and warm the butter beans through in the steamer.
3. Add to the broccoli and while both are still warm, dress with the lemon juice or vinegar, oil and seasoning.
4. Allow to cool to room temperature then add the lamb's lettuce or watercress and toss.
5. Add any extras you wish and serve at once.

Note: Broccoli and beans are both good for those on dairy-free diets as they both contain significant amounts of calcium.

CELERIAC AND BEETROOT REMOULADE

Fresh beetroot, visually, is all pervading but although this salad looks very pink, the flavour of the celeriac and mint are quite strong enough to hold their own with the beetroot. | Serves 6

3 tbsp	mayonnaise — home-made or ready-made	3 tbsp
	but check the ingredients if you are buying ready-made	
	juice of 1 lemon or 2 tbsp cider vinegar	
1 tbsp	plain goat's, sheep's milk or soya yogurt	1 tbsp
2 tbsp	boiling water	2 tbsp
	sea salt and freshly ground black pepper	
450g	celeriac	1 lb
2	medium-size fresh beetroots	2
2	large handfuls fresh mint leaves	2

1. Put the mayonnaise in a small bowl and add the lemon juice or vinegar, yogurt, water, salt and pepper and adjust to taste.
2. Peel the celeriac and top and tail the beetroots.
3. Grate them both, by hand or in a food processor and turn into a salad bowl.
4. Add the dressing and mix well then adjust seasoning to taste if needed.
5. Just before serving, chop the mint leaves and mix into the salad.

Note: The beetroot is roughly the same size, shape and colour as the human heart. It is said that if two people eat from the same beetroot, they will fall in love with each other...

BROWN RICE WITH FENNEL

You can serve this as a vegetable for 6 or you could add 75g/3 oz of roasted, salted cashew nuts and serve it as a main meal for 4.

2 tbsp	olive oil	2 tbsp
2	leeks, trimmed and sliced thinly	2
2	medium heads of fennel, trimmed and cut small	2
6 heaped tbsp	wholegrain brown rice	6 heaped tbsp
1 litre	wheat/ gluten-free stock	1¾ pints
200g	fine green beans	7 oz
	juice of 2 lemons	
	sea salt and freshly ground black pepper	
75g	roasted salted cashews (optional)	3 oz

1. Heat the oil in a wide pan and add the leeks and fennel.
2. Fry gently for around 10 minutes or until they are both beginning to soften.
3. Add the rice and cook for a minute or two. Add the stock, bring to the boil and simmer gently for 20-25 minutes or until the liquid is absorbed and the rice is cooked. Add more liquid if needed.
4. Meanwhile, top and tail the beans and cut them in half. Steam them for 3-5 minutes or until they are just beginning to soften but are still a bit crunchy and have not lost their colour. Remove from the heat.
5. When the rice is cooked add the beans and salt, pepper and lemon juice to taste. Serve hot or at room temperature.

Note: Since fresh fennel is not always available you could substitute 4 sticks of celery.

ARTICHOKE AND RED ONION RISOTTO

Jerusalem artichokes are delicious (although can have a 'windy' effect on the digestion) but are only available in season. Although the flavour is quite different, water chestnuts make a good substitute in this dish. I used an exotic black rice which tasted delicious and turned the whole dish black! You could also use red Camargue rice, brown wholemeal rice or a white basmati. However, cooking times will vary according to the type you use. | Serves 6

2	red onions, sliced thinly	2
6	spring onions, chopped small	6
3	large cloves of garlic, peeled and sliced thinly	3
250g	rice	9 oz
2 tsp	coriander seeds	2 tsp
200g	Jerusalem artichokes, scrubbed or tinned water chestnuts, drained and halved horizontally	7 oz
750ml	gluten/wheat-free vegetable stock	1 ¼ pints
50g	pine nuts, lightly toasted under the grill or in a dry frying pan	2 oz

1. Heat the oil in a wide pan and gently cook the red onion, spring onion and garlic until they are just starting to soften.
2. Add the rice and continue to cook for a few minutes.
3. Meanwhile bruise the coriander seeds with a wooden spoon and slice the artichokes into moderately thin rounds.
4. Add the coriander seeds, artichokes and stock to the rice.
5. If you are using water chestnuts, only add them when the rice is half cooked.
6. Bring to the boil and simmer gently for 15-35 minutes, depending on the variety of rice used. Check it frequently as, depending on the rice used, you may need to add extra liquid.
7. Adjust seasoning to taste, pile onto a serving dish and sprinkle with the pine nuts.
8. Serve warm or at room temperature with a green salad.

Note: The Jerusalem artichoke is neither from Jerusalem nor is it an artichoke although it is from the same family (asteraceae). It is the root of a flower related to the sunflower. Jerusalem artichokes contain high levels of inulin, a carbohydrate that promotes good intestinal health due to its prebiotic properties.

NORI RICE

This is a truly international dish. Nori is one of the many Japanese seaweeds. There are lots of different varieties of nori — dark green is the most common, but it also can be black, purple or dark red and comes in varying thicknesses. Although it's commonly used to roll sushi, it can also be crumbled over dishes and salads as a garnish. You will be able to buy it in speciality delicatessens or some health food stores. It gives a delicious but delicate flavour to the rice. Dried limes are an essential ingredient in Middle Eastern cooking and if you can get them (most Arab food shops will stock them) will add a further subtle flavour to your rice. Dried shrimp (shrimp and salt only) are a common ingredient in much Chinese cooking and if you can find them (any Chinese food shop will stock them) are very useful to keep in the store cupboard as they keep for years and add lots of flavour to all kinds of dishes.

200g	white basmati rice	7 oz
2 tbsp (10g)	nori	2 tbsp
3	dried limes, pierced with a few holes	3
900ml	water	1½ pints
1 tbsp	dried shrimp or, if you want to make it	1 tbsp
	vegetarian use 2 tbsp roasted pumpkin or sunflower seeds	
	juice from 1-2 lemons	
	sea salt and freshly ground black pepper	
2-3 tbsp	cold pressed sunflower oil	2-3 tbsp

1. Rinse the rice then put it in a pan with the seaweed, the dried limes, the water and the shrimp. Bring to the boil and boil briskly for 7-8 minutes or until the rice is cooked and the liquid absorbed. If it is boiling dry add a little more water; if the rice is cooked before the water is entirely absorbed, drain off the excess. Add the seeds if you are not using the shrimp. Mix well then add the oil, lemon juice, salt and black pepper to taste. Serve at room temperature, decorated with some strips of red pepper if you wish.

Note: Seaweeds are one of the best anti-ageing foods in the world, and they have enormously high vitamin and mineral content. High in iodine, they can aid thyroid conditions.

GINGER, PUY LENTIL AND CASHEW NUT LOAF

A classic vegan nut loaf which you may feel does not really need a tomato sauce so feel free to include it or not as you wish.

The mixture makes a soft loaf so be careful when unmoulding it. | Serves 8

3 tbsp	olive oil	3 tbsp
2	large onions, peeled and puréed in a food processor	2
4	cloves garlic, peeled and sliced	4
50g	piece of fresh ginger, peeled and cut into thin matchsticks	2 oz
1 heaped tsp	ground coriander	1 heaped tsp
250g	Puy lentils	9 oz
600ml	gluten/wheat-free vegetable stock	1 pint
6 tbsp	port or Marsala	6 tbsp
400g	sweet potato, peeled and diced	14 oz
500g	hazelnuts	18 oz
100g	cashew nuts	4 oz
	sea salt and freshly ground black pepper	
700g	curly kale or spring greens	1½ lbs
	Recipe for simple tomato sauce page 156	

1. Heat the oil and add the onions, the garlic, ginger and coriander.
2. Stir well then cover and sweat over a low heat for at least 20 minutes or until they are quite soft.
3. Add the lentils, stock and port or Marsala, bring back to the boil and simmer for 30 minutes or until the lentils are cooked (but not mushy) and the liquid absorbed.
4. Meanwhile, steam the sweet potato for 10-15 minutes or until it is soft and mash.
5. Chop the hazelnuts and cashew nuts roughly in a food processor and then toast under the grill or in a dry frying pan until lightly tanned all over.
6. Heat the oven to 180C/350F/gas mark 4.
7. Mix the sweet potato and nuts into the lentil mix and season to taste. Line a loaf tin with oiled greaseproof paper and spoon in the mixture. Bake uncovered for 45 minutes.
8. Remove from the oven and cool slightly.
9. Meanwhile chop and steam the kale or greens lightly for a few minutes or until it is lightly cooked but still has a little bite.
10. Heat the tomato sauce if you are using it.
11. Arrange the greens on your dish. Unmould the loaf carefully into the middle of the greens and spoon over the tomato sauce if you are using it.

Note: Ginger has been used for treating illnesses and ailments for centuries; indeed many mothers will have eaten ginger biscuits or sipped ginger tea as a way to combat pregnancy nausea. Ginger is used widely in Asian and ayurvedic medicines, treating such conditions as arthritis, blocked arteries and anorexia. It also helps digestion.

CHILAU RICE

Persia has always been famous for the delicacy of its rice dishes and the wonderful sauces or *khoresht* that are served with them, although to a European many of these are closer to stews than sauces — see the Khoresh on p113.

    The chilau rice is perfect with them and certainly repays the small extra effort in preparing it. It can, of course, also be used with any other meat or fish dish. | Serves 6

350g	basmati rice — rinsed or soaked for 1-3 hours in lukewarm water — opinions differ but soaking seems to give a slightly lighter texture	12 oz
	salt	
75g	approx goat's butter	3 oz

1. Fill a large pan with plenty of boiling water and salt generously.
2. Sprinkle in the rinsed or soaked rice, bring back to the boil and cook briskly for 4-8 minutes or until the rice is almost but not quite cooked.
3. Drain and rinse again under hot water.
4. Put half the butter in the bottom of a pan, allow it to melt then put in the rice and stir.
5. Put the remaining butter over the top, cover the pan with a cloth to absorb the steam, and a tight fitting lid and cook over a very low heat for 30-40 minutes. The rice on the bottom should form a crisp golden crust. This is called *tahdig*, is delicious and is usually served separately and normally to the guest of honour. The rest of the rice is served with the appropriate stew or khoresh.

Note: The Hindi word basmati means 'fragrant' and refers to its aroma and nut-like taste. Brown basmati is more nutritious than white as it has only had the outer husk removed, leaving the germ and bran layer which makes it higher in B vitamins.

SIMPLE TOMATO SAUCE

4	medium leeks	4
2 x 400g	tins tomatoes	2 x 14 oz
175ml	dry red wine	6 fl oz
	salt and pepper	
3 sprigs	fresh dill	3 sprigs

1. Chop the leeks finely and put in a pan with tomatoes and wine.
2. Bring to the boil and simmer, covered, for 30 minutes. Purée in a food processor, season to taste with salt and pepper and add finely chopped fresh dill just before serving. Thin with a little filtered water if necessary.

Note: The lycopene in tomatoes is a powerful antioxidant, and recently there has been much research into the tomato's anti-cancer properties. Serious tomato enthusiasts can journey to the town of Buñol in Spain to take part in La Tomatina — a week-long food festival including a squashed tomato fight!

RED CABBAGE AND BUTTER BEAN BAKE

This is a good substantial winter dish and very quick to make if you use tinned beans. However, it is even better if you make it in advance and leave for a few hours so that the flavours can amalgamate. Although it is designed to be eaten hot it is also good cold, ideal for a lunch box. | Serves 6

3 tbsp	olive or sunflower oil	3 tbsp
2	leeks, sliced	2
2 tsp	coriander seeds, lightly crushed	2 tsp
200g	red cabbage, sliced thinly	7 oz
200g	Savoy or other green cabbage, sliced thinly	7 oz
½	medium Bramley or other sharp cooking apple cored, peeled and sliced into thin fingers	½
90ml	miso or gluten/wheat-free vegetable stock	3 fl oz
1 x 400g	can cannellini beans, drained	1 x 14 oz
1 x 400g	can butter beans, drained	1 x 14 oz
150g	salted, roasted cashew nuts (optional) large handful of fresh coriander leaves	5 oz

1. Heat the oil in a deep pan and gently cook the leeks for 5 minutes or until they have softened.
2. Add the coriander seeds and continue to cook for a minute or two.
3. Add the cabbages, apple and stock. Cover the dish and continue to cook for 5-8 minutes or until the cabbage is slightly softened but still crunchy.
4. Add the beans and cashew nuts if you are using them.
5. Mix carefully so that you do not break up the beans and continue to cook for another 4-5 minutes or until the beans are warmed through and have had a chance to absorb the other flavours in the dish.
6. Adjust the seasoning to taste and serve warm.

Note: Cannellini beans look, and taste, rather like a small, milder flavoured kidney bean. Like all beans they are very nutritious and high in fibre, iron, magnesium and folate.

BAKED SHALLOTS WITH CHERRY TOMATOES

This is a very simple and quite delicious way to get the most possible flavour out of both the shallots and the tomatoes. You can serve it as it is or combine it with some rocket leaves and buffalo mozzarella for the most delicious summer lunch. | Serves 6

4 tbsp	olive oil	4 tbsp
30	shallots, peeled but left whole	30
	(if you cannot find shallots, use very small onions)	
6	cloves garlic, peeled but left whole	6
20	plum or cherry tomatoes, whole	20
	sea salt and freshly ground black pepper	
½ tsp	muscovado sugar	½ tsp

1. Put the oil into a heavy, lidded pan with the shallots, garlic and tomatoes.
2. Grind over a little salt and black pepper and sprinkle in the sugar.
3. Cover the pan tightly and cook very gently for 45-60 minutes or until the onions are cooked and the juices slightly caramelised.
4. Serve warm or at room temperature.

BEETROOT WITH QUINOA AND RED CABBAGE

This dish is the most wonderful dark red colour as well as tasting delicious.
Serves 6

450g	young beetroots, with their stalks and leaves	1 lb
2 tbsp	olive oil	2 tbsp
2	cloves garlic	2
1	medium leek	1
175g	quinoa	6 oz
200g	red cabbage	7 oz
500ml	water or gluten/wheat-free vegetable stock	18 fl oz
50g	pistachio nuts	2 oz
	sea salt and freshly ground black pepper	

1. Remove the beets from their stalks and leaves.
2. Wash the stalks and leaves then chop them roughly.
3. Steam the beetroots until nearly cooked (15-20 minutes) then remove and halve or quarter them, depending on their size.
4. Meanwhile heat the oil in a heavy based pan, add the leek and garlic and cook gently for a few minutes.
5. Add the quinoa, red cabbage and liquid and bring to the simmer. Add the beetroots and their stalks and leaves.
6. Cover the pan and simmer gently for 15-20 minutes or until the quinoa has swelled and is cooked and most of the liquid absorbed.
7. Add the nuts, season to taste and serve warm or at room temperature.

Note: The combination of the quinoa and the beetroot makes this a nutrient-laden dish.

BEETROOT WITH PAK CHOI AND BLACK OLIVES

Every time I serve beetroot there is a chorus of 'Oh why don't more people cook beetroot, it is wonderful stuff' — so here goes with another beetroot supper dish. | Serves 6

12	small fresh beetroot	12
6 tbsp	olive oil	6 tbsp
750g	pak choi, or, if you cannot get it, Chinese leaf, sliced	1¾ lbs
6 tbsp	black olives, stoned and halved	6 tbsp
2 x 400g	tins butter beans	2 x 14 oz
3 tbsp	pumpkin seeds	3 tbsp
	juice 2 lemons	
	sea salt and freshly ground black pepper	

1. Par cook the beetroot by steaming them for 10-15 minutes then slice them into thick batons.
2. Heat 2 tbsp of the oil in a wide pan and add the beetroot and pak choi (or cabbage) and cook moderately briskly for 5 minutes or until the pak choi is just wilting.
3. Add the olives, butter beans and pumpkin seeds and continue to cook for a further couple of minutes only.
4. Remove from the heat and dress with the remaining oil, lemon juice and salt and pepper to taste.
5. Serve hot or at room temperatures as a vegetarian main course or side dish.

Note: Pak choi and Chinese cabbage are good sources of folate, vitamin C, calcium, beta-carotenes and nitrogen compounds known as indoles which appear to lower the risk of cancer. Green olives are unripe black olives and black olives are ripened green olives. They cannot be eaten straight off the tree, but are processed in a variety of different ways to make them edible. Olives are high in monounsaturated fats and vitamin E.

CREAMED TURNIPS WITH AUBERGINE

This makes a deliciously creamy vegetable dish. You can use it as just that or you can add the seeds to make it into a more substantial vegetarian main dish.
| Serves 6

8	medium turnips, peeled and diced	8
2	large potatoes, scrubbed and diced	2
2	medium aubergines, wiped and diced	2
1 tbsp	olive oil	1 tbsp
6	large cloves garlic, peeled and finely sliced	6
25-50g	fresh ginger root, depending on how keen you are on ginger, peeled and finely chopped	1-2 oz
	sea salt and freshly ground black pepper	
2 tbsp	goat's, sheep's milk or soya yogurt or oat or soya cream	2 tbsp
2 tbsp	each sunflower and pumpkin seeds (optional)	2 tbsp

1. Steam the turnips with potatoes for 10-15 minutes or until both are nearly cooked.
2. Add the aubergine and continue to cook for a further 5 minutes. Meanwhile gently cook the garlic and ginger in the oil.
3. Purée the turnips, potato and aubergine in a food processor, add the oil, garlic and ginger and purée again.
4. Add the yogurt or cream and season to taste with salt and pepper.
5. If you are using them, lightly chop the sunflower and pumpkin seeds in a food processor and then roast them gently in a dry frying pan for 4-5 minutes, taking care that they do not burn.
6. Fold half of the seeds into the vegetable mixture, turn into a serving dish and sprinkle the remaining seeds over the top to serve.

Note: Roasting seeds, nuts and spices always brings out the flavour and is well worth the extra effort. Aubergine belongs to the Nightshade family of plants and can cause irritation to arthritis sufferers.

TOFU 'MOUSSAKA'

A traditional moussaka would include both lamb and cheese but this is a pleasant if somewhat unorthodox alternative. | Serves 6

2	large aubergines	2
	olive oil, sea salt and freshly ground black pepper	
2	largish onions, roughly chopped	2
200g	open mushrooms, sliced thickly	7 oz
350g	smoked tofu, cut in small cubes	12 oz
4 tsp	fresh rosemary leaves (or 3 teaspoons dried)	4 tsp
450g	large tomatoes (beef if possible), sliced horizontally	1 lb
25g	cornflour	1 oz
500ml	unsweetened soya milk	18 fl oz
2	eggs	2

1. Trim and slice the aubergines fairly thinly.
2. Drizzle with olive oil, grind over some sea salt and black pepper and grill briskly until they are lightly tanned. Turn over the slices and repeat on the other side. Lay aside and continue until all the slices are grilled.
3. Lay half of them out in the bottom of an ovenproof dish.
4. Heat the oven to 180C/350F/gas mark 4.
5. Heat another 2 tbsp of oil in a heavy pan and add the onions; cook for several minutes, then add the mushrooms.
6. Fry both briskly until the mushrooms start to give their liquid then transfer them to the pie dish and spread out.
7. Add the tofu and half of the rosemary. Lay the tomatoes over the tofu, sprinkle with the remaining rosemary and a little salt and pepper.
8. Put the pie dish back under the grill for 4-5 minutes to par cook the tomatoes.
9. Meanwhile, mix the cornflour with a little of the soya milk in a pan, gradually add the rest of the soya milk and heat, stirring continually until the mixture thickens slightly.
10. Remove from the heat and allow to cool slightly.
11. Beat the eggs and add to the sauce and season.
12. Remove the pie dish from the grill.
13. Lay the remaining aubergine slices over the tomatoes and then pour the sauce over the top. Bake uncovered for 1 hour.
14. Serve hot or warm accompanied by a crisp green salad.

Note: Rosemary is high in iron, vitamin B6 and calcium, and is reputed to improve memory. It can be used as a tonic for depression and anxiety.

STIR FRIES

Stir fries are excellent for anyone with food intolerance as you need only include the foods that you are happy with. Remember that the essence of a stir fry is that it should be cooked very quickly so as to retain the maximum number of nutrients in the ingredients — so if you are using vegetables that need long cooking they need to be cut very thin. You need to prepare everything that you require in advance so that the actual cooking can be speedy and last minute.

Here are some suggestions for a very basic stir fry to get you enthused.

Allow 225g/8 oz vegetables per person and make it up of as many different vegetables as you choose. Many of the supermarkets now sell ready mixed packs of stir-fry vegetables.
Root vegetables are fine but must be cut very thin to allow quick cooking.
Juicy vegetables such as cucumber and beans shoots are particularly good.
Spring onions, cut lengthways and added at the last minute look and taste great

If you like it spicy, 1 tsp each of finely chopped garlic, fresh chilli, fresh ginger root or fresh turmeric root are all excellent additions

Allow 50g/2 oz of protein to go with your vegetables —
nuts (cashews, peanuts, flaked almonds), seeds (sunflower, pumpkin or sesame) or tofu (plain, smoked or marinated)

2 tbsp oil — rapeseed, groundnut or special stir-fry oil are best, wheat/gluten-free soya sauce, sea salt and freshly ground black pepper

---

1. Cut your vegetables into very thin slices or matchsticks but leaving vegetables such as bean shoots whole.
2. Heat the oil in a wok until nearly smoking. If you do not have a wok you can make a very successful stir fry in a frying pan.
3. Add garlic, turmeric and ginger root; cook for a few minutes stirring continually.
4. Add the harder vegetables, turn the heat down a bit and allow them to cook for 3 minutes or until just softening.
5. Add the softer vegetables, turn the heat up again and cook briskly for a couple of minutes, stirring continuously.
6. Add nuts (you can brown these in an oven or on a dry pan for extra flavour), seeds or tofu and the spring onions, if you are using them.
7. Season to taste with soya sauce and salt and pepper if you need it.
8. Serve at once.

CASHEW AND SPROUT STIR FRY

This is a very colourful stir fry. If Jerusalem artichokes are not in season, substitute water chestnuts — they do not have the same very distinctive flavour but do have much the same texture.

You can serve it with rice although it is really substantial enough to serve on its own. | Serves 6

4 tbsp	stir-fry olive or coconut oil	4 tbsp
6	cloves garlic, peeled and sliced	6
1-2	red or green chillies, depending on how hot you want your stir fry, with the pips removed and thinly sliced	1-2
50g	peeled fresh ginger, cut into thin matchsticks	2 oz
2	large red peppers, de-seeded and cut in strips	2
4	sticks celery, sliced thinly	4
550g	Brussels sprouts, trimmed and sliced thinly	1 ¼ lbs
4	Jerusalem artichokes, peeled and cut in thin matchsticks or 1 x 200g/7oz tin water chestnuts drained and sliced horizontally	4
200g	purple sprouting broccoli, stems cut thinly across and florets left whole	7 oz
4-5 tbsp	wheat/gluten-free soya sauce	4-5 tbsp
150 ml	water	¼ pint
1	head radicchio, sliced	1
20	spring onions, halved and cut in thirds	20
150g	roasted, salted cashew nuts	5 oz
1 pack	bean sprouts	1 pack
	sea salt and freshly ground black pepper	

1. In a wok or wide frying pan heat the oil and add the garlic, chilli and ginger.
2. Fry briskly but without burning for a couple of minutes then add the peppers, celery, sprouts, artichokes or water chestnuts and broccoli.
3. Cook briskly for a couple of minutes then add the soya sauce and the water.
4. Cover the wok and continue to cook for 5 minutes.
5. Add the radicchio, spring onions and cashew nuts and cook for another minute or two.
6. Season further to taste with soya sauce, sea salt and freshly ground black pepper if needed and serve at once.

STEWED CUCUMBER WITH ONIONS

Cucumbers are rarely served hot which is a shame as they cook surprisingly well, retaining lots of 'crunch' despite their very high water content.

Fresh mint tastes much better but if you cannot get it you can use dried, but you need to add it to the sauce along with the liquids. | Serves 6

50g	goat's butter or dairy-free spread or 2 tbsp olive oil	2 oz
2	large cucumbers, unpeeled and grated	2
4	medium onions, sliced thickly	4
1 heaped tbsp	well seasoned cornflour	1 heaped tbsp
150ml	gluten/wheat-free vegetable stock	¼ pint
150ml	goat's, oat or soya cream	¼ pint
	large handful fresh mint, chopped small or	
	2 heaped tsp dried	
	sea salt and freshly ground black pepper	

1. Heat the butter, spread or oil in a wide pan and add the cucumber and onions.
2. Sauté the vegetables gently for 10-15 minutes or until the onions are softening.
3. Mix the stock gradually into the cornflour to make a smooth paste then add the cream.
4. Add this mixture to the vegetables, stir and bring back to simmer. Cook gently, stirring, until the sauce thickens slightly.
5. Add the mint and season to taste before serving.

Note: Cucumber is a diuretic whose watery flesh can help relieve skin irritations and ease inflammations. It also contains silica, which plays a vital role in ensuring healthy connective tissues.

HERBY PARSNIP, CORN AND TOMATO BAKE

A nice filling bake, most of which can come out of the store cupboard.
| Serves 6

550g	parsnips, sliced thinly	1¼ lbs
2	bay leaves	2
2 tbsp	virgin olive or sunflower oil	2 tbsp
2	cloves garlic, chopped or finely sliced	2
1	medium onion, finely chopped	1
1 tsp	each dried marjoram, oregano and basil	1 tsp
250g	sweet corn	9 oz
1 x 400g	tin chickpeas, drained	1 x 14 oz
1 x 400g	tin chopped tomatoes	1 x 14 oz
150ml	wheat/gluten-free vegetable stock	¼ pint
	sea salt and freshly ground pepper	
1	small packet plain potato crisps	1

1. Heat the oven to 180C/350F/gas mark 4.
2. Steam the sliced parsnips for 8-10 minutes or until they are nearly cooked.
3. Lay them in the bottom of an ovenproof casserole or baking dish and lay the bay leaves over them.
4. Meanwhile, heat the oil in a heavy pan and gently cook the garlic and onion with the dried herbs until the onion is soft.
5. Add the sweet corn, chickpeas, tomatoes and stock and season lightly.
6. Mix all well together then spoon over the parsnips.
7. Crumble the crisps over the top, then bake, uncovered, for 30 minutes to thoroughly amalgamate the flavours and finish cooking the parsnips.

Note: Parsnips can be eaten raw, grated into salads, and are good sources of vitamin C, fibre, folate and potassium. Bay leaves can be used in pantries as a moth repellent to protect your grains.

WARM PARSNIPS WITH OKRA AND CORIANDER

This dish can be served hot as a vegetable or warm or at room temperature as a salad or lunch dish. Rather unusual in the winter when parsnips are in season.
| Serves 6

1 ¼ kg	parsnips, scrubbed and sliced thinly	3 lbs
225g	okra, topped and tailed and sliced, not too thinly	8 oz
6 tbsp	olive oil	6 tbsp
	juice from 2 large lemons	
2-3	large handfuls fresh coriander	2-3 handfuls
	coarsely ground sea salt and freshly ground black pepper	

1. Steam the parsnips until they are cooked but not mushy.
2. Meanwhile, heat the oil in a small pan and fry the okra slices fairly briskly for 4-5 minutes until they are just beginning to brown — take them off the heat. They will lose their stickiness as you cook them.
3. As soon as the parsnips are cooked, mix them gently with the okra and the oil they were cooked in.
4. Season with plenty of salt and pepper and add the lemon juice to taste.
Add the chopped coriander just before serving. The salad does not need to be served hot but is very nice, rather unusual and more suitable for February if served warm.

Note: Apart from being delicious, okra is a great source of folate, calcium, vitamin K, vitamin C, magnesium and manganese. The longer you cook okra, the less slimy it becomes — a good tip since their sliminess can be off-putting.

QUINOA WITH CHARD AND PINE NUTS

A very flexible combination, you can use it as a vegetable, a salad or a vegetarian dish. Whichever way, it is excellent and extremely nutritious. | Serves 6

4 tbsp	olive oil	4 tbsp
3	medium onions, peeled and sliced	3
3	sticks celery, cleaned and chopped	3
3 tsp	fennel seeds, lightly crushed	3 tsp
350g	quinoa	12 oz
1½ litres	wheat/gluten-free vegetable stock	2½ pints
600g	chard	1¼ lbs
300g	baby spinach leaves, washed	10 oz
	sea salt and freshly ground black pepper	
75g	pine nuts	3 oz

1. Heat the oil in a wide, heavy pan and add the onions, celery and fennel seeds.
2. Fry gently for 10-15 minutes or until they are quite soft.
3. Add the quinoa and stir around for a few minutes then add the stock and bring slowly to the boil.
4. Meanwhile wash the chard and chop the stalks roughly.
5. Add these to the quinoa and cook all together for around 15 minutes or until the quinoa is nearly cooked.
6. Chop the chard leaves roughly and add to the mixture.
7. Mix in well, cover the pot and continue to cook gently for a further 10-15 minutes or until both the quinoa and the chard are cooked.
8. Remove from the heat and stir in the spinach leaves. Leave the pot covered for a few minutes to allow the spinach leaves to wilt.
9. Meanwhile, dry fry the pine nuts carefully until lightly browned but not burnt.
10. Season the mixture to taste and stir in the pine nuts.
11. Serve warm or at room temperature on its own, with a green salad or as an accompaniment to cold meats or fish.

Note: Quinoa originated in South America. It has become an important grain for vegetarians in recent years due to its high protein content, as well as its balanced essential amino acid content. Fennel seeds are eaten raw on the Indian subcontinent, to improve eyesight.

SWEDE AND CHICKPEA MASH

This is certainly a tasty mash. You can serve it by itself as a vegetarian dish or with a meat or fish dish. | Serves 6

4 tbsp	olive oil	4 tbsp
550g	swede, peeled and grated	1¼ lbs
2	large leeks, trimmed and sliced thinly	2
1 x 400g	tin chickpeas, drained	1 x 14 oz
200g	fresh spinach, washed and trimmed	7 oz
	sea salt and freshly ground black pepper	

1. Heat the oil in a heavy pan and add the swede and leeks.
2. Fry gently for a couple of minutes then cover the pan, turn down the heat and sweat for 30-40 minutes or until the vegetables are well cooked.
3. Add the chickpeas. Roughly purée the vegetables in a food processor then return to the pan, add the spinach and mix in well.
4. Continue to cook for a few minutes to allow the spinach to wilt.
5. Season to taste with sea salt and freshly ground black pepper before serving.

Note: The humble swede is high in minerals such as calcium, phosphorus, potassium, manganese, magnesium, and is low in saturated fat. In Scotland, swede is known as neeps and served alongside tatties and haggis on Burns Night.

LENTIL-STUFFED PEPPERS

These peppers are particularly good with the 'many cabbages' recipe on page 170. | Serves 6

2 tbsp	olive oil	2 tbsp
1	medium onion, peeled and chopped finely	1
	1 small red and 1 small green chilli, seeded and sliced finely	
150g	sun-dried tomatoes, chopped	5 oz
200g	Puy lentils	7 oz
	4 bay leaves and 10 peppercorns	
1 litre	wheat/gluten-free vegetable stock	1¾ pints
75g	pumpkin seeds	3 oz
100g	fresh spinach	4 oz
	sea salt	
	2 red, 2 yellow and 2 green medium-size peppers, cored	

1. Heat the oil in a heavy pan and add the onion and chillies and cook for 3-4 minutes.
2. Add the tomatoes, lentils, bay leaves, peppercorns and stock.
3. Bring to the boil, cover and simmer for 20-30 minutes.
4. Meanwhile, dry fry the pumpkin seeds until they pop.
5. Add the pumpkin seeds and spinach, mix well and season to taste.
6. Heat the oven to 190C/375F/gas mark 5.
7. Stuff the peppers with the mixture and drizzle with olive oil.
8. If there is any stuffing left over, roll it into little balls and bake alongside the peppers.
9. Bake for 25-30 minutes or until the peppers are cooked then serve hot, warm or at room temperature.

MANY CABBAGES!

Cavolo nero is a very fancy and rather sought-after cabbage, (tall, like a Cos lettuce, very dark green/black and rather bitter) which I think works better in a combination like this than on its own. | Serves 6

3 tbsp	olive oil	3 tbsp
2	large onions, peeled and sliced	2
2 heaped tsp	coriander seeds, lightly bruised	2 heaped tsp
½	medium red cabbage, finely sliced	½
200g	cavolo nero, sliced	7 oz
300ml	wheat/gluten-free vegetable stock	½ pint
1	small spring cabbage, sliced	1
	sea salt and freshly ground black pepper	

1. Heat the oil in a heavy pan and gently fry the onions with the coriander seeds for 8-10 minutes or until the onions are nearly cooked.
2. Add the red cabbage, cavolo nero and the stock, cover and cook gently for 5 minutes. Then add the spring cabbage and continue to cook, covered for a further 5 minutes or until the cabbages are just cooked but still a little crunchy.
3. Season to taste before serving.

GREEN THAI TOFU CURRY

Not a classic green Thai curry but with the right kind of 'feel'... | Serves 6

2 tbsp	olive oil	2 tbsp
4	hot green chillies, de-seeded and sliced very finely	4
	(take care to wash your hands very well afterwards, before	
	touching your face or eyes)	
1/2	bulb garlic, the cloves skinned and sliced thinly	1/2
1	head fennel, trimmed and sliced thinly	1
1	yellow pepper, cored and sliced thinly	1
550g	plain tofu, cubed	1 1/4 lbs
250ml	coconut milk	8 fl oz
	juice of 2 limes	
1x 200g	tin water chestnuts, halved horizontally	1 x 7 oz
	sea salt and freshly ground black pepper	
12 tbsp	basmati rice	12 tbsp
150g	mangetout	5 oz
3 tbsp	goat's butter, dairy-free spread or olive oil	3 tbsp
6	spring onions, trimmed and chopped small	6
2	handfuls fresh coriander leaves, chopped fairly small	2

1. Heat the oil in a wide, heavy pan and add the chillies and garlic.
2. Fry gently for a few minutes taking care not to breathe in the chilli fumes.
3. Add the fennel and yellow pepper and continue to fry gently until the latter is starting to soften.
4. Add the tofu, the coconut milk, lime juice, water chestnuts and some seasoning.
5. Bring to the boil, cover, turn down the heat and simmer gently for 15 minutes.
6. While the curry is cooking, bring a large pan of cold water to the boil. Add the rice and boil briskly for 7-8 minutes or until the rice is cooked but not mushy.
7. Cut the mangetout in half and steam for 3-4 minutes in a steamer — they should be only partially cooked so that they retain some of their crunch.
8. Drain the rice, stir in the butter or oil and the mangetout and keep warm.
9. When the curry is ready to be served, adjust the seasoning to taste, then add the spring onions and coriander, chopped quite small, and stir in lightly.
10. Serve with the rice and a green salad.

Note: Fennel powder can be used as a flea repellent, and fennel water is used in gripe water for infants with flatulence. Fennel is rather difficult to grow in the UK, and thrives best in the south and coastal areas, as it likes limestone soils.

VEGETABLE PIE

The red cabbage gives the most wonderful colour to the juices in this pie. If you do not want to bother with the pastry lid, you can just serve it as a vegetable casserole — it is still delicious. | Serves 6

2	medium onions	2
200g	celeriac	7 oz
200g	sweet potato	7 oz
1	large head fennel	1
	1 medium red and 1 medium green pepper	
½	small red cabbage	½
6	field mushrooms	6
2 tbsp	olive oil	2 tbsp
3	large sprigs fresh thyme or 3 tsp dried	3
	sea salt and freshly ground black pepper	
1 x 400g	tin chopped tomatoes	1 x 14 oz
250g	short crust pastry, see p122	9 oz
1	egg (optional)	1

1. Peel the onions, celeriac and sweet potato. Cut the onions in quarters and the celeriac and sweet potato into large dice.
2. Trim the fennel and cut into quarters or eights if it is a large head.
3. Remove the pips from the peppers and cut into large pieces.
4. Chop the red cabbage coarsely.
5. Halve or quarter the mushrooms depending on size.
6. Heat the oil in a heavy pot and add the vegetables. Stir to mix and cook for 4-5 minutes without burning.
7. Add the thyme and some seasoning and then pour the tomatoes over the vegetables.
8. Cover tightly and cook very gently for 25 minutes or until the root vegetables are cooked but not mushy.
9. If you are making the pie, transfer to a pie dish.
10. Heat the oven to 180C/350F/gas mark 4.
11. Roll out the pastry between two sheets of greaseproof paper. Wet the edges of the pie dish with water and use the trimmings from the pastry to line the edges then wet the edges.
12. Carefully lift the pastry lid onto the pie and press down the edges. Repair any tears with extra pastry trimmings and then decorate with pastry balls or leaves.

13. If you are using pastry, brush the top of the pie with egg and bake for 25-35 minutes or until the pastry is crisp and tanned.

14. Serve hot or at room temperature.

Note: It is important to keep the pieces of vegetable large for this pie so that each different vegetable retains its own texture and flavour in the context of the whole.

SAUTÉED SPROUTS WITH WALNUTS

This is a very exotic way to serve Brussels sprouts and quite transforms them.
| Serves 6

4 tbsp	olive oil	4 tbsp
6	large cloves garlic, peeled and halved	6
350g	small Brussels sprouts, trimmed and halved if large	12 oz
400g	button mushrooms, wiped and halved if large	14 oz
150g	broken walnuts	5 oz
	sea salt and freshly ground black pepper	
	pumpkin oil and fresh coriander/flat parsley	

1. Heat 2 tbsp of the oil in a heavy pan and add the garlic.
2. Fry gently for a couple of minutes then add the sprouts.
3. Continue to cook fairly briskly for 4-5 minutes then add the mushrooms and the remaining tablespoon of oil.
4. Continue to cook briskly for another 4-5 minutes or until the mushrooms are just cooked.
5. Add the walnuts, stir around for a couple of minutes and then remove from the heat and season with sea salt and freshly ground black pepper.
6. Just before serving drizzle with pumpkin oil and sprinkle with a little chopped fresh coriander or flat parsley.

Note: Pumpkin oil is the dark, rich oil from roasted pumpkin seed and is quite delicious. If you cannot find it you could substitute a nut oil or a good olive oil. Badly cooked Brussels sprouts are a notorious Christmas feast let-down, and children will be delighted to know that they are justified in disliking them as overcooking releases unpleasant sulphurous compounds.

DESSERTS

Coconut and Cardamom Rice Pudding
Kiwi with Pomegranate Seeds
Prune and Cranberry Jelly
Date, Kiwi and Banana Upside-down Cake
Pear and Date 'Clafoutis'
Strawberry Meringue
Lemon Sponge with Apricots
Chocolate Pots
Apricot and Redcurrant Flan
Baked Lemon Cheesecake
Chocolate, Orange and Coconut Mousse
Coconut Milk Crème Brulée
Chocolate Hazelnut Roulade
Raw Apple Flan
Gingerbread Trifle
Steamed Gooseberry and Teff Pudding
Fruit Crumbles
Stuffed Pancakes with Chocolate Sauce
Mince Pies
Christmas Upside-down Cake
Winter Fruit Compote
Hot Chocolate Soufflé Flan
Plum Tart
Nut and Apple Flan
Melon and Ginger Salad
Autumn Pears with Figs, Ginger Wine and Grapefruit Juice
Peach Flambé
Kiwi Ice
Stem Ginger Ice Cream
Banana and Coconut Smoothie Ice Cream
Coffee and Coconut Ice Cream
Blackberry and Apple Ice Cream
Creamy Strawberry Sorbet

COCONUT AND CARDAMOM RICE PUDDING

The coconut milk gives a lovely creamy texture to the pudding — almost as if you had used single cream. To get the full flavour it needs to be cooked very slowly — the bottom of an Aga is ideal. | Serves 6

75g	pudding rice	3 oz
600ml	coconut milk	1 pint
8-12	cardamom pods	8-12
2	slivers of lemon or lime rind	2

1. Put the rice into a smallish bowl with the other ingredients and cook it slowly in a low oven (150C/275F/gas mark 2) for 1-2 hours or till the rice is totally soft. Stir it now and then to ensure that the cardamom seeds are well buried.
2. Serve warm, at room temperature, or chilled.

Note: *Elettaria cardamomum* is the botanical name for the green cardamom usually used in Indian cooking, although it can also be smoked and the seeds are often chewed rather like chewing gum. This makes sense as, in traditional medicine cardamom is used to treat infections in teeth, throat and lungs. It is also reportedly used as an antidote for snake and scorpion bites.

KIWI WITH POMEGRANATE SEEDS

Pomegranate seeds are so pretty and so tasty that it is well worth the effort of prising them out of their shells — although you can buy fresh seeds already shelled in some supermarkets. If you cannot get fresh pomegranates, you can also use dried seeds (obtainable in most Middle Eastern stores) that you soak in a little boiling water for 10 minutes. If you are using fresh pomegranates, use rubber gloves when removing the seeds as the juice stains and you will have charcoal grey fingers for days. | Serves 6

6	ripe kiwi fruit, peeled and sliced	6
50ml	grand marnier or cointreau	2 fl oz
100ml	apple or elderflower juice	4 fl oz
	seeds from half a fresh pomegranate	

1. Put the kiwi fruit in a pie dish with the liqueur and juice, cover with clingfilm and cook for 2 minutes in a microwave on high. Remove from the oven and transfer to a serving dish.
2. To get at the pomegranate seeds, knock the pomegranate hard on the kitchen counter to help loosen the seeds.
3. Cut it in half with a sharp knife and prise out the seeds taking care to remove all the membrane from between the seeds.
4. Scatter the pomegranate seeds over the top of the kiwi and allow to marinate for several hours before serving.

Note: Cooking the kiwi fruit really brings out its flavour giving it a delicious tartness sometimes lacking in the fresh fruit.

PRUNE AND CRANBERRY JELLY

This makes a very pretty but light dessert to end a heavy meal. | Serves 6

400ml	cranberry or cranberry and apple juice	14 fl oz
10	cardamom pods (optional)	10
10g	gelatine (or 1 x 11g pack)	½ oz
100ml	cherry brandy or crème de cassis	4 fl oz
100g	very soft prunes	4 oz
150ml	sheep's, goat's, soya or oat cream	¼ pint

1. Heat the cranberry juice with the cardamom pods till they just reach boiling point.
2. Take off the heat, cool for a minute or two then sprinkle in the gelatine and stir till it is quite dissolved. Add the liqueur.
3. Chop all but 3 prunes into small pieces and put them in the bottom of 6 wine glasses. Pour the cranberry mixture over the prunes and put in the fridge to chill. Before serving whisk the cream lightly. The goat's, oat and soya creams will whip better if they are well chilled. A teaspoon of sugar will also help. Spoon the cream over the top of each jelly and top with a halved prune.

Note: Cranberries are now popular because of their high antioxidant properties while the tannins they contain have anti-clotting properties which may be why they seem so helpful in treating urinary tract infections. The name cranberry is thought to derive from 'craneberry', a name given to the plants by early settlers in America who thought that the expanding stem and flower of the cranberry resembled the neck, head, and bill of a crane bird.

DATE, KIWI AND BANANA UPSIDE-DOWN CAKE

This is a delicious warming winter pudding. You can successfully substitute plums for the kiwis if they are available. | Serves 6

1	banana	1
2	kiwi fruit	2
6-8	fresh or soft dried dates	6-8
200g	goat's butter or dairy-free spread	7 oz
115g	dark molasses sugar	4 oz
3	eggs	3
200g	your favourite gluten/wheat-free flour or 100g/4 oz gram flour and 100g/3 oz rice flour	7 oz
½ tsp	xanthan gum	½ tsp
1 heaped tsp	wheat/gluten-free baking powder	1 heaped tsp
3-4 tbsp	orange or apple juice enough to make a soft dropping consistency	3-4 tbsp

1. Heat the oven to 180C/350F/gas mark 4.
2. Cut out a piece of greaseproof paper the size of your cake tin — a 20cm/8 inch round tin would be fine. Grease it well and lay it in the bottom of the tin, greased side up.
3. Peel and slice the banana and kiwi fruit and halve the dates. Arrange in a pattern in the bottom of the cake tin.
4. Beat the butter or spread with the sugar until very soft. Add the eggs, one by one, with a tablespoon of flour with each. Fold in the rest of the flour with the baking powder, adding juice as needed to make a soft dropping consistency.
5. Spoon over the fruit, smooth out the top and bake for 40 minutes or until a skewer comes out clean.
6. Cool slightly then turn out onto a plate and carefully remove the greaseproof paper.
7. Serve warm with whatever cream, yogurt or ice cream you can eat.

Note: Upside-down cakes are usually made in a curved bottom baking tin with the fruit laid out in a pattern which is only revealed when the cake is up-ended onto a serving dish — assuming, of course, that it does not stick to the bottom of the baking tin.

PEAR AND DATE 'CLAFOUTIS'

This is a great way of using up some of those pears that simply will not ripen. You can use a fizzy elderflower drink or champagne or else make one up with a little elderflower cordial and some fizzy water. | Serves 6

3	large pears, peeled and quartered	3
6	soft dates, stones removed	6
150ml	elderflower 'champagne'	¼ pint
3	eggs	3
3 tbsp	maize flour or polenta	3 tbsp
1 ½ tbsp	rice flour	1 ½ tbsp
½ tsp	vanilla essence	½ tsp
10	walnut halves	10

1. Slice the pears thinly and put them in a pan.
2. Slice then chop the dates into small pieces and add the pears along with the elderflower drink. Cover the pan, bring to the boil and simmer for 10-15 minutes or until the pears are soft — how long this takes will depend on how ripe they are.
3. Strain the juices out and reserve them.
4. Heat the oven to 180C/350F/gas mark 4.
5. Beat the eggs in an electric beater. Add the flours and the vanilla essence and beat again till well amalgamated and smooth. Beat in the juices from the pears.
6. Pour this mixture into the bottom of a flan or pie dish.
7. Arrange the pears and dates over the top and dot with the walnut halves.
8. Cover the dish and bake for 15 minutes. Uncover and continue to bake for a further 10 minutes to crisp the nuts.
9. Serve warm, alone or with whatever yogurt or cream you can eat.

Note: As any gardener will know, you cannot stop an elder bush once it gets going so it is just as well that you can use its flowers and its berries to make such delicious wines. A quick Google trawl will find you lots of recipes if you fancy brewing your own.

STRAWBERRY MERINGUE

This is sort of like a Baked Alaska but without the ice cream, so it's much less nerve-wracking to make. The juicy strawberries under the sweet meringue make a lovely contrast.

Depending on whether you like your meringue to be cooked through or still gooey in the middle you will need to cook it for more or less time. | Serves 6

	18 large or 24 medium strawberries	
2	egg whites	2
50g	pale muscovado or caster sugar	2 oz

1. Heat the oven to 170C/325F/gas mark 3.
2. Hull the strawberries and arrange them, hulled side down, in a flattish oven-proof dish of such a size as to allow them entirely to cover the bottom.
3. Whisk the egg whites in a bowl until they are very stiff and stand up in sharp peaks. Whisk in the sugar and continue to whisk until the mixture is very stiff and shiny.
4. Spoon carefully over the strawberries making sure that there are no gaps.
5. Whirl the meringue into peaks with a fork.
6. Bake in the oven for 30-40 minutes or till the meringue top is set. Serve hot or at room temperature.

Note: If you only splash out on two organic fruits, one of them should be strawberries as non-organic strawberries have one of the highest pesticide uses of all soft fruits. (The other fruit is banana, also very high usage in non-organic fruit.)

LEMON SPONGE WITH APRICOTS

A very simple but lovely dessert. You could use fresh peaches or plums instead of apricots, or some of those deliciously soft and flavoursome Agen prunes. | Serves 6

	15 soft dried apricots – or 10 stoned fresh apricots, in season	
4 tbsp	brandy	4 tbsp
5	eggs	5
150g	soft brown sugar	6 oz
	rind and juice of 1 large lemon	
150g	rice flour	6 oz

1. Chop the apricots into fairly small pieces and soak them for up to 24 hours in the brandy. They should absorb most of it.
2. Heat the oven to 180C/350F/gas mark 4.
3. In an electric mixer beat the eggs with the sugar till they are very light, fluffy and creamy.
4. Gently fold in the lemon rind, rice flour and lemon juice.
5. Line a 20cm/8 inch cake tin with greased greaseproof paper and pour in the cake mix. Bake for 30 minutes or till a skewer comes out clean. Cool slightly in the tin then turn out onto a rack.
6. When entirely cold, cut the cake in half horizontally. Spread the brandy soaked apricots over the cake and top it with the other half.
7. Sprinkle with extra lemon zest and icing sugar to decorate.
8. Serve either by itself or with whatever cream, yogurt or ice cream you can eat.

CHOCOLATE POTS

This amazingly simple little recipe comes from my schools' allergy catering manual but despite its simplicity, it is remarkably good. | Serves 6

25g	cornflour	1 oz
400ml	soya, oat or rice milk	14 fl oz
75g	dairy-free chocolate	3 oz
	a couple of berries, a little icing sugar or some grated chocolate to decorate	

1. In a pan mix the milk gradually into the cornflour until it is a smooth paste then heat slowly, stirring continually until it thickens.
2. Break the chocolate into the pan and stir until it melts.
3. Pour into 6 individual pots or ramekin dishes and chill.
4. Decorate with berries, a little sifted icing sugar or a little extra grated chocolate to serve.

APRICOT AND REDCURRANT FLAN

A delicious summer flan with no added sugar. The almonds add a delicate sweet-ness to the pastry. | Serves 6

10	fresh apricots, de-stoned and quartered	10
6 tbsp	amaretto, cointreau or redcurrant/cranberry juice	6 tbsp
100g	of your favourite gluten/wheat-free flour or 100g/4 oz of maize flour	4 oz
50g	ground almonds	2 oz
75g	dairy-free spread	3 oz
4 tbsp	cold water	4 tbsp
2	eggs	2
180ml	rice milk	6 fl oz
75g	redcurrants	3 oz

1. Put the apricots in a saucepan with the liqueur or juice and heat gently but do not boil. Turn off the heat, cover and allow to 'marinate' for at least 2 hours.
2. Heat the oven to 180C/350F/gas mark 4.
3. By hand or in a food processor rub the butter into the mixed flours and al-monds.
4. Add enough cold water to make a soft dough then press out into the bottom of a 20cm/8 inch flan dish.
5. Weight with foil and beans and bake blind for 30 minutes, removing the beans for the last 10 minutes.
6. In a bowl, mix the eggs, and rice milk. Add the apricots, soaking juices and the redcurrants and spoon into the flan case.
7. Lower the oven to 160C/325F/gas mark 3 and bake for a further 40 minutes or until the filling is set and slightly risen.
8. Serve warm or at room temperature.

Note: You could also make this flan in the winter with soft dried apricots (you would need a few more as they shrink as they dry) and dried pomegranate seeds. Increase the marinating liquid to 150ml/5 fl oz and heat and soak both fruits.

BAKED LEMON CHEESECAKE

Soya soft cheeses tend to be much more successful than the hard cheeses so work quite well in a cheesecake — especially a lemony one like this when any residual 'beany' flavour gets disguised by the lemon.

Obviously, if you can eat goat's or sheep's cheese, you may prefer to use one of them, but be sure that it is a mild flavoured one. | Serves 6 | Picture page 175

	1 thin gluten/wheat-free sponge base to fit inside a 20cm/8 inch cake tin with a loose bottom — bought or see p225	
200g	sheep's, goat's, buffalo or soya cream cheese	7 oz
3	eggs	3
	grated rind and juice of 2 large lemons	
50g	light muscovado sugar	2 oz
6 tbsp	sheep's, goat's, soya or rice milk	6 tbsp
50g	toasted flaked almonds (optional)	2 oz

1. Heat the oven to 150C/350F/gas mark 2.
2. Fit the sponge base into the bottom of the loose-bottomed cake tin.
3. Put the cheese in a food processor with the eggs, lemon rind and juice, sugar and milk, and purée the mixture.
4. Pour the mixture into the cake tin and, if you are using them, carefully sprinkle the almonds over the top.
5. Bake for 40-50 minutes or until the custard is set and lightly tanned.
6. Remove from the oven and allow to cool completely.
7. Run a knife round inside the tin to loosen it and then remove it by carefully pressing the base upwards.
8. Serve alone or with a fresh fruit purée.

Note: You can make a fresh fruit purée very simply from any fresh fruit that is in season. Take 200-300g/8-12 oz of stoned and peeled (if necessary) fruit or combination of fruits. Purée in a food processor or liquidiser and add sugar, honey or a syrup of your choice to taste. You may also want to add a little lemon or lime juice to 'sharpen' it and possibly a little extra liquid (water, liqueur or fruit juice) although most fruits are naturally juicy enough.

CHOCOLATE, ORANGE AND COCONUT MOUSSE

There is no sugar in the original of this recipe, which is great for heavy-duty chocolate fans and those with 'un-sweet' teeth. However, it may be too bitter for some so you need to taste it before folding in the egg white and add sugar to taste if you think it needs it. | Serves 6

225g	dairy-free dark chocolate	8 oz
	grated rind and juice of 1½ large oranges	
5g	gelatin	¼ oz
4	large eggs, separated	4
6 tbsp	full fat coconut milk	6 tbsp
6 tbsp	brandy	6 tbsp
1-2 tsp	pale muscovado sugar (optional)	1-2 tsp
	chopped pistachio nuts, to decorate	

1. Melt the chocolate in a bowl over hot water or for 2-3 minutes in a microwave on high and then cool slightly.
2. Melt the gelatine in the orange juice.
3. Beat the orange rind, egg yolks, coconut milk and brandy together with a fork.
4. Stir them gently into the chocolate and then add the gelatine melted in the orange juice.
5. Taste at this point and add sugar if you think it needs it.
6. Whisk the egg whites till they hold their shape in soft peaks. Stir around a third of the egg whites into the chocolate mixture and then fold in the rest.
7. Pour into 6 glasses or sundae dishes.
8. Cover and refrigerate till the mousse sets.
9. Decorate with the chopped pistachio nuts.

Note: Once upon a time chocolate was either milk or 'dark' but life is no longer so simple. 'Dark' chocolate should, by definition, be milk free in terms of ingredients although, if it does not claim to be 'dairy free' you should still check the ingredients list and, even if there is no milk in it, be aware that it may have been made in a factory which also manufactures milk chocolate so there is a small possibility of contamination.

Moreover, 'dark' chocolate is no longer just 'dark' as you can now buy chocolate with different levels of cocoa solids (the bit which makes it taste chocolatey) — 50-60% cocoa solids will be quite mild, 70% cocoa solids will give a really good dark chocolate taste, but real chocolate lovers will go for the 85% cocoa solids, dark, bitter and strong, if you like that sort of thing.

COCONUT MILK CRÈME BRULÉE

For those on a dairy-free diet crème brulée always seems a distant and no-longer-obtainable dream — but no more!   The richness of the coconut milk is an excellent substitute for the richness of dairy cream while the coconut flavour is gentle and not overpowering. The result is delicious. | Serves 6

600ml	coconut milk	1 pint
	1 vanilla pod or 1 tsp vanilla essence	
25g	pale muscovado sugar	1 oz
6	large egg yolks	6
50g	approx dark muscovado sugar for topping	2 oz

1. Heat the oven to 150C/300F/gas mark 2.
2. Heat the coconut milk with the vanilla pod or essence and the sugar till just below boiling point. Remove the vanilla pod.
3. Whisk the egg yolks thoroughly with a fork (a whisk makes them too frothy) and, whisking all the time, add the coconut milk.
4. Pour into six small ramekin dishes and place in a low oven in a bain marie for 30-40 minutes or till they are just set. This may take a long time but it is worth cooking them very slowly so that they cannot possibly curdle.
5. Allow to cool and refrigerate.
6. To finish, spread a thin layer of muscovado sugar over the top of each and place as close underneath a very hot grill as you can get them.
7. The sugar should melt, bubble and caramelise without melting the cream.

Note: Coconut products can be quite confusing so, for the uninitiated: coconut water is the natural clear juice found inside the coconut; coconut milk is made by boiling equal amounts of water and shredded coconut together until foamy, then straining; coconut cream is made the same way but with a ratio of four parts of shredded coconut to one part water. However, do not confuse the latter with cream of coconut which is a rich, sweet drink made from fresh coconuts, and added sugar and stabilisers.

CHOCOLATE HAZELNUT ROULADE

Chocolate roulade was a real favourite in the 1960s and not only very delicious but naturally gluten and wheat free. However, in the original it was filled with whipped double cream — not so good for dairy intolerants. But by substituting chopped nuts and a thin layer of yogurt or cream cheese for the cream not only does it become dairy free but it takes on a whole new life as a dessert.
| Serves 6

150g	dairy-free dark chocolate (minimum 70% cocoa solids)	5 oz
4	eggs	4
150g	caster sugar	5 oz
2 tbsp	water	2 tbsp
150g	hazelnuts or mixed hazelnuts and almonds	5 oz
	icing sugar to decorate	
	thick sheep's or goat's yogurt, thick soya fruit yogurt, plain goat's, sheep's or soya cream cheese	

1. Preheat the oven to 180C / 350F / gas mark 4.
2. Line a Swiss roll tin with greaseproof paper and brush it well with oil.
3. Break the chocolate into a double boiler or basin over hot water or in a microwave and melt it slowly.
4. Meanwhile separate the eggs and whisk the yolks with the caster sugar till the mixture is lemon coloured.
5. Remove the chocolate from the heat, stir in the hot water, then mix the chocolate with the egg yolk mixture.
6. Whisk the whites till they hold their shape then fold them into the chocolate mixture. Pour this into the Swiss roll tin, make sure it is evenly spread and bake it for 15 minutes or till it holds its shape when lightly pressed with the finger.
7. Make sure the oven shelf is level or you will get a lopsided roll.
8. Once the roulade is cooked, take it out of the oven, cover it with a clean sheet of greaseproof paper and then with a wet tea towel. Leave it for at least a couple of hours.
9. Meanwhile chop the nuts coarsely in a food processor then toast them in a dry pan, under a grill or in the oven but take care that they do not burn.
10. To finish the roulade, remove the tea towel and greaseproof on top and turn it onto a third piece of greaseproof paper, lightly dusted with icing sugar. Carefully peel off the lower sheet of paper — as long as you greased it well it should come off quite easily.
11. Lightly 'butter' the roulade with whichever yogurt or cream cheese you can eat then sprinkle over a thick layer of nuts reserving a few to decorate. (Cont.)

12. Carefully roll it up using the lower sheet of paper and turn it onto a serving dish.
13. Decorate by shaking a little icing sugar and the remaining nuts over the top.
14. Chill it for a couple of hours before serving alone or with more of whatever cream, yogurt or ice cream you can eat.

RAW APPLE FLAN

This is a raw take on a traditional dessert but delicious and filling. You could make individual pies in old yogurt pots and use them for lunch-box treats.
| Serves 6

200g	soft pitted dates	7 oz
100g	broken walnuts or pecan nuts, ground in a food processor	4 oz
100g	ground almonds	4 oz
6	sharp eating apples, cored but with the skins left on	6
1 scant tsp	cinnamon	1 scant tsp
¼ tsp	nutmeg	¼ tsp
	rind and juice of 1 small lemon	
100g	sultanas or soft prunes, chopped small	4 oz

1. Chop the dates roughly in a food processor with the broken walnuts or pecans and the almonds.
2. Press this mixture out into the bottom of a flan dish.
3. Coarsely grate 2 of the apples.
4. Put the rest of the apples in a food processor with the spices and the lemon juice and blend briefly.
5. Mix with the grated apples and the sultanas or prunes and spread over the nut base.
6. Smooth out, cover and leave for several hours for the flavours to amalgamate.

Note: Raw food enthusiasts maintain that cooking foods destroys much of its nutritional value, killing off the natural enzymes which are so important to our digestive systems and altering the nature of the fats, vitamins and minerals that it contains. They maintain that we are the only animal species that cooks its food — and that we are the sickest.

GINGERBREAD TRIFLE

You can do this the lazy way or the energetic way. Use a ready-made gluten and wheat-free gingerbread (several nice ones now on the shelves) and a ready-made soya custard or make both yourself. | Serves 6

1	small gluten/wheat/dairy-free gingerbread, bought or see p226	1
4-6 tbsp	sweet sherry, ginger wine, brandy or a combination of any or all of them	4-6 tbsp
	raspberry jam	
	1 large tin of pears, drained, or 3 fresh pears, cored and peeled	
300ml	dairy-free custard, bought	½ pint
300ml	well-chilled soya, oat or coconut cream	½ pint
1-2 tsp	light muscovado sugar	1-2 tsp
3-4	pieces stem or crystallised ginger to decorate	3-4

1. Break up the gingerbread in the bottom of a trifle dish and sprinkle over whichever of the liqueurs you are using.
2. Spread a layer of jam over the gingerbread.
3. Slice the pears and lay them over the jam.
4. Spoon the custard over the pears.
5. If you are using the soya or oat cream, make sure they are well chilled then whisk vigorously. They will not thicken like dairy cream but will start to hold their shape. Sweeten to taste with the sugar and then spread over the custard.
6. If you are using the coconut cream, stir vigorously, sweeten if it needs it and spread over the custard.
7. Decorate the top with the sliced pieces of ginger.

Note: Pears are an excellent source of natural dietary fibre (one pear will provide 24% of the recommended daily allowance) and are high in pectin, a soluble fibre that binds to fatty substances in the digestive tract and helps to eliminate them. Pears also have a low glycaemic load, are high in vitamin C (one pear provides 10% of your recommended daily allowance) and in potassium (one pear provides 5% of your recommended daily allowance).

STEAMED GOOSEBERRY AND TEFF PUDDING

Gooseberries are one of the pleasures of the summer so I am always happy to use them but you could use any soft summer fruit for this pudding.

If you cannot find any teff flour (see Note below) this would also work well with polenta. | Serves 6

400g	gooseberries, topped, tailed and washed	14 oz
1 tbsp	agave syrup or pale muscovado sugar	1 tbsp
100g	dairy-free spread	4 oz
50g	light muscovado sugar	2 oz
100g	gluten-free teff flour or polenta	4 oz
1 heaped tsp	gluten-free baking powder	1 heaped tsp
¼ tsp	xanthan gum	¼ tsp
2	eggs	2

1. Put the gooseberries in a pan with the agave syrup or sugar and 100ml/4 fl oz water, bring slowly to the boil, cover the pan and turn off the heat. Leave for 15 minutes then taste and add extra syrup or sugar if they are too sharp.
2. Strain the gooseberries, squashing the fruit gently to get out most of the juices but not crushing it. Reserve the juices.
3. Beat the spread in a mixer with the sugar until fairly light and fluffy.
4. Sieve the flour with the baking powder and xanthan gum.
5. By hand beat the eggs into the mixture alternatively with a tbsp of the flour.
6. Fold in the rest of the flour and then the gooseberries.
7. Turn the mixture into a well greased bowl, cover with greaseproof paper and tie tightly like a Christmas pudding and steam in a steamer or in a pan of hot water (half way up the bowl) for 1 hour.
8. Serve hot with the gooseberry juice.

Note: Teff is an ancient gluten-free Ethiopian seed grown high in the mountains and used to make the flat injera bread which is used as an edible 'plate' in Ethiopia. It is extremely nutritious (and delicious) with very high levels of protein and calcium among other nutrients. The seeds are now also grown in the Midwest of the USA and the flour is becoming more available.

FRUIT CRUMBLES

Fruit crumbles are excellent for anyone on a dairy-, gluten- or wheat-free diet as the topping can be so flexible. Go with the season and use whatever fresh fruits are currently available — fresh and dried fruits, apples, pears, dried apricots, raisins, blackberries, gooseberries, currants, bananas, dates etc.

I make the crumble topping without either sugar or fat as I find that the fruit is sweet enough with extra sugar and I rather like the dry texture you get without the fat, but feel free to add either if you prefer. | Serves 6

900g	any fresh fruit or combination	2 lbs
approx 100ml	water (how much you need will depend on the fruit but make sure that the bottom of the pan is covered)	3 fl oz
100-150g	muscovado sugar or alternative natural sweetener (agave syrup, maple syrup, honey etc. How much you need will depend on the fruit that you use and how sweet you like it. It is better to add it when the fruit is at least partially cooked and has released some of its own sugar)	4-6 oz
100g	rolled or porridge oats	4 oz
25g	sunflower seeds, lightly crushed	1 oz
50g	ground almonds	2 oz
50g	pine nuts	2 oz
25g	dark muscovado sugar (optional)	1 oz
25g	dairy-free spread (optional)	1 oz

1. Wash or peel the fruit as appropriate, chop roughly and put in a large pan with the sugar and water.
2. Bring to the boil, reduce the heat and simmer, covered, for 3-10 minutes, depending on the fruit.
3. Heat the oven to 180C/350F/gas mark 4.
4. Drain off any excess juice from the cooked fruit which will make the top go soggy (reserve to serve with the crumble) and transfer the fruit to a baking dish.
5. In a food processor whizz the oats and sunflower seeds with the spread, if you are using it.
6. Mix into the ground almonds, pine nuts and sugar (if you are using it) and spread over the fruit.
7. Bake in a moderate oven for 30-40 minutes to brown the top.
8. Serve alone or with whatever cream, custard, yogurt or ice cream you can eat.

STUFFED PANCAKES WITH CHOCOLATE SAUCE

This is a real kids dish and was originally devised for an allergy catering manual I wrote for schools. Not that there is anything to stop the rest of the family enjoying the pancakes too. | Serves 6

125g	gluten- and wheat-free flour or or 75g/3 oz gram flour and 50g/2 oz rice flour	5 oz
pinch	salt	pinch
½ tsp	xanthan gum	½ tsp
1	egg (optional)	1
250ml	water, soya or oat milk	8 fl oz
750g	any of the following fruit either fresh, cooked or tinned, sliced or lightly mashed: apple, pear, banana, mandarin or satsuma segments, pineapple, peaches, plums, nectarines, strawberries or blackberries	1 ¾ lbs

Sauce

50g	cornflour	2 oz
900ml	soya, oat or rice milk	1 ½ pints
150g	dairy-free chocolate	6 oz

1. To make the pancakes, whizz the flour, salt, gum, egg (if you are using it) and water or milk in a food processor.
2. Heat a pancake pan with a dribble of sunflower oil.
3. Pour one ladleful of the mixture into the pan, swirl it round and cook quickly on both sides. You should get 12 pancakes from the mixture.
4. Lay the pancakes out and fill with a tablespoonful of whatever fruit mixture you are using. Fold over.
5. In a bowl mix the milk gradually into the cornflour until it is a smooth paste.
6. Turn the mixture into a saucepan and heat slowly, stirring continually until the sauce thickens.
7. Break the chocolate into the sauce and stir until it melts. Pour a spoonful over each pancake.

Note: Don't forget that pancakes freeze well so if you want to double or treble up on the pancake ingredients you can make an extra batch or two for the freezer. Just remember to interleave each pancake with greaseproof paper to prevent them sticking together and allow you to take out as many/few as you need.

MINCE PIES

This amount of filling makes approximately 12 pies but you may wish to multiply it up as it stores well in tightly closed jars or in the freezer. It is better to make the mix a few days before you need it to give it a chance to mature.

	Filling	
75g	raisins	3 oz
75g	currants	3 oz
50g	sultanas	2 oz
25g	dried apricots, chopped small	1 oz
25g	soft dried figs, chopped small	1 oz
25g	soft prunes, chopped small	1 oz
25g	dried blueberries (optional)	1 oz
½ scant tsp	ground cloves	½ scant tsp
1 heaped tsp	dried ginger	1 heaped tsp
1 level tsp	ground nutmeg	1 level tsp
75g	sharp eating or cooking apple, cored but not skinned	3 oz
	grated rind and juice of ½ lemon	
4 tbsp	brandy or whisky	4 tbsp
4 tbsp	fruit juice – I used pomegranate	4 tbsp
	but you could use orange or apple or juice of your choice	

1. In a large bowl mix the raisins, currants, sultanas, apricots, figs, prunes and blueberries, if you are using them, with the spices.
2. Chop the apple into very small pieces (but not to a mush) in a food processor and add to the mix.
3. Grate the peel from the lemon and add to the fruit mix.
4. Cut the lemon into small pieces, remove all the pips and then chop finely in the food processor.
5. Mix into the dried fruit along with the brandy or whisky and fruit juices. Mix well, cover and leave to stand for 24-48 hours.

	Pastry, enough for 12	
150g	gluten/wheat-free flour	6 oz
75g	goat's butter or dairy-free spread	3 oz
2-3 tbsp	water	2-3 tbsp
1	egg, to glaze	1

1. To make the pies, heat the oven to 180C/350F/gas mark 4.
2. Mix the flour and rub in the fat (by hand or in a food processor). Add the water to make a soft dough.
3. Roll out and line your mince pie tins. Fill with the fruit mixture and top with pastry lids. Paint with beaten egg and bake for 25-30 minutes.
4. Remove from the tins when still warm and cool on a rack.

CHRISTMAS UPSIDE-DOWN CAKE

Gluten, nightshade, nut, soya and wheat free; can be dairy and lactose free.

For those who want a hint of the Christmas spirit but who cannot do with Christmas pud. It is delicious warm out of the oven — but also excellent cold as a cake. You can serve it with whatever cream, yogurt or ice cream you can eat, but we felt that they would rather mask its delicate — and yummy — flavours.
| Serves 6

2	medium-size ripe eating apples, cored, peeled and sliced	2
40g	raisins	1½ oz
2	soft dates, stoned and chopped	2
½ tsp	each of ground ginger and cinnamon	½ tsp
pinch	of cloves	pinch
¼	ground fresh nutmeg or ¼ tsp ready ground rind and juice 1 lemon	¼
1 generous tbsp	brandy	1 generous tbsp
150g	goat's butter or dairy-free spread	6 oz
150g	pale muscovado sugar	6 oz
50g	each gram flour, rice flour and coarse polenta	2 oz
½ tsp	each ground ginger and cinnamon	½ tsp
1 level tsp	gluten/wheat-free baking powder	1 level tsp
3	eggs	3

1. Put the apple in a small bowl with the raisins, dates, spices, lemon rind, half the lemon juice and the brandy. Stir well around until the fruit is well coated in the spices and the liquid then cover and leave to steep for 1-3 hours.
2. Heat the oven to 180C/350F/Gas mark 4.
3. Line a 20cm/8 inch loose-bottomed cake tin with foil and oil lightly. Spread the fruit mixture out over the bottom of the cake tin, flattening it out as much as possible.

4. Beat the butter or spread with the sugar in an electric mixer until light and creamy.

5. Sieve the three flours with the baking powder.

6. With a wooden spoon, beat the eggs into the butter and sugar mixture alternately with tablespoons of the flours then fold in the rest of the flour with the remaining lemon juice.

7. Spoon carefully into the tin and flatten out by banging the cake tin gently on the counter.

8. Bake for 35 minutes or until a skewer comes out clean.

9. Carefully turn out onto a serving dish and then, also carefully, peel off the foil.

WINTER FRUIT COMPOTE

This is a wonderful old-fashioned compote — excellent warm or cold, for breakfast, lunch or supper, by itself or with whatever cream, yogurt or ice cream you can eat. Use dried fruits in any combination that you fancy — prunes, figs, dates, sultanas, cherries, raisins etc. Ideally they will be pre-softened but if not you may need to simmer them for 45-60 minutes to make sure that they are really soft. | Serves 6

400g	dried fruit	14 oz
1 litre	water	1 ¾ pints
½	lemon, sliced	½
1	stick of vanilla or cinnamon	1

1. Put all the ingredients together in a pan, cover and bring very slowly to the boil. Simmer for 30 minutes.

2. Strain the fruit, reserving the cooking liquid, and put it in a serving bowl.

3. Return the juices to the heat and continue to simmer briskly for 5-10 minutes till they are slightly reduced.

4. Pour over the fruit and allow to cool.

5. Serve warm, at room temperature or chilled, as you prefer.

Note: In Eastern Europe a compote (or compot, or kompott) refers to a refreshing chilled fruit drink made from dried fruits which have been boiled in water with sugar and then left to infuse. In either guise it is delicious and health giving.

HOT CHOCOLATE SOUFFLÉ FLAN

This is very luscious but very quick to make. If you are doing it for a party you can make the chocolate filling, including folding in the egg whites, ahead of time and just leave it in the fridge. When you are ready to cook it, spoon the filling into the pastry case — and cook. | Serves 6

	Pastry	
100g	rice flour	4 oz
100g	ground almonds	4 oz
100g	dairy-free spread	4 oz
1 level tsp	pale muscovado sugar	1 level tsp
1	egg	1 egg

1. Heat the oven to 170C/325F/gas mark 3.
2. Put the rice flour, almonds, spread and sugar in a food processor and whizz briefly to mix in the fat.
3. Add the egg and whizz briefly again.
4. Press the mixture out into the base and up the sides of a 20cm/8 inch flan dish, getting it as even as you can.
5. Prick the base with a fork.
6. Bake for 25 minutes or until the paste is lightly tanned.

	Filling	
100g	dark dairy-free chocolate	4 oz
1 dessert spoon	agave syrup or dark muscovado sugar	1 dessert spoon
3	large eggs	3

1. Turn the oven up to 180C/350F/gas mark 4.
2. Melt the chocolate in a microwave or over hot water then stir in the syrup or sugar. Meanwhile, separate the eggs.
3. Off the heat, stir the egg yolks into the chocolate mixture.
4. Whisk the egg whites until they hold their shape in soft peaks.
5. Stir approximately a third of the whites into the chocolate mixture then fold in the rest.
6. Spoon into the pastry case and bake for 25-30 minutes or until the chocolate soufflé filling has risen and is firm. Serve at once.

Note: Agave syrup, produced from a central American aloe vera type plant, has become very popular recently because of its low glycaemic load. However, its GL is only low because the glycaemic index measures glucose rather than fructose (thought by some to be as bad or worse than glucose for diabetics); agave is high in fructose. However it also contains significant quantities of calcium, potassium, iron and magnesium and tastes really good.

PLUM TART

A warming autumnal tart. You could also make it in the summer with peaches, nectarines, apricots or greengages. The buckwheat flour and ground almonds make a lovely nutty base. | Serves 6

75g	ground almonds	3 oz
75g	brown rice flour	3 oz
75g	buckwheat flour	3 oz
½ tsp	xanthan gum	½ tsp
100g	goat's butter or dairy-free spread	4 oz
30g	cornflour	1½ oz
300ml	coconut milk	½ pint
1 dessertspoon approx	date, rice or agave syrup or molasses	1 dessertspoon
30 approx	Victoria or other well flavoured plums	30 approx

1. Heat the oven to 180C/350F/gas mark 4.
2. Sieve the flours and the gum together and turn into a food processor with the ground almonds. Chop the butter or spread, add and whizz until they are like breadcrumbs. Add a couple of tbsp very cold water and whizz again briefly until the pastry comes together in a ball.
3. Roll out on a floured board and line a 20cm/8 inch flan dish and bake for 25-30 minutes or until quite crisp.
4. Meanwhile, mix the cornflour with the coconut milk then heat slowly, stirring continually until it thickens and boils. Cook for one minute then remove from the heat and add the sweetener of your choice to taste. Stir well in and pour into the prepared flan dish.
5. Wipe, halve and stone the plums and arrange tightly on top of the custard.
6. Return to the oven for 20 minutes or until the plums are cooked. Serve at once.

NUT AND APPLE FLAN

This is really delicious and very easy to do and you can make it with nuts or with seeds.

If you pre-cook the base, it is quite biscuity; some people prefer not to pre-cook it, in which case it is quite chewy and tastes more strongly of the nuts.

If you like the apple slightly crunchy, bake uncovered; if you prefer your apples softer, cover the apples with another piece of foil when you bake them.
| Serves 6

	a little sunflower oil	
75g	each of hazelnuts, almonds and cashew nuts, or for the seed version, 75g/3 oz each of pumpkin, sunflower and sesame seeds	3 oz
2	egg whites	2
1-2	Bramley cooking apples, depending on size	1-2
	agave syrup, maple syrup or dark muscovado sugar	
	a little redcurrant, raspberry or other smooth-ish jam	

1. Heat the oven to 180C/350F/gas mark 4.
2. Double some aluminium foil to about the size of the flan you want to make and grease it with a little oil. Lay it on an oven tray.
3. Pulverise the nuts or seeds in a food processor.
4. Beat the egg whites till stiff but not peaky and mix them into the nuts.
5. With your hands, press the mixture out on the foil into a round or square shape.
6. If you want your base biscuity cook uncovered for 30 minutes in the oven, then remove.
7. Core the apples and remove the skin or not, as you prefer. Slice them thinly and arrange them on the flan base.
8. Drizzle with agave or maple syrup or sprinkle lightly with muscovado sugar and return to the oven, covered or uncovered (depending on whether you want the apples to stay slightly crunchy or to be quite soft), for a further 30 minutes.
9. If you prefer your base softer and nuttier, then do not pre-cook the base but lay the apples straight on it and cook as above for 30 minutes.
10. In either case, remove from the oven and allow to cool slightly.
11. Melt the jam and brush over the apples.
12. Serve warm or at room temperature, alone or with whatever cream, yogurt or ice cream you can eat.

MELON AND GINGER SALAD

This is a very simple but refreshing salad. | Serves 6

15-25g	piece fresh ginger, depending on how gingery you want your salad	½-1 oz
400ml	pink fruit juice — I used an apple and raspberry but you could use a cranberry mixture or any other combination that you like; the juice does not need to be pink for flavour, it just looks prettier	14 fl oz
	1 large or 2 small Ogen or Charentais melons	

1. Peel and slice the ginger into very thin matchsticks.
2. Put them in a pan with the juice and heat to a simmer.
3. Cook just below a simmer for 3-4 minutes to soften the ginger.
4. Deseed the melons and scoop or spoon out the flesh into one large or six small bowls.
5. Spoon over the ginger and fruit juice and leave to cool in the juices before serving either chilled or at room temperature.

Note: If you cannot get any fresh ginger you could also make this dessert with crystallised or stem ginger but be careful to remove most of the syrup or sugar or it will be too sweet.

AUTUMN PEARS WITH FIGS, GINGER WINE AND GRAPEFRUIT JUICE

Serves 4

3	ripe pears, it does not matter which breed	3
3	ripe figs	3
6 tbsp	fresh pink grapefruit juice	6 tbsp
6 tbsp	ginger wine or ginger liqueur	6 tbsp
25g	dairy-free chocolate	1 oz

1. Peel the pears and cut them in quarters, laying them out on a serving dish. Slice the figs and arrange them with the pears on the dish. Mix the grapefruit juice with the ginger wine or liqueur and pour over the fruit.
2. Melt the chocolate in the microwave (45 seconds-1 minute on high) or in a bowl over hot water. Take a spoon and drizzle the chocolate over the pears — having decided, before you start, what pattern you want to make! If you have already decided, it is quite easy (if you have not, it can look rather a mess as mine does). However, it tasted delicious.

PEACH FLAMBÉ

To get the full flavour of the rather delicate juices you may prefer not to cover it with cream or ice cream. Both of the syrups give a pleasant, slightly smoky sweetness to the juices. | Serves 6

6	large ripe peaches	6
400ml	water	14 fl oz
2 tbsp	agave or maple syrup	2 tbsp
	1 large soup ladle of brandy	
	handful of redcurrants	
	whatever cream, yogurt or ice cream you can eat	

1. Carefully cut the peaches into wedges and put into a saucepan.
2. Add the water and agave or maple syrup and bring gently to a simmer. Depending on how ripe the peaches are, simmer gently, covered, for 3-8 minutes or until they are just cooked.
3. Transfer to a serving bowl and sprinkle over the redcurrants.
4. When you are ready to serve it, heat the brandy gently in the soup ladle. Light the brandy and immediately pour over the peaches and serve.

KIWI ICE

A really refreshing ice cream-sorbet for a hot summer's day. | Serves 6

6	kiwi fruit, peeled	6
	juice 1 lemon	
150ml	rice milk	¼ pint
1 tbsp	Grand Marnier or other orange-based liqueur	1 tbsp

1. Purée the kiwis with the lemon juice and milk in a food processor or, if you want a very smooth purée, in a liquidiser.
2. Add the liqueur and turn into an ice-cream maker and churn freeze.
3. Soften in the refrigerator for at least 30 minutes before serving

STEM GINGER ICE CREAM

A really yummy ice cream.

300ml	goat's, soya or oat cream	½ pint
50g	stem ginger, finely sliced	2 oz
1-2 tbsp	ginger syrup	1-2 tbsp
50g	toasted, nibbed almonds	2 oz
2 tbsp	brandy	2 tbsp
	pinch salt	

1. If you have an ice-cream maker mix all the ingredients together, tasting it as you do so. If the ginger is too strong substitute 1 tbsp muscovado sugar for the syrup. Turn the mixture into it and churn freeze according to the instructions.
2. If you do not have an ice-cream maker, whisk the cream until it thickens a bit. Fold in the ginger, the nuts and the brandy and then the syrup to taste. Put in the freezer and when it is just starting to freeze take it out and whisk hard. Repeat this several times until the ice cream is solid.
3. To serve, remove from the freezer to the fridge at least half an hour before you want to serve it. Pile into glasses. You can also top it with more toasted nibbed almonds or some sliced ginger.

BANANA AND COCONUT SMOOTHIE ICE CREAM

A great recipe which you can either use as a smoothie or pop into the ice-cream machine and turn into an ice cream. | Serves 6

3	medium bananas	3
600ml	tinned coconut milk	1 pint
75g	blueberries or raspberries	3 oz
100g	pitted cherries, halved (optional)	4 oz

1. Purée the bananas in a food processor with the coconut milk.
2. You can then either whizz the blueberries and raspberries in the processor with the milk or you can add them separately so that the basic smoothie/ice cream remains creamy coloured with lots of fruity bits.
3. Similarly, you can whizz the cherries with the mixture, or keep them separate.
4. The bananas should give you the smooth texture of a creamy ice cream and provide lots of sweetness.
5. For the smoothie, you can add some crushed ice and serve in a long glass. For the ice cream, turn the mixture into an ice-cream maker and churn freeze.
6. However, be warned that if you use whole or half cherries in the ice cream they will freeze very hard and crunchy so you might do better to chop them up even if you do not process them.

COFFEE AND COCONUT ICE CREAM

I use shots of espresso coffee from my local Costa but if you have a home espresso machine you can make your own. Without the sugar the ice cream has a quite 'adult' taste which you may not find sweet enough for ice cream.

   The flavour matures in the freezer so try to make it a bit ahead of time.
| Serves 6

600ml	coconut milk	1 pint
6 shots (approx 150ml)	strong espresso coffee	5 fl oz
150ml	Tia Maria or other dairy-free coffee-flavoured liqueur	¼ pint
1 heaped tbsp	dark muscovado sugar (optional)	1 heaped tbsp
75-100g	pecan nuts (optional)	3-4 oz

1. Mix the coconut milk, coffee, liqueur and sugar, if you are using it, and put them into an ice-cream maker.
2. Churn/freeze until it has reached 'slush' texture then add the pecan nuts if you are using them.
3. If you are serving the ice cream at once, continue to churn freeze until it is frozen but not frozen hard.
4. If you are not using it immediately continue to churn freeze until it is frozen but remember to take it out of the freezer and 'defrost' in the microwave for two minutes on 'defrost' or leave it in the fridge for at least 30 minutes before you want to serve it.

BLACKBERRY AND APPLE ICE CREAM

A nice seasonal change from blackberry and apple crumble — or, or course, you could serve the ice cream with a blackberry and apple crumble. | Serves 6

200g	sharp eating apples	7 oz
200g	blackberries	7 oz
6 tbsp	water	6 tbsp
1-2 tbsp	dark muscovado sugar, depending on how tart the fruit is and how sweet you like it	1-2 tbsp
300g	plain goat's, sheep's milk or soya yogurt	½ pint

1. Core the apples and chop them, leaving the skins on. Put them in a pan with the blackberries, water and sugar and bring to the boil. Cover and simmer gently for 5 minutes or until the fruit is soft.
2. Purée the fruit in a food processor — just a little bit if you like to keep some texture in the ice cream, for a bit longer if you want it totally smooth. Pour into a bowl and mix in the yogurt.
3. Churn freeze in an ice-cream maker if you have one.
4. If not put into the freezer for 20-25 minutes or until it is starting to freeze, then remove and beat hard. Return to the freezer and repeat the operation in another 20 minutes. Return to the freezer.
5. Remove from the freezer into the fridge 25 minutes before you want to eat it to allow it to soften slightly.

CREAMY STRAWBERRY SORBET

The oat milk gives a slightly nutty flavour to this very simple but tasty sorbet/ice cream. | Serves 6

3	large, ripe bananas	3
750g	ripe strawberries plus 4 for decoration	1¾ lbs
450ml	oat milk	15 fl oz

1. Purée the bananas, strawberries and oat milk in a food processor.
2. Turn into an ice-cream maker and churn freeze.
3. Remove from the freezer and place into the refrigerator at least 30 minutes before you want to serve the sorbet.
4. Spoon into individual serving dishes and decorate with the fresh strawberries.

Note: Oat milk is made mainly in Sweden and is now fairly easily available. It is quite creamy with a faint, background taste of oats. You can also get oat cream — a thicker version of the milk which is excellent as a pouring cream and can be lightly whipped although it will never get really thick.

If you cannot get oat milk you can use either a soya milk or a rice milk.

BAKING

BREAD

Quick White Loaf

White Loaf with Coconut Milk

Brown Loaf with Ground Almonds

Coconut Milk Soda Bread

Fruit Malt Loaf

Corn Bread

BISCUITS

Oatcakes

Almond Biscuits

Meringues

Chocolate Biscuits

Lemon Biscuits

Ginger and Sultana Flapjacks

Strawberry Crunchies

CAKES

Almond Cake

Very Rich Chocolate Gateau-Cake

Wholemeal Cinnamon Muffins

Summer Fruit Cake

Luscious Apple Cake

Seedy Christmas Cake

Sponge Cakes

Sticky Gingerbread

Classic Chocolate Cake

Lemon Poppy Seed Cake

Chocolate Brownies

Coffee Cake

Fig, Banana and Cashew Nut Cake

Carrot and Walnut Cake

Some notes about gluten-free bread

Because gluten is such an intrinsic part of a normal loaf, any bread made without it is going to involve compromises and changes in technique.

For example, kneading gluten-free flour is pointless as there is no gluten to stretch (the point of kneading). Indeed, kneading gluten-free dough will just make it tough. Gluten-free flours (especially buckwheat) also tend to need more liquid than regular flour.

There is some disagreement among gluten-free bakers as to whether it is better to 'prove' the mixture (as with normal yeast breads) before you cook it or not. The chemical structure of gluten-free flours, even with the addition of xanthan gum, does not 'hold up' as well as flours containing gluten so it may be better to skip the proving stage and go straight to the cooking.

I have found that both methods are moderately successful but that you need to use rather more yeast if you are not giving it time to rise.

Gluten-free breads do not, on the whole, keep as well as 'normal' breads so are best eaten freshly baked. Alternatively, slice them and freeze the slices to be defrosted as needed.

QUICK WHITE LOAF

This mixture makes a quite light and pleasant loaf which keeps relatively well and is good for sandwiches. | Makes 1 small loaf

100g	rice flour	4 oz
100g	potato flour	4 oz
50g	gram flour	2 oz
50g	millet flakes	2 oz
1 tsp	sea salt	1 tsp
1 tsp	pale muscovado sugar	1 tsp
1 heaped tsp	xanthan gum	1 heaped tsp
7g pack	quick acting yeast	¼ oz pack
2 tbsp	oil (olive or sunflower)	2 tbsp
300ml	lukewarm water	½ pint

1. Heat the oven to 200C/400F/gas mark 6.
2. Grease a small loaf tin.
3. In an electric mixer with a beater combine the dry ingredients. Add the oil and then, gradually, the warm water.
4. Continue to beat for 1-2 minutes or until you have a smooth dough.
5. Transfer it to the loaf tin (you do not need to knead the dough) smooth the

top with the back of a wet spoon and put into the oven.

7. Bake for 45 minutes or until the loaf is well risen. Remove, knock out of the tin and cool on a rack.

WHITE LOAF WITH COCONUT MILK

Some people find it much easier to use a proprietary gluten-free flour mix than making up a mix of their own, so, for this loaf I have used Doves Farm gluten-free flour which is a combination of rice, potato, tapioca, maize and buckwheat flours.

Some flour makers (such as Doves Farm) are now offering specific mixes for bread making, most of which already include xanthan gum. So you need to check the ingredients of the flour and, if it does include xanthan gum, do not add extra.

Obviously, the make-up of the mix that you use will affect the taste and texture of your bread but hopefully, this will prove a reasonably successful recipe for most.

This loaf uses an egg as well as the yeast to help it rise and is proved for an hour before being cooked. | Makes 1 large loaf

400g	gluten-free flour	14 oz
1 tbsp	xanthan gum (if not already in the flour mix)	1 tbsp
7g sachet	quick acting yeast	¼ oz sachet
1 heaped tsp	sea salt	1 heaped tsp
4 tbsp	olive or sunflower oil	4 tbsp
1	egg	1
200ml	coconut milk	7 fl oz
180ml	warm water	6 fl oz

1. Mix the dry ingredients together in the bowl of an electric mixer with a beater.
2. Add the oil and egg.
3. Mix the coconut milk and the water ensuring that their combined temperature is lukewarm. Gradually beat this into the mixture and continue to beat for 3-4 minutes until you have a smooth dough.
4. Transfer to a well greased loaf tin, smooth the top with the back of a wet spoon, cover with clingfilm and leave in a warm place (an airing cupboard or an oven on 'warm') for 45-60 minutes or until it has risen to the top of the tin. Meanwhile, heat the oven to 200C/400F/gas mark 6.
5. Remove the clingfilm from the top and transfer the bread to the oven. Bake for 1 hour or until the bread sounds hollow when tapped.
6. Knock out of the tin and cool on a rack.

BROWN LOAF WITH GROUND ALMONDS

This is another loaf which needs time to rise. It has a very slight and rather pleasantly sweet aftertaste thanks to the dark muscovado sugar and the almonds, which also help to keep it moist. | Makes 1 large loaf

100g	buckwheat flour	4 oz
100g	gram flour	4 oz
100g	rice flour	4 oz
50g	ground almonds	2 oz
1 tsp	sea salt	1 tsp
2 heaped tsp	dark muscovado sugar	2 heaped tsp
1 heaped tsp	xanthan gum	1 heaped tsp
1 x 7g sachet	easy bake yeast	1x ¼ oz sachet
3 tbsp	olive oil	3 tbsp
400ml	lukewarm water	14 fl oz

1. Mix the flours, almonds, salt, sugar, xanthan gum and yeast in the bowl of a mixer then beat in the olive oil and warm water. Continue to beat till you have a smooth dough.
2. Turn the dough into a well greased loaf tin, smooth the top with a wet spoon, cover with clingfilm and prove for 30-45 minutes in an airing cupboard or a warming oven.
3. Heat the oven to 200C/400F/gas mark 6.
4. Remove the clingfilm and bake for 45 minutes or until the bread sounds hollow when tapped.
5. Turn out onto a rack to cool.

COCONUT MILK SODA BREAD

This mixture makes a really tasty, coarse brown soda bread — not the same as the original but a good substitute. | Picture page 205

100g	buckwheat flour	4 oz
150g	gram flour	6 oz
50g	millet flakes	2 oz
50g	potato flour	2 oz
1 level tsp	salt	1 level tsp

2 level tsp	bicarbonate of soda	2 level tsp
2 level tsp	cream of tartar	2 level tsp
1 heaped tsp	xanthan gum	1 heaped tsp
300ml	coconut milk	½ pint
	juice ½ lemon	

1. Heat the oven to 190C/375F/gas mark 5.
2. Flour a baking tray.
3. Mix all the dry ingredients together well.
4. Form a well in the centre and add the coconut milk and lemon juice. Incorporate it quickly and lightly into the dough which will be quite 'wet'.
5. Form the dough into a round loaf shape and cut a cross on the top with a wet knife.
6. Bake for 40 minutes then remove from the oven, ease gently off the tray with a spatula and cool on a rack.

FRUIT MALT LOAF

A classic for tea on its own, or with a skimming of goat's butter, dairy-free spread or raspberry jam.

200g	gram flour	7 oz
50g	rice flour	2 oz
2 heaped tsp	gluten-free baking powder	2 heaped tsp
1 level tsp	xanthan gum	1 level tsp
50g	raisins	2 oz
50g	sultanas	2 oz
50g	soft prunes, chopped roughly	2 oz
1 tbsp	malt extract	1 tbsp
240ml	skimmed sheep's, goat's, soya, or oat milk	8 fl oz

1. Heat the oven to 160C/325F/gas mark 3.
2. Sift the flour with the baking powder and xanthan gum then mix in the fruit.
3. Heat the malt extract with the milk in a pan or a microwave then stir into the dry mixture.
4. Spoon the bread into a well greased loaf tin and bake for 45 minutes or till a skewer comes out clean.
5. Cool on a rack and serve alone or with goat's butter or dairy-free spread.

CORN BREAD

This is the traditional bread of the deep south of America where corn is (or was) the staple grain. Because of the inclusion of the eggs it is more like a pudding than a conventional bread and is best eaten warm, straight out of the oven!

200g	coarse maize meal or polenta	7 oz
50g	fine cornflour	2 oz
50g	potato flour	2 oz
1 heaped tsp	gluten/wheat-free baking powder	1 heaped tsp
1 scant tsp	salt	1 scant tsp
1 tbsp	light muscovado sugar	1 tbsp
20g	goat's butter or dairy-free spread	¾ oz
1 tbsp	olive oil	1 tbsp
2	eggs	2
240ml	goat's, sheep's or soya milk soured with the juice from ½ lemon	8 fl oz

1. Heat the oven to 200C/400F/gas mark 6.
2. Mix the dry ingredients thoroughly in the bowl of an electric mixer.
3. Melt the butter or spread then add the oil, eggs and soured milk and mix well together.
4. Beat this into the dry ingredients.
5. Line a small square or rectangular oven dish with greased greaseproof paper and pour in the batter. The mixture should be approximately 2.5cm/1 inch deep.
6. Bake for 20 minutes or until the corn bread is firm to the touch and golden.
7. Remove from the oven and serve in squares.

Note: There are many varieties of corn bread across the southern states of the US, many of which are cooked in a skillet or frying pan rather than the oven.

OATCAKES

Provided that you can eat oats (which most people on wheat/gluten-free diets now can) oatcakes are the most delicious, nutritious and sustaining of biscuits. Good for eating on their own, with pâté, with cheese, with dips or, with some added fruit or spice, as a sweet biscuit with coffee. You can also make mini oatcakes as a base for cocktail snacks or finger food. There are a number of excellent proprietary oatcakes on the market but they never taste quite as good as your own, warm and crisp out of the oven. | Makes approximately 10 regular-size oatcakes

100g	rolled oats	4 oz
50g	rice flour	2 oz
½ tsp	gluten/wheat-free baking powder	½ tsp
¼ tsp	xanthan gum	¼ tsp
¼ tsp	salt	¼ tsp
1 tbsp	dairy-free spread	1 tbsp
	for sweet oatcakes leave out the salt and add 1 level tsp pale muscovado sugar and 1 tbsp currants or 1 heaped tsp ground ginger	

1. Heat the oven to 180C/350F/gas mark 4.
2. Pulverise the oats in a food processor as finely as you wish your oatcakes to be — fine or coarse.
3. Mix the oats with the rice flour, baking powder, xanthan gum and salt or sugar plus currants or ginger.
4. Rub in the spread. Add enough cold water to mix to a soft dough then roll it out. You can make the oatcakes as thick or thin as you want but no thinner than a £1 coin. Cut into whatever shape you wish.
5. Transfer the oatcakes to a baking tray and bake for 10-15 minutes, depending on how thick you made them. Cool on a rack before eating.

Note: Oatcakes have always been considered to be a staple food in Scotland where medieval chieftains and their followers on raids across the border would carry small sacks of oatmeal strapped to the saddles of their horses and an iron plate slung over their back. The plate was used as a shield in combat and for cooking their oatcakes over an open fire when they made camp.

ALMOND BISCUITS

These are an alternative version of a macaroon. Macaroons, along with meringues (see below), are the perfect biscuits for anyone on a gluten-, wheat- or dairy-free diet. | Makes around 6 regular size biscuits or 10 mini ones.

100g	ground almonds	4 oz
75g	rice flour	3 oz
75g	pale muscovado sugar	3 oz
25g	dairy-free margarine	1 oz
2	egg whites	2

1. Heat the oven to 180C/350F/gas mark 4.
2. Mix the almonds, rice flour and 50g/2 oz of the sugar together and rub in the dairy-free spread followed by the egg whites.
3. With your hands form the mixture into small balls and roll in the remaining sugar. Place on a lightly oiled baking tray and press flat with a fork.
4. Bake for 15-20 minutes, or until the biscuits are just turning golden.
5. Remove to a wire rack and allow to cool.

MERINGUES

Surprisingly, if you can manage not to eat them all, cooked meringues freeze well, but freeze them in containers not in bags or they will get broken. | Makes 6-8 large meringues or 12 minis

3	egg whites	3
150 g	sugar	6 oz
	a few drops vanilla or almond essence (optional)	
15-25 g	grated dark chocolate, ground hazelnuts or any other basically dry and light flavouring you fancy	½-1 oz

1. Whisk the egg whites until they are pretty stiff, then add the sugar and continue to whisk until they are very shiny and stiff enough to stand in very spiky peaks.
2. If you are whisking by hand this can take some time but it is very important that they are sufficiently whisked; too little and the texture will be granular.
3. Fold in your flavouring and spoon or pipe the mixture onto a sheet of foil. Cook in a very low oven — 120C/250F/gas mark ½ for 2-4 hours (or the lower

oven of an Aga all night) to give you a light, crisp meringue.

4. If you prefer them sticky in the middle you need to cook them at a higher temperature (150C/300F/gas mark 2) for less time, approximately 45 minutes.

5. Remove from the oven and peel gently off the foil.

Note: Meringue mixtures come in many forms including the partly cooked meringue toppings for pies, poached meringue floating islands, whisked-over-hot water meringues for Pavlova and even, apparently, as an accompaniment to curried chicken in Serbia.

CHOCOLATE BISCUITS

These are very tasty little biscuits — ideal for coffee — but you need to be careful not to burn them. Because they are so dark it is not easy to see when they are cooked. | Makes 15-20 mini biscuits

75g	dairy-free spread	3 oz
75g	dark muscovado sugar	3 oz
50g	rice flour	2 oz
50g	gram/chickpea flour	2 oz
½ level tsp	xanthan gum	½ tsp
50g	gluten/wheat-free cocoa powder	2 oz
1 tsp	gluten/wheat-free baking powder	1 tsp

1. Heat the oven to 190C/375F/gas mark 5.

2. Beat the spread and sugar together till they are light and fluffy.

3. Sift together the flours, xanthan gum, cocoa and baking powder and beat them into the mixture.

4. Roll teaspoons of the mixture into balls with your hands then squash them flat and decorate with the back of a fork.

5. Transfer carefully onto a baking tray and bake for 10-15 minutes, taking care that they do not burn.

6. Remove the biscuits from the oven, cool slightly then transfer them carefully onto a rack to cool completely.

Note: You could vary the flavouring of the basic biscuit mix by substituting 50g/2 oz ground and toasted almonds, walnuts or hazelnuts or the grated rind of 2 lemons, for the chocolate.

LEMON BISCUITS

These are sort of lemon shortbreads — and very tasty. If you have a favourite gluten-free flour mix, you can substitute 200g/7 oz of it for the three flours.
| Makes 12 biscuits

75g	rice flour	3 oz
50g	potato flour	2 oz
50g	gram flour	2 oz
75g	light muscovado sugar	3 oz
1 level tsp	wheat/gluten-free baking powder	1 level tsp
½ tsp	xanthan gum	½ tsp
75g	dairy-free spread	3 oz
	grated rind of 1-2 lemons, depending on how lemony you like your biscuits	
3 tbsp	soya, oat or coconut milk, soured with a good squeeze of lemon juice	3 tbsp

1. Heat the oven to 160C/325F/gas mark 3.
2. Mix the flours, sugar, baking powder and xanthan gum together in a bowl, then rub in the fat. You can do this in a food processor if you prefer.
3. Make a well in the middle of the mixture, add whichever milk you are using and mix to a soft dough.
4. Line a small Swiss roll tin with greased greaseproof paper and press the mixture into it — it should not be more than 1cm / ½ inch thick.
5. Bake for 20 minutes. Remove and cut into biscuit shapes (wedges, rounds, squares) then return to the oven for a further 10 minutes.
6. Cool in the tin then remove carefully with a spatula and finish cooling on a rack.

Note: Lemons are a great source of B6, iron, potassium, not to mention vitamin C, calcium, folic acid, manganese, magnesium and zinc. They are also rich in antioxidants and pectin so may protect us from free radicals, prevent heart disease, lower cholesterol, lower blood sugar levels, and act as a natural antibacterial.

GINGER AND SULTANA FLAPJACKS

Everyone has their own pet flapjack recipe. I prefer mine not to be too sticky or too sweet. If you would rather not use oats, substitute millet flakes. If you like a bit of crispier chewiness in your flapjack, add some sunflower seeds.
| Makes approximately 16 flapjacks

175g	dairy-free spread	6 oz
75g	dark molasses sugar	3 oz
75g	demerara sugar	3 oz
2 heaped tsp	ground ginger	2 heaped tsp
225g	rolled porridge oats (or millet flakes)	8 oz
75g	sultanas	3 oz
50g	sunflower seeds (optional)	2 oz

1. Heat the oven to 180C/350F/gas mark 4.
2. Melt the spread and sugars over a low heat — the brown sugars will be slower to dissolve than ordinary white sugar but give the flapjacks a much better flavour.
3. Mix the ginger into the porridge oats or millet flakes and, when the sugar is melted, stir them both into the butter and sugar mixture.
4. Finally stir in the sultanas and sunflower seeds, if you are using them, and press the flapjacks out into a greased, shallow baking tray, either round or oblong. They should be 0.5-1 cm / ¼-½ inch thick.
5. Bake for 25-30 minutes until tanned but not burnt.
6. Remove from the oven and cut into triangles or fingers while they are still hot. Leave them to cool in the tin and then remove with care.

Note: To get the best flavour be sure you use unrefined molasses sugar. Many of the 'brown' sugars on the shelves are in fact white sugars dyed brown, not genuine brown sugar.

And, did you know... that flapjack is also a brown seaweed found in New Zealand.

STRAWBERRY CRUNCHIES

These are sort of fresh strawberry flapjacks. Like flapjacks they would traditionally be made with porridge oats but those who would prefer not to eat oats can substitute millet flakes. | Makes approximately 12

225g	porridge oats or millet flakes	8 oz
50g	gram flour	2 oz
50g	potato flour	2 oz
75g	unrefined demerara sugar	3 oz
75g	honey	3 oz
150g	dairy-free spread	6 oz
550g	strawberries	1 ¼ lbs
2 heaped tsp	arrowroot	2 heaped tsp

1. Heat the oven to 180C / 350F / gas mark 4.
2. Mix the oats or millet flakes, the flours and sugar.
3. Warm the honey with the spread until both are melted then stir them well into the dry mixture.
4. Purée 225g/8 oz of the strawberries and chop the rest fairly roughly.
5. Put the arrowroot in a small pan and add a little of the purée, stir till smooth, then add the rest of the purée.
6. Heat gently till the sauce thickens then amalgamate it with the chopped strawberries.
7. Spread half of the crumble mixture over the bottom of an oiled baking tray — you need it to be at least 1cm / ½ inch thick.
8. Mix the remaining crumble into the strawberry mixture and spread over the crumble base.
9. Bake for 30 minutes, remove and cool slightly, then cut, in the tin, into whatever size and shape pieces you want.
10. Allow the crunchies to cool completely in the tin before removing them.

Note: These can be eaten as biscuits but are also rather delicious warm, as a dessert, topped with dairy-free vanilla ice cream.

ALMOND CAKE

This is a really delicious cake which can be served by itself or used as a base for a gateau, filled or topped with fresh fruit.

6	eggs	6
225g	light muscovado sugar	8 oz
300g	ground almonds	11 oz
	juice of 1 and the rind of 2 lemons	

1. Heat the oven to 190C/375F/gas mark 5.
2. Separate the eggs and beat the yolks with the sugar until they are light and fluffy.
3. Fold in the almonds, the lemon rind and juice.
4. Whisk the egg whites until they are stiff but not dry and fold them into the almond mixture.
5. Thoroughly grease a 20cm/8 inch cake tin or round baking ring. If you are concerned about it sticking, line the tin with greased greaseproof paper.
6. Pour in the mixture and bake it for 40 minutes or until a skewer comes out clean.
7. Turn the cake out onto a rack to cool. When cold decorate or fill with fresh fruits. You can use a thin layer of plain soya cream 'cheese' or a thin layer of jam to 'hold' the fruits in place.

VERY RICH CHOCOLATE GATEAU-CAKE

This is an extremely luscious but very rich mixture so a little goes a long way. You may wish to eat it exactly as it is but if you wish to decorate it further I suggest a layer of tart fruit jam in the middle and a sprinkling of icing sugar over the top — or, if you want to use it as a dessert, a thick fresh (or frozen) raspberry coulis poured over the top and served with soya ice cream.

325g	dairy-free dark chocolate	12 oz
9	eggs	9
275g	pale muscovado sugar	10 oz
5 tbsp	hot water	5 tbsp

1. Heat the oven to 180C/350F/gas mark 4.
2. Line a 20cm/8 inch tin with greased greaseproof paper.
3. Break up and melt the chocolate in a bowl over hot water or in a microwave.
4. Separate the eggs and whisk the yolks with the sugar until pale, fluffy and lemon coloured.
5. When the chocolate is melted, carefully stir in the hot water then add the chocolate to the egg and sugar and mix well.
6. Whisk the whites until they hold their shape (but are not dry and pointy as for meringues) and fold them into the chocolate and egg mixture.

7. Pour into the prepared tin and bake for 50 minutes or until a skewer comes out clean — unless you want the cake to have a slightly gooey centre (rather delicious) in which case, bake it for 40 minutes.

8. Serve as it is or split horizontally, fill with a tart raspberry jam and sprinkle with icing sugar.

9. You can also serve the cake as a dessert with a fruit purée and accompanied by a dairy-free ice cream, or cream. Puréed raspberries, strawberries or passion fruit, sweetened very lightly to taste, are all delicious and, when the fruit are no longer available fresh, you can use frozen.

WHOLEMEAL CINNAMON MUFFINS

A nice treat for a Sunday breakfast. | Makes 6 muffins

75g	dairy-free spread	3 oz
50g	pale muscovado sugar	2 oz
1	small egg	1
150ml	coconut milk	¼ pint
50g	gram flour	2 oz
50g	buckwheat flour	2 oz
50g	rice flour	2 oz
1 heaped tsp	baking powder	1 heaped tsp
½ tsp	xanthan gum	½ tsp
1 heaped tsp	cinnamon	1 heaped tsp
generous pinch	salt	generous pinch
100g	raisins or sultanas	4 oz

1. Heat the oven to 190C/375F/gas mark 5.
2. Beat the spread and sugar together till pale and creamy.
3. Gently beat in the egg and coconut milk.
4. Sieve the flours with the baking powder, xanthan gum, cinnamon and salt and gradually beat them into the liquid mixture with a wooden spoon.
5. Fold in the raisins or sultanas and spoon the dough into 6 greased mince pie or tart pans.
6. Bake the muffins for 20 minutes or until a skewer comes out clean.
7. Remove from the tins and cool slightly on a rack. The muffins are also good cold and freeze well.

Note: Although many people love blueberry and other soft fruit muffins, I find that the soft fruit ones are rather 'wet' and that dried fruits work better.

SUMMER FRUIT CAKE

A lovely, fresh-tasting cake — just right for tea on the lawn. To convert it into a dessert, serve it warm in wedges with a fresh fruit purée.

100g	soft dairy-free spread	4 oz
50g	light muscovado sugar	2 oz
1	ripe banana, mashed	1
50g	soft dried apricots, chopped	2 oz
100g	strawberries, chopped	4 oz
100g	redcurrants	4 oz
3	medium eggs	3
100g	gluten/wheat-free flour – your own favourite brand or mixture or 50g/2 oz each of gram and rice flour	4 oz
½ tsp	xanthan gum – if you are using a flour mix which does not already contain it	½ tsp
1 tsp	gluten/wheat-free baking powder	1 tsp
100g	rolled oats or millet flakes pulverised in a food processor juice of ½ a large lemon	4 oz

1. Heat the oven to 180C/350F/gas mark 4.
2. Beat the butter with the sugar till light and fluffy.
3. Meanwhile purée the banana with the apricots, strawberries and half of the redcurrants and then beat into the butter and sugar mixture.
4. Beat in the eggs, adding a spoonful of flour with each egg, then fold in the rest of the flour, xanthan gum and baking powder, the oats or millet flakes and the remaining redcurrants along with the lemon juice.
5. Line an 20cm/8 inch loose-bottomed cake tin with greaseproof paper and oil well.
6. Spoon in the mixture and bake for 40 minutes or until the cake is firm and a skewer comes out clean. Cool on a rack before cutting.

Note: Using fresh fruit in a cake can make it quite 'wet' which is why there is no extra liquid in this cake. However, fresh fruit does give it a 'fresh' flavour quite different from cakes made with dried fruits, delicious though those are.

LUSCIOUS APPLE CAKE

Try to use really sharp-tasting apples for this cake, preferably Bramley cooking apples as they give it such a great flavour. The recipes also uses dates rather than sugar for sweetening which gives the cake more texture and a deeper sweetness.

150g	dairy-free spread	6 oz
150g	softened and roughly chopped dates	6 oz
300g	cooking or sharp eating apples, cored and roughly chopped but with the skin still on	11 oz
75g	your favourite gluten/wheat-free flour or 50g/2 oz gram flour and 25g/1oz rice	3 oz
2 heaped tsp	gluten/wheat-free baking powder	2 heaped tsp
3	eggs	3
75g	ground almonds	3 oz
50g	fat sultanas	2 oz

1. Heat the oven to 180C/350F/gas mark 4.
2. In a food processor, purée the spread with the dates and apples.
3. Sieve the flour with the baking powder.
4. Transfer the dates and apples to a bowl and mix in the eggs, alternately with the flours and almonds.
5. Stir in the sultanas.
6. Spoon into a greased 20cm/8 inch cake tin with a removeable bottom or lined with greased greaseproof paper and bake for 45 minutes or until a skewer comes out clean.
7. Remove the tin and cool the cake on a rack.

Note: The first Bramley apple tree grew from pips planted in a Nottinghamshire garden by a little girl in 1809 and, despite being blown over by a violent storm in 1900, the original tree is still producing apples. The apple got its name from the village butcher, Matthew Bramley, who lived in the cottage in the 1850s and who allowed a local nurseryman, Henry Merryweather, to take cuttings from his tree and to sell the seedlings.

Today growing Bramley apples is a £50 million pound business with commercial growers across the midlands and south east of England. The flavour of the Bramley apple remains unique.

SEEDY CHRISTMAS CAKE

This cake is also good for those with nut allergies as it uses seeds rather than the more traditional nuts. If you think Christmas would not be the same without a nutty Christmas cake you can substitute a similar quantity of your favourite nuts for the seeds. Because there is so much fruit in the cake, I have not added any sugar. If you have a sweet tooth add 50g/2 oz dark muscovado sugar to the initial purée.

These amounts make a fairly modest-sized cake — if you have a large family, double the ingredients and increase the cooking time by 40 minutes.

Fortunately for traditional Christmas enthusiasts, neither marzipan nor royal icing have either dairy products or gluten so classic recipes are given below.

100g	soft dried dates, chopped roughly	4 oz
	rind and juice 2 lemons	
100g	dairy-free spread or coconut oil	4 oz
1	medium, ripe banana	1
75g	each raisins and sultanas	3 oz
150g	soft dried apricots, chopped roughly	6 oz
25g	each sesame seeds and golden linseeds	1 oz
50g	each sunflower and pumpkin seeds	2 oz
2	eggs	2
75g	rolled oats or millet flakes, lightly pulverised in a food processor	3 oz
75g	rice flour	3 oz
2 level tsp	gluten/wheat-free baking powder	2 level tsp
2 level tsp	ground nutmeg, freshly grated if possible	2 level tsp
1 heaped tsp	ground cinnamon	1 heaped tsp
1 x 25g	piece fresh ginger, peeled and grated or	1x1 oz
	1 heaped tsp ground ginger	
2 tbsp	brandy / orange / apple juice	2 tbsp

1. Heat the oven to 160C/325F/gas mark 3.
2. If the dates are hard, put them in a small pan with the lemon juice and gradually heat for 5 minutes to help soften them.
3. Purée the dairy-free spread with the banana and lemon rind in a food processor.
4. Turn into a bowl and stir in the dates and lemon juice, the dried fruits and seeds, followed by the eggs, the flours, baking powder, spices and fresh ginger and, finally, the brandy or fruit juice. Mix well.
5. Line a 15cm/6 inch cake tin with greased greaseproof paper and spoon in the mixture. Smooth out and bake for 1 hour or until a skewer comes out clean. (Cont.)

6. Cool slightly in the tin then turn out and leave to get completely cold before cutting.

MARZIPAN

The lemon juice in this recipe is optional — it just slightly tempers the richness and sweetness of the icing. | To cover one small cake

400g	ground almonds	14 oz
200g	icing sugar	7 oz
200g	caster sugar	7 oz
2	egg whites	2
	juice ½ lemon (optional)	

1. Mix the almonds and sugar then add the egg whites and lemon juice and mix thoroughly.
2. To ice the cake, spread it with a thin layer of jam of your choice.
3. Dust your worktop with icing sugar then roll out the marzipan and lift it onto the cake. Don't worry if it tears as it is easy to patch.

ROYAL ICING

2	egg whites	2
450g	approx icing sugar	1 lb
	juice ½ lemon	

1. Put the egg whites in the bowl of a mixer and gradually beat in the sugar and lemon juice. If they are particularly large egg whites you may need a little extra sugar. Keep beating until the icing is stiff and smooth.
2. Using a spatula, spread the icing over the marzipan and decorate as you fancy.
3. If you are not going to use the icing immediately, cover it with wet kitchen paper and clingflim to stop it drying out.

SPONGE CAKES

I have two classic sponge cake recipes which I use as a base for fruit gateaux, trifles, tiramisu or just as simple cakes on their own layered with jam and sprinkled with icing sugar. The first is made with rice flour and is very light — an American angel cake; the second uses fat and is more like a traditional Madeira cake.

'ANGEL' CAKE

6	medium eggs	6
150g	caster sugar	6 oz
150g	rice flour	6 oz

1. Heat the oven to 170C/325F/gas mark 3.
2. Line a loose-bottomed 20cm/8 inch cake tin with lightly floured greaseproof paper.
3. Whisk the eggs and sugar together with an electric whisk until they are light and fluffy. Sift the flour into the bowl and fold it very carefully into the egg mixture making sure that you do not get any lumps of flour.
4. Pour the mixture into the tin and bake for 20-30 minutes or till the cake is firm to the touch.
5. Remove from the oven and then carefully remove from the tin. Peel off the greaseproof paper and allow to cool on a rack.
6. If you are to use the cake in another recipe (trifle or tiramisu) and do not want to use it all, the remains will freeze well.

'MADEIRA' CAKE

200g	dairy-free spread	7 oz
200g	light muscovado sugar	7 oz
3	medium eggs	3
150g	sifted gram/chickpea flour	6 oz
50g	rice flour	2 oz
2 level tsp	gluten/wheat-free baking powder	2 level tsp
1 tsp	vanilla essence	1 tsp

1. Heat the oven to 180C/350F/gas mark 4.
2. Beat the spread with the sugar until light and fluffy.
3. Beating slowly add the eggs alternately with a spoonful of the flour.
4. Fold in the remaining flour, baking powder and vanilla essence. Spoon into a well oiled or lined 20cm/8 inch tin and bake it for 30 minutes or until the cake is firm to the touch and a skewer comes out clean.
5. Cool on a rack and when cold, split and fill with jam of your choice. If you wish you can also dust the top with icing sugar or soft muscovado.

STICKY GINGERBREAD

I normally make this with rolled oats but those who would rather avoid oats could also use a coarse maize flour.

You can use dairy-free spread or coconut oil as the fat for this 'bread'. For those who normally find the flavour of the coconut a bit strong, you will find the flavours of the gingerbread will successfully conceal it.

If you a real ginger fan you can include bits of chopped crystallised ginger.

100g	dairy-free spread or coconut oil	4 oz
100g	unrefined demerara or dark muscovado sugar	4 oz
350g	black treacle	12 oz
4	eggs	4
225g	rolled or porridge oats, powdered in a food processor or coarse maize flour	8 oz
1 heaped tsp	wheat/gluten-free baking powder	1 heaped tsp
2 heaped tsp	ground ginger	2 heaped tsp
1 heaped tsp each	mixed spice and ground cinnamon	1 heaped tsp each
50g	crystallised ginger, chopped roughly (optional) – or finely if you do not like large chunks of ginger in your cake	2 oz

1. Heat the oven to 160C/325F/gas mark 3.
2. Line a loaf tin with oiled greaseproof paper.
3. Melt the spread or coconut oil, sugar and treacle together in a pan.
4. Draw off the heat.
5. Beat the eggs into the melted mixture followed by the oats or maize flour, baking powder and spices. Also crystallised ginger if used.
6. Pour into the tin and bake for 45-60 minutes or till a skewer comes out clean.
7. Remove and cool on a rack.

CLASSIC CHOCOLATE CAKE

This is my fall back for visiting children — or adults. Very simple to make and totally reliable. It usually gets eaten before it gets a chance to get iced but if you wish to ice it you could do so with a standard chocolate butter icing or just with melted chocolate.

175g	dairy-free spread	6 oz
200g	dark muscovado sugar	7 oz
50g	cocoa powder	2 oz
6 tbsp	boiling water	6 tbsp
175g	of your favourite gluten/wheat-free flour or 100g/4 oz gram flour and 75g/3 oz rice flour	6 oz
1 level tsp	wheat/gluten-free baking powder	1 level tsp
3	medium eggs	3
2 tbsp	sheep's, goat's, soya, oat or rice milk	2 tbsp
225g	dairy-free chocolate for icing (optional)	8 oz

1. Heat the oven to 180C/350F/gas mark 4.
2. Grease a 20cm/8 inch tin with a removeable bottom or line a cake tin with greased greaseproof paper.
3. In an electric mixer beat the spread with the sugar until they are light and fluffy.
4. Meanwhile, mix the cocoa powder with the boiling water until you have a smooth paste and beat into the spread and sugar.
5. Sift the flours with the baking powder.
6. Slowly beat in the three eggs, each accompanied by a spoonful of flour. Fold in the rest of the flour with the baking powder and the 2 tablespoons of milk.
7. Pour the mixture into the cake tin and bake for 30 minutes or until it is firm to the touch and a skewer comes out clean from the middle.
8. Cool slightly and then turn onto a rack to get cold before cutting.
9. If you want to 'ice' the cake, move it onto the serving plate while it is still warm.
10. Melt the chocolate over hot water or in a microwave. When it is entirely melted and runny pour it in a slow stream onto the middle of the cake and allow it to gradually flow over the top of the cake and down the sides as with glacé icing. It should be quite thin.
11. Allow to get completely cold before cutting.

Note: As with any cake, especially any chocolate cake, you can quickly convert it into a dessert by warming it in a microwave for 20-30 seconds and serving it with dairy-free ice cream.

LEMON POPPY SEED CAKE

A very simple but very refreshing cake.

200g	dairy-free spread	7 oz
200g	light muscovado sugar	7 oz
	coarsely grated rind and juice of 2 lemons	
2 tsp	poppy seeds	2 tsp
3	medium eggs	3
125g	polenta or coarse maize flour	5 oz
75g	potato flour	3 oz
2 level tsp	wheat/gluten-free baking powder	2 level tsp

Glacé icing

300g	icing sugar	12 oz
	finely grated rind and juice of 1 lemon	
	water	

1. Heat the oven to 180C/350F/gas mark 4.
2. Beat the spread with the sugar until light and fluffy.
3. Beating slowly, add the lemon rind and juice and poppy seeds, then the egg alternately with a spoonful of the flours.
4. Fold in the remaining flours, and baking powder.
5. Spoon into a well oiled or lined 20cm/8 inch tin and bake it for 30 minutes or until the cake is firm to the touch and a skewer comes out clean. Cool on a rack.

To make the icing:
1. Put the icing sugar into a bowl with the lemon rind and juice and mix well. Put the bowl into a pan with hot water half way up the bowl. Keep hot over a low heat but do not boil.
2. Slowly add water to the icing sugar, stirring with a wooden spoon, until it is the consistency of thick cream. Continue to stir until it is lukewarm.
3. Pour about ¾ of the icing over the middle of the cake — it should spread naturally over the top of the cake and run down the sides but you can help it along with a spatula. Use the remaining icing to 'patch' any bits not properly covered.

CHOCOLATE BROWNIES

Brownies can be relatively light and cakey or seriously gooey and rich. This one comes somewhere in the middle. Dark and yummy. If you want to make them even more chocolatey, add 50g/2 oz dairy-free chocolate, grated or in small lumps along with the walnuts. | Makes 12 brownies

150g	dairy-free spread	6 oz
150g	dark muscovado sugar	6 oz
50g	cocoa powder	2 oz
50g	porridge oats, whizzed in a processor to a coarse powder	2 oz
50g	sifted gram (chickpea) flour or	2 oz
	100g/4 oz gram flour, if you do not want to use oats	
50g	buckwheat flour	2 oz
3 level tsp	wheat/gluten-free baking powder	3 level tsp
150ml	goat's, sheep's, soya, oat or rice milk	¼ pint
50g	broken walnuts	2 oz
50g	dairy-free chocolate, grated or in drops (optional)	2 oz

1. Preheat the oven to 160C/325F/gas mark 3.
2. In an electric mixer beat the spread thoroughly with the sugar and the cocoa.
3. Fold in the flours and baking powder alternately with the milk and then fold in the walnuts and the extra chocolate if you are using it.
4. Spoon the mixture into a well oiled square or rectangular tin, as thick or as thin as you want your brownies, smooth out with a spatula and bake for 30 minutes or till a skewer comes out clean.
5. Cool for a few minutes in the tin then cut into brownie shapes.
6. Remove them carefully from the tin with a spatula and cool on a rack.

COFFEE CAKE

The figs give this cake a rather different texture and flavour from your standard coffee cake, while the dark sugar and the dry instant coffee give a slightly crunchy texture to the icing. However, be warned, the icing does make it very rich.

300g	coconut oil or dairy-free spread	11 oz
200g	dark muscovado sugar	7 oz

6 tbsp	very strong black coffee	6 tbsp
6	eggs	6
100g	teff flour (or buckwheat flour)	4 oz
100g	rice flour	4 oz
100g	hazelnuts ground in a food processor	4 oz
	(how fine you grind them will depend on how crunchy a texture you want your cake to have)	
2 heaped tsp	gluten/wheat-free baking powder	2 heaped tsp
200g	soft figs, cut in small pieces	7 oz
2 tbsp	coconut or other dairy-free milk	2 tbsp

'Butter' icing

250g	soft coconut oil or dairy-free spread	9 oz
200g	dark muscovado sugar	7 oz
2 tbsp	dark roast instant coffee	2 tbsp
75g	finely grated dairy-free chocolate	3 oz

1. Heat the oven to 180C/350F/gas mark 4.
2. Beat the coconut oil or spread with the sugar in an electric mixer until it is creamy. Beat in the coffee.
3. Add the eggs one by one, each with a spoonful of the mixed flours, hazelnuts and the baking powder.
4. Beat well with a wooden spoon then stir in the figs and the extra milk.
5. Line a 20cm/8 inch cake tin with greased greaseproof paper (or use a tin with a removable bottom) and spoon in the mixture.
6. Bake for 50-60 minutes or until the cake is firm to the touch and a skewer comes out clean.
7. Remove from the oven and cool completely on a rack.

Icing
1. Beat the coconut oil or spread together with the sugar, coffee and chocolate in an electric mixer until it is soft and creamy. It will retain a slight crunch from the sugar and the coffee.
2. When the cake is quite cold, split it and spread a layer of icing in the middle. Use the rest of the icing to cover the cake and chill slightly to firm up the icing.

Note: If you have time, roast or toast the hazelnuts after you have ground them as it really brings out their flavour — as it does with any nut, seed or spice.

FIG, BANANA AND CASHEW NUT CAKE

A perfect cake for the winter.

150g	dairy-free spread or coconut oil	6 oz
100g	soft dried figs	4 oz
1	large banana	1
50g	broken cashew nuts	2 oz
100g	rolled oats or millet flakes	4 oz
1 heaped tsp	gluten/wheat-free baking powder	1 heaped tsp
3	eggs	3
50g	rice flour	2 oz
2 tbsp	milk (sheep's, goat's, soya, oat, coconut or rice)	2 tbsp
50g	sultanas	2 oz
24	approx whole almonds (optional)	24

1. Heat the oven to 180C/350F/gas mark 4.
2. Put the spread, figs, banana, cashew nuts, oats and baking powder in a food processor and whizz for 2-3 minutes or until they are all well puréed and amalgamated.
3. Remove to a bowl and stir in the eggs alternately with the rice flour, milk and sultanas.
4. Spoon the mixture into a 15cm/6 inch cake tin lined with greased greaseproof paper.
5. If you are using them, press the almonds into the top of the cake in a pattern, as for a Dundee cake.
6. Bake for 35 minutes or until a skewer comes out clean.
7. Cool on a rack before cutting.

CARROT AND WALNUT CAKE

A lovely spicy carrot cake. You can ice it or not as you feel inclined.

100g	dairy-free spread or coconut oil	4 oz
100g	light muscovado sugar	4 oz
150g	sharpish eating apples, cored but not peeled	6 oz
150g	carrots, grated	6 oz
3	medium eggs	3
150g	polenta or coarse maize meal	6 oz
2 heaped tsp	gluten-free baking powder	2 heaped tsp
2 level tsp	ground cinnamon	2 level tsp
1 level tsp	ground nutmeg	1 level tsp
pinch	salt	pinch
6 tbsp	apple juice	6 tbsp
100g	broken walnuts	4 oz
	Topping	
200g	plain soya cream cheese	7 oz
1 tsp	pale muscovado sugar	1 tsp
	rind and juice of 1 lemon and 1 orange	

1. Preheat the oven to 180C/350F/gas mark 4.
2. Purée the spread or coconut oil in a processor with the sugar and the apples.
3. Transfer to a bowl and mix in the carrot.
4. Beat in the eggs, alternately with the polenta, the baking powder and the spices along with the apple juice.
5. Finally stir in the walnuts.
6. Pour into a greased 20cm/8 inch cake tin with a removable bottom or a tin lined with greased greaseproof paper.
7. Bake for 60 minutes or until the cake is firm to the touch and a skewer comes out clean.
8. Remove from the oven and allow to cool on a wire rack.
9. To make the topping, beat the sugar, and rind into the cream cheese, then add the juices until you are happy with the flavour and the texture — some brands of soya cheese will be softer than others so will need less juice.
Use a spatula to ice the cake.

RESOURCES DIRECTORY

USEFUL ORGANISATIONS

Foods Matter websites
The author's own very extensive websites dealing with every aspect of food allergy and intolerance and freefrom food.
5 Lawn Road, London NW3 2XS, 020 7722 2866, www.foodsmatter.com and www.freefromfoodsmatter.com

Allergy
Action Against Allergy: support group, PO Box 278, Twickenham TW1 4QQ, Tel 020 8892 2711, www.actionagainstallergy.co.uk

AllAllergy.net: allergy sites worldwide, www.allallergy.net

Allergies Explained: general information on allergy, www.allergiesexplained.com

Allergy Action: useful advice for serious food allergies, 01727 855294, www.allergyaction.org

Allergy Clinic: advice site run by mainstream allergists, www.allergyclinic.co.uk

AllergyFreeDirect, www.allergyfreedirect.com

The Allergy Bible: excellent blog by a severe nut and dairy allergic, www.theallergybible.com

The Allergy Site, www.theallergysite.co.uk

Allergy UK: support group, Tel 01322 619898, www.allergyuk.org

The Anaphylaxis Campaign: support group, Tel 01252 542029, www.anaphylaxis.org.uk

Children's Allergy Services: Paediatric Allergy, Evelina Children's Hospital, St Thomas' Hospital, Westminster Bridge Road, London SE1 7EH, Tel 020 7188 3300, http://www.guysandstthomas.nhs.uk/services/childrens/paediatricallergy/clinics.aspx

Coeliac UK: support group, Tel 01494 437 278, www.coeliac.co.uk

Food-Info: information site run by Wageningen University in Holland, www.food-info.net

FreeFrom Food Awards: www.freefrom-foodawards.co.uk. Annual UK industry award for the best freefrom (gluten, wheat, dairy, egg, nut etc) food.

MedicAlert: medical identification bracelets, etc, 1 Bridge Wharf, 156 Caledonian Road, London, N1 9UU Tel 0800 581420, www.medicalert.org.uk

Nambudripad's Allergy Elimination Techniques: complementary approach to allergy, Tel 00 33 4 50 51 31 50, www.naet.co.uk

Truly Gluten Free: website for those allergic to grains, www.trulyglutenfree.co.uk

Allergy Testing
Biolab Medical Unit: via a practitioner only, The Stone House, 9 Weymouth St, London W1W 6DB Tel 020 7636 5959, www.biolab.co.uk

Food Detective/Cambridge Nutritional Sciences Ltd: intolerance and allergy testing, Tel 01353 863279, www.food-detective.com

Home Coeliac Test, www.myeasydiet.co.uk

Home Gluten Test, www.tepnel.com

York Test: intolerance and allergy testing, www.homeinonhealth.com

Children
Foresight: preconceptual nutrition, www.foresight-preconception.org.uk

Health and Nutrition, www.healthandnutrition.co.uk

Hyperactive Children's Support Group: Tel 01243 539966, www.hacsg.org.uk

Kids Allergies: information site on allergies in kids, www.kidsallergies.co.uk

Medical Conditions at School: help to create a safe school environment for allergic kids, www.medicalconditionsatschool.org.uk

(Freefrom) Cookery Courses

Ashburton Cookery School, www.ashburtoncookeryschool.co.uk

Ballymaloe Cookery School, www.cookingisfun.ie

Bread Matters, www.breadmatters.com

Green Cuisine, Penrhos Court, Kington, Herefordshire, HR5 3LH, Tel 01544 230720, www.greencuisine.penrhos.com

Lucy Cook's Cookery School, Mill Yard, Staveley, Nr Kendal, Cumbria, LA8 9LR Tel 015394 32288, www.lucycooks.co.uk

Dairy

Dairy-free UK Forums, www.dairyfreeuk.com

Go Dairy Free, www.godairyfree.org

Milkfree, www.milkfree.org.uk

No Cow's Milk for Me Thanks!, www.lactoseintolerance.co.uk

Digestive/IBS

Core, 3 St Andrews Place, London, NW1 4LB UK, www.corecharity.org.uk

The Gut Trust: support group (IBS), Unit 5, 53, Mowbray Street, Sheffield, S3 8EN UK 0114 272 32 53, www.theguttrust.org

The Register of IBS Therapists, P.O. Box 57, Warrington, WA5 1FG, UK 01925 629437, www.ibsregister.com

Irritable Bowel Syndrome Treatment, www.irritable-bowel-syndrome.ws

National Association for Colitis and Crohn's Disease: support group 01727 844296, www.nacc.org.uk

Eating Out and Travel

AllergyText, www.allergytext.co.uk

Eat Well, Be Well: Food Standard Agency advice, www.eatwell.gov.uk

Dietary Card: translation travel cards, www.dietarycard.co.uk

Gluten Free on the Go: Coeliac UK hotel/restaurant guide, www.gluten-free-onthego.com

Leave It Out: freefrom restaurant guide, www.leaveitout.com

Select Wisely: translation travel cards, etc, www.selectwisely.com

Products and Suppliers
Dairy and Lactose Free

Alpro 08000 188 180: soya milk, cream, yoghurt, desserts, www.alprosoya.co.uk

Billy Goat Stuff 01326 566315: goat's milk chocolate, www.billygoatstuff.co.uk

The Booja-Booja Company Ltd 01508 558888: dairy-free truffles and ice-cream, www.boojabooja.com

Caprilatte Ice Cream 01206 736121: goat's milk ice-cream, www.caprilatteicecream.co.uk

Delamere Dairy 01565 750528: goat's milk products, www.delameredairy.co.uk

D and D Chocolates 02476 370909: dairy-free chocolate and carob, www.danddchocolates.com

Droppa and Droppa Specialist Foods 01237 421874: gluten-free baked goods, www.droppaanddroppa.com

High Weald Dairy 01825 791636: goat and sheep products, www.highwealddairy.co.uk

Kinnerton Confectionery 020 7284 9503: dairy-free chocolate, www.kinnerton.com

Lactofree: lactose-reduced milk, www.lactofree.co.uk

Nannycare: goat's milk infant formula and follow-on milk, www.vitacare.co.uk

Oatly: oat-based milk and cream, www.oatly.com

Plamil Foods Ltd 01303 850588: dairy-free chocolate, www.plamilfoods.co.uk

Pure 0800 028 4499: dairy-free spread, www.puredairyfree.co.uk

The Redwood Wholefood Co. Ltd. 01536 400557: dairy-free soya cheese, www.redwoodfoods.co.uk

St Helen's Farm 01430 861715: goat's milk products, www.sthelensfarm.co.uk

Swedish Glace 01270 589311: dairy-free soya ice-creams, www.fayrefield.com

Tofutti, Triano Brands 020 8861 4443: dairy-free soya cheese and ice-cream, www.trianobrands.co.uk

Woodlands Park Dairy 01202 822 687: goat and sheep products, www.woodlands-park.co.uk

Wheat and Gluten Free

Against the Grain Ltd 020 8876 6247: gluten-free biscuits, www.againstthegrainfoods.com

Artisan Bread Ltd: gluten-free breads, www.artisanbread-abo.com

Biona, Windmill Organics Ltd 0208 547 2775 : wheat-free products, www.windmillorganics.com

Orgran 01455 55687: gluten-free products, www.naturallygoodfood.co.uk

Dietary Needs Direct 01453 790 999: online gluten- and dairy-free products, www.dietaryneedsdirect.co.uk

Dietary Specials 01925 865100: wide range of gluten-free goods, www.dietaryspecials.co.uk

Doves Farm Foods Ltd: gluten- and wheat-free flours, www.dovesfarm.co.uk

Dr Schaer: gluten-free products, www.schaer.com

EnerG 020 8336 2323: gluten-free goods — many on prescription, www.generaldietary.com

Everfresh Natural Foods: gluten-free breads, www.everfreshnaturalfoods.com

G Free Ltd: 01404 47904: gluten-free baked goods, sweet and savoury, www.gfree.co.uk

Glebe Farm 01487 773282: gluten-free bread and cake mixes, www.glebe-flour.co.uk

Glu2go 01324 717273: gluten-free fish and chips, www.glu2go.co.uk

Glutafin 0800 988 2470: gluten-free food on prescription, www.glutafin.co.uk

Gluten Free Foods Ltd 0208 953 4444: gluten-free bread, biscuits, pasta etc, some on prescription, www.glutenfree-foods.co.uk

Glutenfree Foods Direct 01757 289200: online gluten-free shop — wide range of goods, www.gffdirect.co.uk

The Gluten-Free Kitchen 01969 666 999: gluten-free baked goods, www.theglutenfreekitchen.co.uk

Goodness Direct 0871 871 6611: online shop, very extensive range of gluten- and dairy-free goods, www.goodnessdirect.co.uk

Green's Gluten Free Beers 01274 714664: gluten-free beer, www.glutenfreebeers.co.uk

Hambleton Ales: gluten-free beer, www.hambletonales.co.uk

Honeybuns 01963 23597: gluten-free cakes and goodies, www.honeybuns.co.uk

Honeyrose Bakery Ltd 020 8960 5567: gluten-free cakes and goodies, www.honeyrosebakery.com

Innovative Solutions UK Ltd 01706 746 713: xanthan gum, etc, www.innovative-solutions.co.uk

The Intolerable Food Company 01825 790090: dairy- and gluten-free ready meals, www.intolerablefood.com

Juvela 0800 783 1992: gluten-free goods on prescription, www.juvela.co.uk

Lifestyle Healthcare Ltd 01491 570000: gluten-free goods, many on prescription, www.gfdiet.com

Meridian Foods Limited: dairy-free sauces and spreads, www.meridianfoods.co.uk

My Exclusive Recipes: recipes adapted to your diet, www.myexclusiverecipes.co.uk

Organico 01189 238767: gluten-free pasta, www.organico.co.uk

Raspberry Creek Foods 07711 538 601: wheat- and gluten-free foods, www.raspberrycreekfoods.co.uk

Rizopia, PGR Health Foods Ltd 01992 581715: gluten-free pasta, www.pgrhealthfoods.co.uk

Stiletto Foods (UK) Ltd 08451 300869: gluten-free biscuits and cakes, www.mrscrimbles.com

The Village Bakery 01768 898437: gluten-free breads and cakes, www.village-bakery.com

Trufree 07041 544 044: wheat- and gluten-free foods, www.trufree.co.uk

Wellfoods Ltd 01226 381712: gluten-free bread mixes, pizzas, etc, some on prescription, www.wellfoods.co.uk

Ulula 01603 308164: gluten- and dairy-free foods for children, www.ulula.co.uk

BOOKS, PUBLICATIONS, BLOGSPOTS AND WEBSITES

Books

The Everyday Wheat-free and Gluten-free Cookbook by Michelle Berriedale-Johnson, Grub Street, London

The Allergy Aware Schools Catering Manual by Michelle Berriedale-Johnson, Berrydales Publishers

Allergy Catering Manual by Michelle Berriedale-Johnson, Berrydales Publishers

Food Allergy and Your Child by Alice Willits and Deborah Carter, Class Publishing

Food Allergies – Enjoying Life with a Severe Food Allergy by Tanya Wright, Class Publishing

The Complete Guide to Food Allergy and Intolerance by Prof. Jonathan Brostoff and Linda Gamlin, Quality Health Press

The Allergy Bible by Linda Gamlin, Quadrille

Bread Matters — The State of Modern Bread and a Definitive Guide to Baking Your Own by Andrew Whitley, Fourth Estate

Active Again by Heather Stott, Tulip Press

The Best Gluten-free, Wheat-free and Dairy-free Recipes by Grace Cheetham, Duncan Baird Publishers

How to Cook For Allergies by Lucinda Bruce-Gardyne, Rodale

Allergy-Free Cookbook by Alice Sherwood, Dorling Kindersley

Cooking Without Made Easy by Barbara Cousins, Thorsons

Tony's Lactose Free Cookbook by Prof. Anthony Campbell and Dr Stephanie Matthews, Welston Press Ltd

The Complete Guide to Gluten-free and Dairy-free Cooking by Glenis Lucas, Duncan Baird Publishers

Cooking Without and Vegetarian Cooking Without by Barbara Cousins, Thorsons